Law and the Islamization of Morocco under the Almoravids

Studies in the History and Society of the Maghrib

Series Editors

Amira K. Bennison (*University of Cambridge*)
Léon Buskens (*University of Leiden*)
Houari Touati (*École des hautes études en sciences sociales, Paris*)

VOLUME 6

The titles published in this series are listed at *brill.com/shsm*

Law and the Islamization of Morocco under the Almoravids

The Fatwās of Ibn Rushd al-Jadd to the Far Maghrib

By

Camilo Gómez-Rivas

BRILL

LEIDEN | BOSTON

Cover illustration: Qubbat al-Bārudiyyīn, Marrakesh, commissioned by ʿAlī b. Yūsuf and finished in 1117.
Photo: Camilo Gómez-Rivas.

Library of Congress Cataloging-in-Publication Data

Gomez-Rivas, Camilo, author.
Law and the Islamization of Morocco under the Almoravids : the fatwas of Ibn Rushd al-Jadd to the far Maghrib / by Camilo Gomez-Rivas.
pages cm. -- (Studies in the history and society of the Maghrib ; volume 6)
Based on author's thesis (doctoral - Yale University, 2009) issued under title: The Fatwas of Ibn Rushd al-Jadd to the Far Maghrib.
Includes bibliographical references and index.
ISBN 978-90-04-27780-9 (hardback : alk. paper) -- ISBN 978-90-04-27984-1 (e-book)
1. Law--Morocco--History--To 1500. 2. Islamic law--Morocco--History--To 1500.
3. Almoravides. 4. Fatwas--Morocco--History--To 1500. 5. Ibn Rushd, Muhammad ibn Ahmad, 1058-1126. I. Title.

KSW130.G66 2014
340.5'9220964--dc23

2014030587

This publication has been typeset in the multilingual "Brill" typeface. With over 5,100 characters covering Latin, IPA, Greek, and Cyrillic, this typeface is especially suitable for use in the humanities.
For more information, please see brill.com/brill-typeface.

ISSN 1877-9808
ISBN 978-90-04-27780-9 (hardback)
ISBN 978-90-04-27984-1 (e-book)

This book is printed on acid-free paper.

For Emmanuelle

Contents

Acknowledgements IX

Introduction 1
1 Introduction 1
2 Historical and Historiographical Background 9
3 The Muftī 21
4 Urban Development of the Far Maghrib 26
5 Mālikī Law and Custom in the Far Maghrib 33
6 The Development of the Network and Its Activity as Seen through al-Wansharīsī's *Mi'yār* and Qāḍī Iyāḍ's *Tartīb al-Madārik* 39
7 Book Structure 42

1 **Fatwās to Marrakesh: Regulation of the City Market and the Symbolic Authority of Mālikī Learning** 46
1 Introduction 46
2 The Founding and Development of Marrakesh 49
3 The Motor of Gold: Two Questions Involving Gold Exchange 59
4 Mediating Exchange: Two Questions over Commercial Disputes 65
5 Transmitting and Developing Juristic Knowledge: Two Questions Resolving Contradictions within the School 70
6 The Symbolic Religious Authority of Cordoba: the Case of the Man who Wouldn't Remove his Turban and the Case of the Apostate 76

2 **Fatwās to the Far Maghrib: Ibn Rushd's Consultations for the Amīr and Cases of Murder and Stolen Cattle** 85
1 Introduction 85
2 Questions from the Almoravid Leadership: On the Permissibility of Ash'arism and the Exceptionalism of the Islamic Maghrib 86
3 Two Technical Questions from al-'Idwa: Ritual and Murder 99
4 The Islamicization of Property: Partitioning and Gifts from Plunder 104

3 Fatwās to Ceuta: Water Rights, Judicial Review, and Ibn Rushd's Correspondence with al-Qāḍī ʿIyāḍ 113
1 Introduction 113
2 Historical Background 113
3 The Qāḍī 116
4 Islamic Water Law 121
5 The First Ruling 122
6 The Case Re-Opened: Judicial Review and Avoiding Harm 127
7 ʿIyāḍ's Case Part II: Riparian Dispute, Avoiding Harm, and Water Rights Adjudication 136

Epilogue 149

Appendix A: Breakdown of the Fatwās in al-Wansharīsī's *Miʿyār* by Subject and Region 153
Appendix B: Fatwās Chapter One 155
Appendix C: Fatwās Chapter Two 167
Appendix D: Fatwā Chapter Three, The Case of the Gardeners vs. the Miller 177
Bibliography 192
Index 203

Acknowledgements

I am deeply thankful to the people who read the manuscript and guided me through the process of writing this book. Paul Freedman, Beatrice Gruendler, David Powers, and María Rosa Menocal–whom I wish I had been able to thank again before her premature passing–guided me through the first stage of this project. Maribel Fierro, Amira K. Bennison, and Delfina Serrano were instrumental in helping me through the revision. I have strived to incorporate and respond to their many generous and careful suggestions and have not always managed. The shortcomings are all my own. Many thanks also to the anonymous reviewers at Brill for their incisive comments. The colleagues, friends, and family members who have helped, insipred, and supported me through this long process are too many to list; I hope for the chance to deliver my unreserved thanks to each and every one, in person.

A summer research grant and a semester leave from the American University in Cairo provided the time and support to complete the revision.

Introduction

1 Introduction

In the middle of the fifth/eleventh century, the religio-political movement of the Almoravids (*al-Murābiṭūn*, 434–530/1042–1147) took root in the western Sahara. Within forty years of its formation, the Ṣanhāja tribal confederation that was at its core unified, for the first time, a region extending from the Senegal and Niger River Valleys in West Africa to the Ebro Valley in northeastern Iberia. The resulting state, which in Maghribī historiography is referred to as an empire,[1] was the first of this magnitude headed by Muslims of Berber ethnicity, historically the dominant demographic of the Maghrib.[2] The prevailing view in the twentieth-century historiography in the West – inspired to an extent by classical Arabic historical writing in and about the Islamic West[3] – perceived these developments from the narrative perspective of barbarian invasion ensued by decline. It focused on the movement's espousal of jihād, its unsophisticated and utterly "surprising" emergence from sparsely populated desert provenance, and the cultural clash it generated in the Iberian Peninsula, where it was perceived to have come up against a more sophisticated civilization. The dominant narrative thus focused on the occupation of a cosmopolitan Hispano-Arab society by a less sophisticated and "intolerant" Berber religious movement, followed by the eventual regional replacement of the diverse civilization

1 Defined as "an extensive territory (esp. an aggregate of many separate states) under the sway of an emperor or supreme ruler; also, an aggregate of subject territories ruled over by a sovereign state." *OED*, 2nd Edition, s.v. Empire.

2 Berbers are a population indigenous to North Africa from antiquity. In Morocco, the North African country with the largest Berber population today, the terms *Amazigh/Imazighen* are used as self-identifiers. For a general historical introduction to the Berbers in history, see Michael Brett, and Elizabeth Fentress, *The Berbers*, The Peoples of Africa (Wiley-Blackwell, 1997).

3 Islamic West (*al-Gharb al-Islamī*) in the pre-modern period generally refers to the Maghrib and al-Andalus together. The Maghrib consists of a group of countries in North Africa, including Tunisia, Algeria, and Morocco, and more marginally Mauritania and Libya. One of the unifying characteristics of the Maghrib as a region is the presence of Berber or Amazigh language and culture. The Maghrib can be further divided into the regions of Middle or Central Maghrib and Far Maghrib. This last term, which coincides with the Arabic, *al-Maghrib al-Aqṣā*, and is roughly coterminous with modern Morocco and the Western Sahara, is widely used below. Al-Andalus is the Arabic term for the Iberian Peninsula, which I use consistently and occasionally substitute with Islamic Iberia, its translation. I do not use the more popular Muslim Spain, because it omits Portugal.

 | DOI 10.1163/9789004279841_002

of al-Andalus by a more homogeneous and conservative Maghrib.[4] This narrative, moreover, was predicated on the grand narrative of *reconquista*, the rise of Europe, and eclipse of Islam – unfortunately and perhaps inevitably current today, even if not among all specialists.

From the mid-1970s several voices have emerged questioning the reductionism of this view, which has tended to omit, among other things, the place of Berbers in history and the fluidity of the relationship between the peninsula and North Africa. These historians have attempted to do justice to the complexity of the region's social development during the period of Islamic rule in Iberia.[5] While the results of these inquiries have been compelling, on the whole, Western scholars have favored the study of Iberia and the interaction and influence that Islam and Islamicate culture had on Europe. As a result, the Maghrib has been cast as a marginal region within Mediterranean and Islamic history. This is true, moreover, not only within Western historiography, but also within the Arab-Islamic historiographical and literary traditions, in which the Mashriq has traditionally claimed centrality.[6] In an effort to counter this trend, *Law and the Islamization of Morocco under the Almoravids* adopts a perspective centered on the Maghrib and seeks to complement the growing understanding of a period that signified a clear historical turning point – the import of which

4 An example from one of the standard histories of medieval Spain reads: The Almoravids, who covered their faces with a veil, were fanatical puritans who insisted upon a rigorous observance of Muslim law, condemning the use of wine, the imposition of taxes not sanctioned by the Koran, and the custom of having more than four wives permitted by law. Under the leadership of Yusuf ibn Tashufin (1061–1106), a rude Berber endowed with great military talent, who called himself emir of the Muslims (*amir al-muslimin*) and acknowledged the supremacy of the Abbasid caliphs of Baghdad, the Almoravids conquered Morocco and western Algeria… The contrast between the Almoravids and the petty kings of al-Andalus could not have been greater. The former were barbarian nomads who viewed the latter as effete lovers of luxury who bore their religious obligations lightly. In summoning the Almoravids to their aid the *reyes de taifas* were running the risk of self-destruction, but they had no other choice. Al-Mutamid of Seville summed up the feelings of his colleagues when he remarked that he preferred to herd camels for the Almoravids than to guard the pigsty of Alfonso VI. Joseph F. O'Callaghan, *A History of Medieval Spain* (Ithaca: Cornell University Press, 1975), 208.

5 Widely seen as one of the pioneering studies investigating the Berber presence in al-Andalus is Pierre Guichard, *Al-Andalus: estructura antropológica de una sociedad islámica en Occidente* (Barcelona: Barral Editores, 1976).

6 Marginalization of the history of the Islamic West in Western and Arab-Islamic historiography is not coincidental. Anglo-American historians of the pre-modern period have focused mostly on the Islamic "central" lands of the Near East. For historical reasons, French and Spanish historians have devoted much more attention to the region.

perhaps only modern Maghribī historians have been aware. Characterized by a marked intensification of urbanization and the development of institutions associated with Islamic urban civilization of the Middle Period,[7] the era spanning from the second half of the fifth/eleventh century to the middle of the sixth/twelfth witnessed not only the rise of the first Berber-Islamic empire (i.e., the region's first large indigenous Islamic state) but also the first articulation of a political community that, in many ways, laid the foundations for the modern state of Morocco. Seen from this perspective, the political experience of the Far Maghrib[8] has been characterized by remarkable institutional longevity, singular in the experience of Arab-Islamic world.

The rise of the Almoravids in the Far Maghrib transformed the region from frontier zone to regional center. Before this, during the first three and a half centuries after the Arab conquests, the Far Maghrib had been overshadowed by Qayrāwan to the east, in Ifrīqiya, and Cordoba to the north, in southern Iberia. There had been cities between Qayrawān and Cordoba in the pre-Almoravid period, to be sure. Several Roman cities, such as Tangier, Ceuta, and Oran, survived into the Islamic era, and the city of Fez was foundational in more ways than one – its appearance in the late second/early ninth century under an alliance of Zanāta tribes and the Sayyid Idrissid family-line created one of the region's spiritual axes.[9] Nevertheless, in the first centuries of the Islamic era, the Far Maghrib lagged behind al-Andalus and Ifrīqiya in terms of economic and urban development. Much of the region was described in contemporary sources as frontier-like, its principal economic activities being slave-raiding and the extraction of a few commodities.[10] Adding to its liminality, during the fourth/tenth century, the Far Maghrib was the site of the proxy struggle between the Umayyad Caliphate of Cordoba and the Fāṭimid

---

7 Following Hodgson's periodization, the Islamic Middle Period is 945–1258. Marshall G. S Hodgson, *The Venture of Islam: Conscience and History in a World Civilization* (Chicago: University of Chicago Press, 1974). On urban development in the Far Maghrib more generally, see Michael Brett, "The Islamisation of Morocco from the Arabs to the Almoravids," in *Ibn Khaldun and the Medieval Maghrib*, ed. Michael Brett, Varorium Collected Studies (London: Ashgate, 1999), chap. 1.

8 *Al-Maghrib al-Aqṣā*, separated from the Middle Maghrib by the Middle and High Atlas Mountains.

9 On this concept, see Amira K. Bennison, "Liminal States: Morocco and the Iberian Frontier between the Twelfth and Nineteenth Centuries," in *North Africa, Islam and the Mediterranean World: From the Almoravids to the Algerian War*, ed. Julia Clancy-Smith (New York: Frank Cass Publishers, 2001), 11–28.

10 Jamil M. Abun-Nasr, *A History of the Maghrib in the Islamic Period* (Cambridge: Cambridge University Press, 1987), 33.

Imamate, based first in Mahdia and later in Cairo.[11] Efforts by each to extend their power into the region, with the consequent alignment of proxies and allies, were powerfully destabilizing forces.[12]

The religio-political bases of the Almoravid movement originated in the missionary activity of Mālikī scholars from Ifrīqiya. The defense of orthopraxy as defined by Mālikism had become invigorated and central to the identity of this group as a result of the ideological contest waged, and ultimate victory against, Ismāʿīlism in Ifrīqiya.[13] In its earliest stages in the western Sahara, the "corrective" Almoravid movement focused its attention on the basics of Sunnī-Mālikī identification through ritual practice.[14] The targets of the initial thrust of Almoravid armed expansion were local unorthoprax/unorthodox communities, such as the Sufrī Khārijīs of Sijilmāsa[15] and the Barghawāṭa of the Atlantic coastal plain. Behind this ideologically-inspired armed struggle for the orthodoxification[16] of territories gradually coming under Almoravid control, lay powerful economic forces that would draw the movement northward, into the historically more urbanized regions of the northern Maghrib and, especially, al-Andalus, almost all of which would be conquered by the Almoravids within forty years of their formation. As noted above, much attention has been devoted to the dynamics of the Almoravid presence in Iberia, especially as it partook in the epic of southward expansion by the Christian kingdoms of the north of the peninsula. These kingdoms would make their most significant advances in the period between 478/1085 and 646/1248, roughly the first half of which took place under Almoravid rule. The Almoravids thus participated as major players in the Mediterranean wars between Muslims and Christians. And, in undeniably significant ways, they embody the combination of religious fervor and militancy that so characterized this struggle. Focusing on this militancy, however, does not do justice to the story.

Historians' preoccupation with the inter-religious struggle related to the Christian expansion or *reconquista* has eclipsed, among other things, the

---

11 The Fāṭimid Dynasty (297–567/909–1171) had its capital at Mahdia from 308/920, moved to Cairo from 358/969.

12 One such alignment was the Maghrāwā and Banū Ifrān (Zanāta) with the Umayyads, and the Ṣanhāja of Ifrīqiya with the Fāṭimids. Jamil M. Abun-Nasr, *A History of the Maghrib in the Islamic Period*, 64.

13 Jamil M. Abun-Nasr, *A History of the Maghrib in the Islamic Period*, 68. On this see also Heinz Halm, *Empire of the Mahdi: The Rise of the Fatimids* (Leiden: Brill, 1996).

14 On social identity construction and ritual, see D. A. Marshall, "Behavior, Belonging, and Belief: A Theory of Ritual Practice," *Sociological Theory* 20, no. 3 (2002): 360–80.

15 Of the Banū Midrār dynasty *c.* 208–366/823–824 - 976–977.

16 Orthopraxification is more correct but unwieldy.

major changes that swept the Far Maghrib as it became the political center of the Almoravid state. Urban centers that would come to define the region – most significantly Marrakesh – appeared in the Almoravid period, as did the principal features of the region's pre-existing cities, including Sijilmāsa, Fez, and Ceuta. Burgeoning long-distance trade brought the Far Maghrib into the Mediterranean as a major political-economic entity; the currency it established would become the gold standard of the western Mediterranean and be traded as far east as China. From these facts alone, it is plain that the economic landscape of the Far Maghrib was profoundly and irreversibly transformed in the Almoravid period. It should come as no surprise, then, that several of the social movements and institutions that would come to define the region are known to have originated in this period. These include the broad spectrum of practices, institutions, and beliefs subsumed under the rubric of "Ṣūfism," as well as the learning network and judicial and administrative institutions associated with the Islamic legal school of Mālikism, to this day an essential component of the region's legal traditions.

In spite of the striking significance of such changes, however, the social history of the Far Maghrib in the Almoravid period remains largely unexplored. Aside from a few pioneering exceptions, the study of the multiple facets of this transformation, and its repercussions in and interaction with the wider region, have been subordinated either to a reductionist narrative whose principal characters are Mālikī fundamentalists fighting Christians and persecuting religious minorities (read: holy war and intolerance), or to the more elaborate but still shallow political and military history of great leaders, conquests, and tribal alliances forged and failed. Even if somewhat overstated here, this description of modern historiography touching on the Almoravids is, on the whole, I believe, fair.[17] One of the principal aims of this book, therefore, is to investigate some of the major facets of this neglected social history; I will do so through the examination of the rich source provided by consultative legal texts (fatwās and *nawāzil*[18]) and the development of the social institutions and discursive practices they entail.

---

17 Especially noticeable when compared to the more sophisticated understanding of other regions of the pre-modern Islamic world, such as Iberia or Mamluk Egypt.

18 Sing. *nāzila*, "case." This term is most often encountered in plural form, which I use throughout, instead of *nāzila*s. Fatwā, pl. *fatāwā*, is a non-binding legal opinion by a jurisconsult or muftī. Compilations of *fatāwā* and *nawāzil* constitute a genre of legal writing, consisting of collections of authoritative and significant opnions and cases (because difficult, influencial, or otherwise notable). The terms are distinct since they refer to different parts of the legal process: 1. an opinion by a muftī (fatwā) and 2. the case as a whole (*nāzila*). This distinction is underscored by the texts of the two jurists who are the subject

The historiographical corpus that provides grounding for this project is that which takes Islamic social institutions – their history and relationship to culture – as its object of study. Once perceived as inscrutable and immutable (even arbitrary), the long history of Islamic institutions, their development and adaptation to an astonishing diversity of environments (producing an equally astonishing diversity of institutional forms and practices) has become better appreciated and more sophisticated over the past few decades, assuming a central place in the study of Islamic societies as a whole.[19] Of particular importance to the present inquiry is the study of the discursive tradition of consultation in Islamic law, a textual practice associated with, but not limited to, the term fatwā.[20] The genre of legal writing associated with this term is particularly compelling for social historians because of its responsiveness to and grounding in changing social conditions. Enthusiasm for Fatwā Studies, which has developed substantially since the early 1990s, has yielded both increasingly sophisticated models for the interaction between Islamic law and society and a growing corpus of textual sources, editions of which are appearing with growing frequency.[21]

---

of this study: the fatwās of Ibn Rushd consist of his judicial opinions, whereas the *nawāzil* of Qāḍī ʿIyāḍ comprise his own opinions as well as the opinions of muftīs he consulted as judge presiding over a case (as can be seen in Chapter Three). A further distinction between the two terms relates to the region and/or dominant legal school or madhhab: the term *nawāzil* is more popular in the Islamic West and in the usage of the Mālikī School (in which, to some extent, the terms are interchangeable), whereas fatwā is current elsewhere and in modern usage.

19 Examples (from a very large bibliography) of such work include P. J. Bearman, et al., *The Islamic School of Law: Evolution, Devolution, and Progress* (Cambridge, Mass: Islamic Legal Studies Program, Harvard Law School: Distributed by Harvard University Press, 2005); Jonathan Berkey, *The Transmission of Knowledge in Medieval Cairo: A Social History of Islamic Education* (Princeton, N.J.: Princeton University Press, 1992); Leonor E. Fernandes, *The Evolution of a Sufi Institution in Mamluk Egypt: The Khanqah*, Islamkundliche Untersuchungen (K. Schwarz, 1988). These focus on the development of legal, educational, and Ṣūfī institutions and their interaction with specific geographical, cultural, and historical contexts. Institutional development is made central to the interpretation of Islamic history in both Jonathan Berkey, *The Formation of Islam: Religion and Society in the Near East, 600–1800* (Cambridge; New York: Cambridge University Press, 2003), and Ira Lapidus, *A History of Islamic Societies*, 2nd ed. (New York: Cambridge University Press, 2002).

20 On the definition and conceptualization of discursive traditions in Islam, see O. Anjum, "Islam as a Discursive Tradition: Talal Asad and His Interlocutors," *Comparative Studies of South Asia, Africa and the Middle East* 2, no. 3 (2007): 656–92.

21 Muhammad Khalid Masud, et al., *Islamic Legal Interpretation: Muftis and Their Fatwas* (Cambridge, Mass: Harvard University Press, 1996). Masud et al. present an important

Law and the Islamization of Morocco under the Almoravids explores the intersection of these two historiographical currents: i.e., the social history of the Almoravid Far Maghrib and the development of the discursive tradition of legal consultation, through an examination of consultative communications between jurists of al-Andalus and the Far Maghrib, that is, through a technical correspondence between a region in which this textual tradition was established and a region in which it was appearing. Each text analyzed below originated from questions that arose in the Far Maghrib in the first quarter of the sixth/twelfth century. The texts are further unified by the authorship of the responses to the questions, as almost all are by one of the preeminent jurisconsults or muftīs of the period, Ibn Rushd al-Jadd of Cordoba. The book is thus an examination and reassessment of the relationship between al-Andalus and the Far Maghrib, viewed from an angle opposite to that which has garnered most scholarly attention. Analysis of the texts from this perspective reveals a process of expansion of Islamic institutions into what had been a borderland or frontier. Through the consultative correspondence analyzed below, the institutional knowledge of the religio-political establishment of al-Andalus can be seen to move into the Far Maghrib, at once mobilized for and adapting to the needs of the transforming region. This book examines the nature of this process; the

collection of studies of fatwās, from diverse periods and across the Islamic world, testament to the interest and diversity of work with this genre of legal document – the fatwā – as principal point of inquiry. Much has been produced since then, overcoming the need to defend and justify such studies (the result of the lingering, and superficial, Weberian view that Islamic law was the "*procedurally* irrational" result of individual considerations based on social context. David S. Powers, *Law, Society, and Culture in the Maghrib, 1300–1500*, Cambridge Studies in Islamic Civilization (Cambridge; New York: Cambridge University Press, 2002), 1. The impressions projected from debates over the reliability of legal documents in the historiography of the Latin West are likely a contributing factor). Studies dealing with the legal tradition of the Islamic West that I have found useful include: Wael Hallaq, "Murder in Cordoba: Ijtihād, Iftā' and the Evolution of Substantive Law in Medieval Islam," *Acta Orientalia* 55 (1994): 55–83; Delfina Serrano, "Legal Practice in an Andalusī-Maghribī Source from the Twelfth Century CE: The Madhāhib al-ḥukkām fī nawāzil al-aḥkām," *Islamic Law and Society* 7, no. 2 (2000): 187–234; David S. Powers, *Law, Society, and Culture in the Maghrib, 1300–1500*; P. Cressier, et al., eds. *L'urbanisme dans l'Occident musulman au Moyen Age: aspects juridiques* (Madrid: Casa de Velázquez Consejo Superior de Investigaciones Científicas, 2000); Kathryn A. Miller, *Guardians of Islam: Religious Authority and Muslim Communities of Late Medieval Spain* (New York: Columbia University Press, 2008). Editions of Ibn Rushd's fatwās appeared in 1987 and 1992 and of 'Iyāḍ's *Nawāzil* in 1990 with a second, corrected edition appearing in 1997. More on my own use of these editions is discussed on the section on the book's structure at the end of the Introduction.

analysis of the microhistories of each question/case opens a window onto the larger socio-historical landscape.

Law and the Islamization of Morocco under the Almoravids argues that, far from serving merely as a religious ideology for mobilization and military expansion (through jihād), the institution of Mālikism in the Far Maghrib developed to meet the specific practical needs of the urban transformation of the fifth/eleventh and sixth/twelfth centuries. These needs, moreover, did not respond to the top-down demands of a military administration (i.e., as a kind of coercion through moral legitimation) but involved, rather, a two-way exchange or interactive process. While the administrative needs of the state were a key component in the development of the, principally, "legal" institution of Mālikism, analysis of the texts below demonstrates how this development consisted, to a significant degree, of incorporating self-regulating practices.[22] Another key dimension to the development of these institutions, as betrayed by the texts, was their role in shaping and cultivating the flow of knowledge through a learning network, the basic social contours of which were defined by the relationship between teachers and students.[23] We thus find that a substantial portion of the consultative correspondence was devoted to learning through debate and clarification of practical and theoretical questions. Furthermore, many of the questions reveal the nature of the changing social practices of a region whose identity was in transformation as it came under a unified polity and was integrated into the larger Islamic world. The success of the social institution of Mālikism, as it was adopted, developed, and transformed in the Far Maghrib, helps to explain important dimensions of the relationship between the Far Maghrib and al-Andalus, from where the Almoravids and their leadership so often took cue and sought guidance.

Neither this relationship nor the larger process it involved were simple. It was complex and fraught with opposition and contestation, both in al-Andalus and the Far Marghib. The social history of the Far Maghrib has long been confused, however, with its dynastic history (i.e., the movement from Almoravids

22 One of the important functions of these practices, and the first encountered below, was to regulate growing commercial exchange.

23 On the formation and context of Islamic learning networks, see George Makdisi, *The Rise of Colleges: Institutions of Learning in Islam and the West* (Edinburgh: Edinburgh University Press, 1981). Jonathan Berkey, *The Transmission of Knowledge in Medieval Cairo: A Social History of Islamic Education.* On the development specifically of Mālikism as the dominant tradition of "teachers and pupils" in al-Andalus, see Maribel Fierro, "Proto-Malikis, Malikis, and Reformed Malikis in al-Andalus," in *The Islamic School of Law: Evolution, Devolution, and Progress*, ed. Peri Bearman, et al. (Cambridge: Harvard University Press, 2005).

to Almohads to Marinids). This has been the result, most likely, of a desire to account for the tribal alliances and reconfigurations these dynastic changes implied, as well as for the significant religio-political and ideological differences that came with dynastic change. *Law and the Islamization of Morocco under the Almoravids* argues that the institutions born with the urban transformation of the fifth/eleventh and sixth/twelfth centuries transcended these dynastic vicissitudes, even while being affected by them.

2 Historical and Historiographical Background[24]

The extent of the spread of Islam into the southern Far Maghrib and western Sahara, the character of Islam practiced there in its earliest form, and the causes for the irruption of the Saharan Ṣanhāja into the Northern Maghrib and al-Andalus have all been subject to debate. Sources for the origins of the Almoravid movement and for the social history of the greater Almoravid Far Maghrib are scant and difficult, to a great extent because the events associated with this social transformation occurred at a turning-point: a historical "beginning," eliciting descriptions such as "true surprise of history,"[25] on the farthest frontier of the Arab-Islamic world, and in a profoundly diglossic environment.[26] The dominance of a classical Arabo-centric historiography along with long-standing partiality toward Roman archeology in the modern period have compounded the problem. The historical narrative that we possess remains largely based on chronicles and geographical writing, little of which is contemporaneous with the events.

In the elite and individually-driven historiography of Maghribī-Andalusī chronicles and biographies, one of the traditional narratives of the Almoravids begins with Yaḥyā b. Ibrāhīm, a Judāla Ṣanhāja who took control of an existing Ṣanhāja tribal confederation in the western Sahara.[27] Historians have

24 The three principal chapters below are all prefaced by historical and historiographical information, relevant to material in each. To avoid repetition, in this section, I present only a general background dicussion.

25 María Jesús Viguera Molíns, "Historia Política," in *El retroceso territorial de al-Andalus: almorávides y almohades, siglos XI al XIII*, ed. María Jesús Vigerua Molíns, Historia de España Menéndez Pidal (Madrid: Espasa Calpe, 1997), 41. For a recent, accessible history of the Almoravids, see Ronald A. Messier, *The Almoravids and the Meanings of Jihad* (Oxford: Praeger, 2010).

26 Diglossia, defined as situations in which two or more languages are separately and systematically employed in certain domains or events.

27 María Jesús Viguera Molíns, "Historia Política," 47. Yaḥyā b. Ibrāhīm appears to have wrested leadership from the Lamtūna, a tribal group that had traditionally exercised

speculated that Yaḥyā b. Ibrāhīm undertook the pilgrimage to Mecca in 427/1035–6 in an effort to shore up his relatively new position of authority (or that of his group) through the vehicle of religious ideological cohesion. For this gesture to be socially intelligible, Islamic religio-political discourse must have been developed to some extent in the region by this time; Islamic practice, on the other hand, appears to have been found "wanting" and was mixed with local customary religious practices in a kind of creative interaction.[28] Of special note is what appears to have been the mounting competition in the region comprised today of Mauritania, the Western Sahara, and southern Morocco, between the groups, broadly defined, of the Soninke Kings of Ghana, the Zanāta Maghrāwa, and the Ṣanhāja confederation of which Yaḥyā b. Ibrāhīm had become leader.[29] This competition was over control of a trade route on which these groups can be said, somewhat schematically, to have exercised influence at three key points: 1.) on the southern edge of the Sahara, where the kings of Ghana had captured the urban center of Awdaghusht[30] sometime in the late fourth/tenth or first half of the fifth/eleventh centuries;[31] 2.) on the northern edge, where the Maghrāwa controlled Sijilmāsa from the middle of the fourth/tenth century;[32] and 3.) the region in between, where Yaḥyā b. Ibrāhīm's confederation was located. The axis on which these three points lay traces a trade route on which the commerce of gold and salt was dominant and growing in this period and defined the space where the Almoravids' political power would first develop.[33]

---

leadership of the confederation. Jamil M. Abun-Nasr, *A History of the Maghrib in the Islamic Period*, 79.

28 Bosch Vilá writes that Yaḥyā b. Ibrāhīm performed the pilgrimage in imitation of Tarsīna, his Lamtūnī predecessor. Jacinto Bosch Vilá, *Los Almorávides*, introductory study by Emilio Molina López (Granada: Universidad de Granada, 1998), 49. Descriptions of the Barghawāṭa and the Ṣufrī Khārijī Midrārids of Sijilmāsa in al-Bakrī and Ibn Hawqal are cited as evidence for such syncretism. For a recent study of the Midrārids see Paul M. Love, "The Sufris of Sijilmasa: Toward a History of the Midrarids," *The Journal of North African Studies* 15, no. 2 (2010): 173–88.

29 María Jesús Viguera Molíns, "Historia Política," 47.

30 North of the Senegal River Valley, 750 km east of modern Nouakchott.

31 The archeological site of Awdaghusht is on the tentative list of UNESCO World Heritage sites. http://whc.unesco.org/en/tentativelists/1547/

32 James A. Miller, "Trading through Islam: The Interconnections of Sijilmasa, Ghana and the Almoravid Movement," in *North Africa, Islam and the Mediterranean World: From the Almoravids to the Algerian War*, ed. Julia Clancy-Smith (London: Frank Cass, 2001), 41.

33 The importance of this trade to West Africa, the Maghrib, and the Mediterranean, as well as its importance to the Almoravids who were seen to have fostered it greatly, has long been appreciated. The classic study is E. W. Bovill, *The Golden Trade of the Moors: West*

The key episode for Almoravid history in Yaḥyā b. Ibrāhīm's pilgrimage did not occur, as might be expected, in the Islamic East, but in Qayrawān, in Ifrīqiya,[34] a city characterized by a vibrant Islamic intellectual milieu. Qayrawān had been on the frontline of the Ismāʿīlī "challenge" from which the Sunnī legal school of Mālikism had emerged as a dominant popular social force with missionary inclinations.[35] Sometime between 427/1035 and 430/1039,[36] on his return from Mecca, Yaḥyā b. Ibrāhīm met with Abū ʿImrān al-Fāsī (d. 430/1039), a key figure in the development of the Mālikī tradition in the Islamic West.[37] Yaḥyā asked him for help in bringing more robust knowledge of Islam to his homeland and al-Fāsī recommended a student, Wajjāj b. Zalwī.[38] The latter, in turn, put Yaḥyā b. Ibrāhīm in touch with his own student, ʿAbd Allāh b. Yāsīn (d. 451/1059). This last is the man credited with founding the Almoravid movement in the western Sahara. A Ṣanhāja of the Judāla tribe, Ibn Yāsīn was said to have been a learned Mālikī jurist or *faqīh* (although al-Bakrī describes him as largely ignorant of the finer points of religious doctrine and Mālikī jurisprudence).[39] An alternate version of events, put forth by Qāḍī ʿIyāḍ, omits Yaḥyā b. Ibrāhīm and al-Fāsī altogether and credits one Jawhar b. Sakkum with performing the pilgrimage and asking for help from Wajjāj. H.T. Norris considered this the most dependable account (he suggested that Yaḥyā and Jawhar traveled together and had a falling out upon their return).[40]

African Kingdoms in the Fourteenth Century, 2nd ed. (Princeton: M. Weiner Publishers, 1995). An engaging recent study of trans-Saharan trade is Ralph A. Austen, *Trans-Saharan Africa in World History*, The New Oxford World History (Oxford: Oxford Uiversity Press, 2010).

34 Modern day Tunisia.

35 Jamil M. Abun-Nasr, *A History of the Maghrib in the Islamic Period*, 77.

36 María Jesús Viguera Molíns, "Historia Política," 48.

37 M. Fierro credits Abū ʿImrān al-Fāsī for playing a major role in diffusion of Ashʿarism in the Islamic West. Maribel Fierro, "La Religión," in *El retroceso territorial de al-Andalus: almorávides y almohades. Siglos XI al XIII*, ed. María Jesús Vigerua Molíns, Historia de España Menéndez Pidal (Madrid: Espasa Calpe, 1997), 437.

38 Or Wajāj b. Zallū. Maribel Fierro, "La Religión." Wajjāj b. Zalwī is said to have established a *ribāṭ* in the Sūs. Jamil M. Abun-Nasr, *A History of the Maghrib in the Islamic Period*, 79.

39 N. Levtzion, and J. F. P. Hopkins, eds. *Corpus of Early Arabic Sources for West African History* (Princeton: Markus Wiener Publishers, 2000), 75. My thanks to the anonymous reviewer who pointed this out and reminded me of the importance of H. T. Norris's article, cited in the following note.

40 H. T. Norris, "New Evidence on the Life of ʿAbdullāh b. Yāsīn and the Origins of the Almoravid Movement," *Journal of African History* 12, no. 2 (1971): 255–68. By the same author, and more generally on Saharan and Berber history, see H. T. Norris, *Saharan Myth*

While there is some uncertainty over the exact dates and personalities involved, what is significant in this general narrative is the second critical axis of Almoravid development that it traces: one following the chain of Islamic learning from Qayrawān to Sijilmāsa – where Wajjāj was said to be from – to the western Sahara, where Ibn Yāsīn began to preach the orthopraxis of the Mālikī tradition that Abū ʿImrān al-Fāsī had championed in Qayrawān. Commercial ties between Qayrawān and Sijilmāsa – political vicissitudes notwithstanding – had been firmly established since the fourth/tenth century. The eleventh century trans-Saharan commercial activity associated with the rise of the Almoravids made these ties stronger.

Once arrived in the western Sahara, Ibn Yāsīn, together with Yaḥyā b. Ibrāhīm (said to have repudiated five of his nine wives to conform with the new ideology),[41] exercised growing political and ideological control over other groups of the western Sahara until the death of Yaḥyā b. Ibrāhīm, when the Judāla banished Ibn Yāsīn (presumably because of the political threat he represented).[42] A Lamtūna leader[43] took him in, thereby establishing what would become the core of the Almoravid movement: a missionary and militarized Mālikī ideological movement led by the Lamtūna. The name Almoravid originated in this early period when the Lamtūna squared off against the Judāla.[44] The question of whether the *ribāṭ* implicit in "*al-Murābiṭ*" refers to a real place or, metaphorically, to an activity (religiously inspired war or struggle) has generated some debate, with recent consensus favoring the latter definition.[45]

Ensuing Almoravid political and military success consisted of consolidating the confederation of western Saharan tribes and conquering Sijilmāsa in 445/1053 after siege,[46] followed by Awdaghusht in 446/1054, as a result securing a monopoly on western trans-Saharan trade. The conquest of the southern end of this trade route was decisive for Almoravid success. The nature and

---

and Saga (Oxford: Clarendon Press, 1972); H. T. Norris, *The Berbers in Arabic literature*, Arab Background Series (London: Longman, 1982).

41 Jamil M. Abun-Nasr, *A History of the Maghrib in the Islamic Period*, 80.

42 María Jesús Viguera Molíns, "Historia Política," 48.

43 Abū Zakariyyāʾ Yaḥyā b. ʿUmar b. Bulankayn.

44 María Jesús Viguera Molíns, "Historia Política," 48. H. T. Norris suggests that it reffers to the *ribāṭ* of Wajjāj b. al-Zalwī in the Sūs, the movement, lead by Wajjāj's student represented an extension of the influence of this *ribāṭ* southward. H. T. Norris, "New Evidence on the Life of ʿAbdullāh b. Yāsīn and the Origins of the Almoravid Movement."

45 Maribel Fierro, "La Religión," 439; María Jesús Viguera Molíns, "Historia Política," 48.

46 Where a sympathetic Ṣanhāja population rebelled against their Maghrāwa/Zanāta leader Masʿūd b. Wanūdī. Jacinto Bosch Vilá, *Los Almorávides*, 66.

consequences of the competition with the kingdom of Ghana, however, as well as the extent of the diffusion of Islam in the Senegal and Niger River Valleys, has been subject to debate – due again to the paucity of textual and material sources. D. Conrad and H. Fisher argued that an Almoravid conquest, in fact, never occurred. This interpretation of events was countered by later scholars, such as S. Burkhlater, who argued that, whatever the nature of the "conquest" in the south, the indisputable influence and success of the Almoravids in securing West African gold and circulating it widely necessitated a high degree of political control.[47]

With the death in 447/1055[48] of the Lamtūnī leader[49] who had embraced Ibn Yāsīn, military leadership passed to the deceased leader's brother, Abū Bakr b. ʿUmar, who was recognized amīr of Sijilmāsa in 450/1058.[50] The conquest of Sijilmāsa, the northern point on the Saharan trade route, had been momentous for the movement's future in the Far Maghrib, as it opened the door to a network of urban centers (many of which until then had been controlled by Maghrāwa Berbers). With armies commanded by Abū Bakr's cousin, the famous Yūsuf b. Tāshufīn, the Almoravids captured the Draʿ and Sūs valleys[51] and moved north of the High Atlas, capturing Aghmāt in 450/1058.[52] From here they pushed northward against the Barghawāṭa: a Berber group of the coastal plain who presented the first significant military challenge for the Almoravids and against whom Ibn Yāsīn, spiritual leader of the movement for seventeen years, died fighting on I Jumāda 451/July 1059.[53] The process by which the Almoravids had conquered most of the areas of the southern Far Maghrib to this point had likely combined the use of force with the building of alliances. This process is illustrated by Ibn ʿIdhārī's account of the foundation

---

47 David Conrad, and Humprey Fisher, "The Conquest that Never was: Ghana and the Almoravids, 1076. I. The External Arabic Sources," *History in Africa* 9 (1982): 21–59; David Conrad, and Humprey Fisher, "The Conquest that Never was: Ghana and the Almoravids, 1076. II. The Local Oral Sources," *History in Africa* 10 (1983): 53–78; Sheryl L. Burkhalter, "Listening for Silences in Almoravid History: Another Reading of "The Conquest That Never Was,"" *History in Africa* 19 (1992): 103–31.

48 María Jesús Viguera Molíns, "Historia Política," 49.

49 Yaḥyā b. ʿUmar b. Bulankayn.

50 María Jesús Viguera Molíns, "Historia Política," 49.

51 Where they took the town of Tārūdānt. Jacinto Bosch Vilá, *Los Almorávides*, 84.

52 Jacinto Bosch Vilá, *Los Almorávides*, 89.

53 María Jesús Viguera Molíns, "Historia Política," 49. Ibn Yāsīn appears to have had a short lived successor named Sulayman b. Addā. Jacinto Bosch Vilá, *Los Almorávides*, 93. For more on the Barghawāṭa see John Iskander, "Devout Heretics: The Barghawata in Maghribi Historiography," *The Journal of North African Studies* 12, no. 1 (2007): 37–53.

of Marrakesh: When Aghmāt had become overcrowded as a result of economic expansion and immigration, Abū Bakr b. ʿUmar reached a compromise in 462/1070[54] with the two most prominent tribal groups of the immediate region and chose the site of what would become the Almoravid capital and most striking example of the region's urban transformation.[55]

As the early Almoravid state expanded northward, it encountered urban societies with a longer experience of Arab-Islamic urban institutions. All of the northern Maghribī cities they conquered – Fez in 455/1063, Tlemcen in Ṣafar 468/October 1075, Tangier in 471/1078–1079, and Ceuta in I Rabīʿ 477/July 1084 – had experience with Islamic urban institutions. Ceuta, an important Mediterranean port, moreover, had been the foothold in the Maghrib of the Andalusī Umayyads, from where they led their campaigns against the Fāṭimids in the fourth/tenth century.[56] But it was across the strait of Gibraltar, in al-Andalus, where the Almoravids would encounter the cities with the most developed Islamic institutions, paramount of which was Cordoba, a major metropolis with commercial ties across the Mediterranean and former caliphal capital with over three and half centuries of life as an Islamic city.

The foundation of Marrakesh followed by the encounter with the more urban civilizations to the north would spell a turning point in Almoravid history, one of the effects of which was to split the Almoravid state into two distinct spheres, northern and southern. This split is illustrated by the reports of the episode that led to Yūsuf b. Tāshufīn's ascension to command: When, soon after founding Marrakesh in 462/1070, Abū Bakr b. ʿUmar was called back south to deal with a rebellion,[57] he felt compelled to repudiate his wife, Zaynab bint Isḥāq al-Nafzāwiyya[58] (d. 464/1071–2), likely due to the local prominence of her family, and marry her to his cousin, Yūsuf b. Tāshufīn. The arrangement was meant to be temporary but proved permanent. Upon Abū Bakr's return in 465/1072–3, Yūsuf b. Tāshufīn met him outside the city and discreetly let Abū Bakr know that he would not be ceding command. Whether in fear of discord or for some other reason, Abū Bakr told Yūsuf, according to the author of the *Qirṭās*, that he was merely visiting and would head back south to lead the expansion along the southern frontier against the Kingdom of Ghana. Abū Bakr

54 María Jesús Viguera Molíns, "Historia Política," 49.

55 Marrakesh would also become the Almohad capital.

56 Halima Ferhat, *Sabta des origines au xivème siècle* (Rabat: Ministère des affaires culturelles, 1993), 70–84.

57 Jacinto Bosch Vilá, *Los Almorávides*, 96.

58 Who had been the wife of the Maghrāwa chief/lord of Aghmāt, Laqqūt b. Yūsuf, and who belonged to an influential family of Qayrawānī origin. Jacinto Bosch Vilá, *Los Almorávides*, 90.

b. ʿUmar would remain nominal leader of the Almoravids. On the whole, however, he, and, in a sense, the entire southern region of the Almoravid state, disappeared from the history our sources privilege. The Kingdom of Ghana is said to have been defeated by the Almoravids but to have later regained the lost territory. Abū Bakr is reported to have died fighting in otherwise unknown circumstances in 480/1087–8,[59] and the institutional landscape of the far south – south of the High Atlas, that is – would remain distinct from that north of the mountains. Certainly the markedly distinct geography of the two regions was a factor; the extreme aridity of the south historically made state formation difficult. And while Bosch Vilá writes that the desert Ṣanhāja confederation fragmented and the Ghanans retook possession of Awdaghusht, it also appears clear that the Almoravids retained enough political influence there to control the flow of gold.[60]

Under the command of Yūsuf b. Tāshufīn, the Almoravid state would turn dynastic and imperial in ambition and extension.[61] The articulation of Berber-Islamic authority under Yūsuf b. Tāshufin (further developed by his son) was the first on this scale and had lasting regional impact. It effectively paved the way for two ensuing dynasties, altogether comprising over four centuries of Berber-Islamic rule.[62] The urban landscape of the Far Maghrib, moreover, would be transformed under the Almoravids, much of it by direct intervention of Yūsuf and his son ʿAlī. Among other projects, they commissioned the first great mosque and the city ramparts of Marrakesh, the expansion of the Qarawiyyīn mosque and unification and fortification of Fez, the great mosque

59 Jacinto Bosch Vilá, *Los Almorávides*, 100–01.

60 Sheryl L. Burkhalter, "Listening for Silences in Almoravid History: Another Reading of "The Conquest That Never Was,"" 119. Burkhalter notes the significant detail that, while the chronicles pay little attention to Abū Bakr and his leadership in the south after leaving Yūsuf in charge in Marrakesh, other sources – including Mauritanian oral traditions and fourteenth-century Catalan maps bearing "giant painted figures" of Abū Bakr in the Sahara – point to his continued and lasting importance as founder of the dynasty and as support for Yūsuf's activities in the north.

61 While the dynasty, after Abū Bakr, consisted of a succession of five leaders, Yūsuf and ʿAlī's reigns (1071–1106 and 1106–1143 respectively) would be the defining ones of the empire's experience. ʿAlī's successor, Tāshufīn, only reigned for two years. Tāshufīn's son, Ibrahīm, was named amīr as a child and was ousted by his uncle Isḥāq b. ʿAlī who died a year an a half later, in 1147, when the Almohads conquered Marrakesh.

62 While the Almoravids' successors, the Almohads and the Marinids, were different from the Almoravids in important ways, there is significant continuity among the three, both in terms of their articulation of religio-political authority (and the specific challenges each faced), the bases of their economies, and the scope of their military activities.

of Tlemcen, and the doubling in size of the great mosque of Ceuta.[63] This transformation was also marked by the appearance of a cosmopolitan architectural style in the Maghrib, much of which occurred as a result of the unification of the Far Maghrib with al-Andalus (the first political unification of the two territories since the days of the Umayyad caliphate of Damascus).[64]

By the last quarter of the fifth/eleventh century, the Almoravids had emerged as a redoubtable regional military power. They would deliberately refashion their image from champions of orthodoxy to defenders of Islam. This function became the centerpiece of their claim to legitimacy in al-Andalus, where they arrived in 479/1086, as well as of their identity in the wider Islamic world. Yūsuf b. Tāshufīn was summoned to al-Andalus to play the role of defender of Dār al-Islam when the leaders of the *taifa* states[65] found themselves increasingly powerless before the advances of Alfonso VI of Castile-Leon, who conquered Toledo in 478/1085 – the fall of the first major Islamic city in the peninsula. Yūsuf's armies received financial support from al-Muʿtamid of Seville[66] and did not cross the strait before receiving sanction by prominent Andalusī *fuqahāʾ*. The Almoravids reached a symbolic high point in their role as defenders of Dār al-Islam in the same year of their first crossing, 479/1086, when Yūsuf lead a combined Andalusī-Maghribī force against combined Christian forces in what is known in Western historiography as the Battle of Zallāqa.[67] Yūsuf returned to al-Andalus in 481/1088 and again in 483/1090 when he conquered most of the *taifas*, arguing that such conquest was justified on grounds that the

63 Even the original fortification of Rabat, the foundation of which is traditionally credited to the first Almohad caliph, was commissioned by Tāshufīn b. ʿAlī. This structure has been recently uncovered during redevelopment. See: http://www.middle-east-online.com/english/?id=19469

64 Umayyad Caliphate of Damascus 661–756; from 756 al-Andalus was practically independent from the Abbasid Caliphate. While politically separate from the Maghrib throughout the first three centuries of the Islamic West, there remained strong cultural and economic ties between al-Andalus and the Maghrib; the Almoravid unification was an intensification, albeit great, of these ties. A survey of Almoravid material culture in al-Andalus and the Far Maghrib is María Marcos Cobaleda, "Los Almorávides: Territorio, Arquitectura, y Artes Suntuarias" (Universidad de Granada, 2010). And a recent special issue explores material and cultural exchange between Iberia and the Maghrib: Miriam Ali-de-Unzaga, and Adam Gaiser, "Facets of Exchange between North Africa and the Iberian Peninsula," *The Journal of North African Studies* 19, no. 1 (2014): 1–6.

65 The collection of city states that appeared after the fall of the Umayyad Caliphate of al-Andalus (Ar. *Mulūk al-Ṭawāʾif*).

66 María Jesús Viguera Molíns, "Historia Política," 50.

67 October 23, 1086; in Arabic sources referred to as "the Battle of Friday." María Jesús Viguera Molíns, "Historia Política," 51.

taifas were unable to defend Dār al-Islam and that they imposed illegal taxes. In spite of the initial military success, however, it is uncertain whether the Almoravids were able to enlist the Andalusīs in their cause or convince them of the legitimacy of the Ṣanhāja as legitimate Muslim leaders and wagers of jihād.[68] The ensuing political history of the Almoravid unification and eventual failure in al-Andalus is complex, as were the day-to-day relations between Almoravids and Andalusīs. This dimension of Almoravid history, however, has received a fair amount scholarly attention (some of it exaggerating the hostility of the local population and thus neglecting the existence of local support that facilitated Almoraivd success in al-Andalus while it lasted).[69]

By the time of Yūsuf b. Tāshufīn's death on 1 Muḥarram 500/2 September 1106, much of al-Andalus had been conquered. Conquest of the Ebro Valley and the Balearic Islands would follow in 503/1110 and 507/1114 under ʿAlī b. Yūsuf,[70] who continued his father's enterprise and was largely successful, at least during the first half of his reign. Serious opposition, however, arose, beginning in the 1120s, leading eventually to the dynasty's foundering.[71] Increased military pressure from the likes of Alfonso I "the Battler," of Aragon and Alfonso VII of Castile-Leon, together with growing Andalusī opposition (including the Cordoban rebellion of 515/1121,[72] the insurrection of Mozarabs[73] who joined Alfonso I's long raid of 519/1125 and, the "Ṣūfī" rebellion of Ibn Qasī in Algarve) sapped the emipre's military resources.[74] But it was a sustained rebellion in the Far Maghrib itself, that would topple the dynasty. From 515/1121, Ibn Tūmart (founder of the Almohad movement) began to contest the Almoravids' legitimacy as Muslim rulers; he is reported to have publicly rebuked ʿAlī b. Yūsuf's sister[75] and contest the court's own *fuqahā*ʾ in open disputation. Ex-

68 Maribel Fierro, "La Religión," 440.

69 As well as the nature of the religio-political investment of sympathetic parties.

70 María Jesús Viguera Molíns, "Historia Política," 54.

71 María Jesús Viguera Molíns, "Historia Política," 56.

72 Sparked by an Almoravid soldier's abduction of a Cordoban woman.

73 A recent collection investigates the cultural identity and practices of the Christian minority of al-Andalus: Cyrille Aillet, et al., eds. *¿Existe una identidad mozárabe? Historia, lengua y cultura de los cristianos de al-Andalus* (*siglos IX-XII*) (Madrid: Casa de Velázquez, 2008).

74 María Jesús Viguera Molíns, "Historia Política," 57. On Alfonso's raid and Mozarab participation, see Vincent Lagardère, "Communautés mozarabes et pouvoir almoravide en 519H/1125 en Andalus," *Studia Islamica* 67 (1988): 99–119. And Delfina Serrano, "Dos fetuas sobre la expulsión de mozárabes al Maghreb en 1126," *Anaquel de Estudios Árabes* 2 (1991): 163–82.

75 Reputedly for riding a horse. Jamil M. Abun-Nasr, *A History of the Maghrib in the Islamic Period*, 87.

pelled from Marrakesh by ʿAlī, Ibn Tumart proclaimed himself *mahdī* and from 518/1124 led the Almohad movement from Tin Māl, directly south of Marrakesh in the High Atlas Mountains. Tāshufīn b. ʿAlī, third dynastic leader and last able military commander of the Almoravids, after meeting some success in campaigns in al-Andalus, was overwhelmed in the Maghrib during his two year reign by the offensive of the Almohads, fighting against whom he fell 27 Shaʿbān 539/22 February 1145.[76] Tāshufīn's brother, Isḥāq b. ʿAlī, wrested power from the intended successor, Ibrāhīm b. Tāshufīn, but was only seventeen or eighteen when the Almohads entered Marrakesh 18 Shawwāl 530/24 March 1147 after several months of siege.[77] Almoravid rule in the Far Maghrib thus came to an end after over just one century; the cities they founded and the urban institutions within them, however, would continue to grow.[78]

•••

Summarizing the state of sociohistorical writing on the Far Maghrib in the Almoravid period, Abdallah Laroui, in his classic 1977 study, *L'histoire du Maghreb: Un essai de synthèse*, wrote that historians had few precise "givens" concerning the period's socio-economic evolution. He speculated that by the beginning of the period, the basic Berber social unit, which he termed "tribal-familial," had lost some cohesion under the combined influence of commerce, gold currency, and religious ideology. The city state was giving way to empire, precisely

76 Jacinto Bosch Vilá, *Los Almorávides*, 262–64.

77 Jacinto Bosch Vilá, *Los Almorávides*, 270–80; María Jesús Viguera Molíns, "Historia Política," 59.

78 The nature of this continuity was by no means simple. Marrakesh is a prime example; the Almohads went to considerable effort to redraw the city and efface the symbols of Almoravid authority. The institution of Mālikism, a bastion of Almoravid support in the region, was aggressively suppressed during the first half of Almohad rule, Maribel Fierro, "The Legal Policies of the Almohad Caliphs and Ibn Rushd's *Bidayat al-Mujtahid*," *Journal of Islamic Studies* 10, no. 3 (1999): 226–48. Eventually it survived and flourished, however. The burgeoning Ṣūfī movements of the Almoravid period, in a sense, fared better, being largely coopted and enlisted to the Almohad (and alter Marinid) identity and cause. In his recounting of the history of the Banū Amghār of Azemmour, V. Cornell presents a good example of such continuity. Vincent J. Cornell, *Realm of the Saint: Power and Authority in Moroccan Sufism* (Austin: University of Texas Press, 1998), 40–49. Kenneth Garden, in his analysis of the reception of al-Ghazālī's *Iḥyāʾ ʿulūm al-dīn* in the Islamic West argues for a similar understanding of this process: i.e., Almohad adoption of Ṣūfī movements which existed from the Almoravid period, and while not anti-Almoravid in their beginnings, were eventually described as such in Maghribī historiography, especially in Ṣūfī *ṭabbaqāt*. Kenneth Garden, "Al-Ghazālī's Contested Revival: *Iḥyāʾ ʿUlūm al-Dīn* and Its Critics in Khorasan and the Maghrib" (PhD diss., University of Chicago, 2005).

because of the "relative homogeneity of social organization" combined with "weak relations between groups and regions."[79] The "decadence" of the Byzantine and eastern Islamic states in the fifth/eleventh century, coinciding with the beginning of a renaissance in the Latin West, "gave the Maghreb its chance":

> Pendant deux siècles et demi, ce dernier [i.e., the Maghrib] pourra jouer un rôle actif, exactement le temps que l'Europe occidentale rattrape son retard. La première expression de cette action positive sera l'épopée almoravide. Pour l'etude de la dynastie almoravide, la premiére de dynasties marocaines d'importance nord-africaine et européene, nous possédons des sources écrites assez nombreuses, mais elles sont toutes centrées sur le rôle qu'elle a joué en Andalousie dans la lutte contre les Castillans... En conséquence, ses origines et sa chute, qui trouvent leurs causes profondes au Maghreb, nous restent peu connues à cause des carence de la documentation.[80]

Laroui emphasizes the deep social transformation the period witnessed and contemporaneity of this transformation with an apparent connection to the sixth/twelfth-century renaissance of the Latin West. Most of the Arabic chronicles, however, have focused on the Almoravid experience in al-Andalus and the struggle against the Christians, a tendency reproduced in Western historiography. The causes of the profound changes involved with the appearance of the Almoravids and their fall – or, as I prefer, the causes behind the rise of a powerful local opposition – are difficult to perceive.[81]

Since 1977, however, a series of historians have taken up the task of compensating for these deficiencies. The following scholars – whose work informs this study - are some of the most significant: Vincent Lagardère has been a vigorous contributor to Almoravid studies, even while at times adhering to a few long-held notions and the biases of the sources, including their Ibero-centricity.[82]

---

79 Abdallah Laroui, *L'histoire du Maghreb: Un essai de synthese*, 2nd ed. (Casablanca: Centre Culturel Arabe, 2001), 147.

80 Abdallah Laroui, *L'histoire du Maghreb: Un essai de synthese*, 148.

81 Abdallah Laroui, *L'histoire du Maghreb: Un essai de synthese*, 148.

82 His work, however – including his topical index of al-Wansharisi's *Miʿyār*, his study of the rural life in al-Andalus, and articles on Ibn Rushd al-Jadd and the Mozarab participation in Alfonso I's incursion – has been of great value to my own research. Vincent Lagardère, *Histoire et société en occident musulman au Moyen Age: analyse du Miʿyār d'al-Wanšarīsī*, Collection de la Casa de Velázquez; 53 (Madrid: Casa de Velázquez, 1995); Vincent Lagardère, *Campagnes et paysans d'Al-Andalus* (*VIII-XVe s.*), Collection Islam et Occident; 9 (Paris: Editions Maisonneuve et Larose, 1993); Vincent Lagardère, "Abū l-Walīd b. Rushd

Halima Ferhat's *Sabta des origines au XIVème siècle* provides a detailed account and analysis of the history of this important Mediterranean port. It highlights the centrality the city gained in the Almoravid period and the key role it played in the economic and intellectual relationship between the Almoravid Far Maghrib and al-Andalus.[83] In *Mabāḥith fī al-taʾrīkh al-ijtimāʿī li-l-Maghrib wa-l-Andalus khilāl ʿaṣr al-Murābiṭīn*, Ibrāhīm Būtshīsh studies the demographic makeup of the territories that came under Almoravid influence. He places special emphasis on the dynamic of the relationship between these groups, as affected by the changing conditions of the period.[84] Maya Shatzmiller, in *The Berbers and the Islamic State: The Marīnid Experience in Pre-protectorate Morocco*, mostly dealing with the thirteenth – fifteenth centuries, tackles the important question of the Berbers' role in history and the nature of their relationship to the Islamic state and its institutions, using a variety of sources, including legal sources such as those this utilized here.[85] Likewise, David S. Powers in *Law, Society, and Culture in the Maghrib, 1300–1500*, explores Maghribī fatwās, unpacking the full complexity of their production in historical context.[86]

Qāḍī al-Quḍāt de Cordue," *al-Qantara* VII (1986): 202–28; Vincent Lagardère, "Communautés mozarabes et pouvoir almoravide en 519H/1125 en Andalus."

83 Halima Ferhat, *Sabta des origines au xivème siècle.* On ʿIyāḍ's *nawāzil,* see also Halima Ferhat, "Famille et societe a Sabta d'apres l'ouvrage du cadi ʿIyāḍ Madhāhib al-ḥukkām (XIIème siecle)," *Hespéris-Tamuda* Vol. XXX, no. 2 (1992): 5–15. Her collection of sources for the urban history of the Maghrib, edited with ʿAbd al-Āḥad al-Sabtī provides encouraging evidence of the growing interest in the history of urban development in the Maghrib in *al-ʿAṣr al-Wasīṭ.* ʿAbd al-Aḥad al-Sabtī, and Ḥalīma Farḥāt, *Al-Madīna fī al-ʿaṣr al-wasīṭ: qaḍāyā wa-wathāʾiq min taʾrīkh al-Gharb al-Islāmī* (Casablanca: al-Markaz al-Thaqāfī al-ʿArabī, 1994).

84 Ibrāhīm al-Qādirī Būtshīsh, *Mabāḥith fī al-taʾrīkh al-ijtimāʿī li-l-Maghrib wa-l-Andalus khilāl ʿasr al-murābiṭīn* (Beirut: Dār al-Ṭalīʿa, 1998). In a follow up, he points to promising textual sources and what he considers are key needs for developing a comprehensive socio-economic history of Islamic West. Ibrāhīm al-Qādirī Būtshīsh, *Iḍāʾāt Hawla turāth al-gharb al-islāmī wa-taʾrīkhihi al-iqtiṣādī wa-l-ijtimāʿī* (Beirut: Dār al-Ṭalīʿa, 2002).

85 Maya Shatzmiller, *The Berbers and the Islamic state* (Princeton, NJ: Markus Weiner Publishers, 2000); Maya Shatzmiller, *Her Day in Court: Women's Property Rights in Fifteenth-Century Granada,* First Edition ed., Harvard Series in Islamic Law (Boston: Islamic Legal Studies Program, Harvard Law School, 2007); Maya Shatzmiller, "Women and Property Rights in al-Andalus and the Maghrib: Social Patterns and Legal Discourse," *Islamic Law and Soceity* 2, no. 3 (1995): 219–57.

86 His work has provided a methodological model and made explicit for me the potential of these texts as sources of social historical inquiry.

From a different angle, Vincent Cornell, in *Realm of the Saint: Power and Authority in Moroccan Sufism*, and while focusing on the development of Ṣūfism and devoting half of the work to the study of a fifteenth-century figure, presents a unique and important study on the development of social institutions in the Far Maghrib. He views these developments as an intersection of wider Islamic intellectual currents with those of the local cultures, a perspective I also assume. Likewise, he identifies the Almoravid period as a turning point and beginning for Moroccan Ṣūfism, a religio-cultural phenomenon marked by the interaction of urban and rural traditions.[87] Maribel Fierro, while chiefly a scholar of al-Andalus, presents great awareness in her work of the dynamic relationship and deep cultural connections between al-Andalus and the Maghrib; in her work she has proven that, indeed, one cannot be studied without the other. Her understanding of the religio-political landscape of the Islamic West is sophisticated and coherent, and I have taken cue from it in many places in this study. Delfina Serrano has written a series of studies using texts, very much like those used here, from the Almoravid period. Her edition and introductory study of the *Nawāzil* of Qāḍī ʿIyāḍ,[88] followed by a series of articles, forms a crucial foundation for the direction of this book.

The above are but a representative selection of major historiographical trends with which this investigation is in conversation. *Law and the Islamization of Morocco under the Almoravids* complements these by benefiting from the use of a source whose theoretical and methodological treatment has achieved a much greater degree of maturity in the last fifteen to twenty years, and which remains rich (with many unpublished manuscripts in existence and new editions appearing frequently). This study complements these major trends by addressing a set of questions, vital to the history of the region, which, for a variety of reasons, alluded to above, have not been sufficiently explored.

3 The Muftī

The jurisconsult whose work is the object of this study – having authored the bulk of the opinions analyzed below[89] – was a preeminent jurist from Cordoba who left a lasting mark in the legal tradition of the Islamic West. Ibn Rushd

87 Vincent J. Cornell, *Realm of the Saint*.

88 Muḥammad b. ʿIyāḍ, *Madhāhib al-ḥukkām fī nawāzil al-aḥkām* (*La actuación de los jueces en los procesos judiciales*), trans. Delfina Serrano (Madrid: Consejo Superior de Investigaciones Científicas, 1998).

89 Except for some included in Chapter Three, which analyses a single long case, to which several jurisconsults provided opinions.

al-Jadd was recognized as such by his contemporaries and his prestige brought him considerable influence with the Almoravid leadership, notably the Amīr ʿAlī b. Yūsuf, whom he advised in writing and in person on more than one occasion. He was recognized as a *mujtahid*[90] and was author of seminal commentaries reconciling Islamic legal theory (*uṣūl al-fiqh*) with some of the principal texts of Mālikism.[91] His legal opinions composed in response to questions from contemporary judges, jurists, and individuals including the amīr, gained widespread and lasting influence by being recopied, compiled, and introduced into the substantive tradition of the school. Ibn Rushd al-Jadd was, furthermore, an active participant in some of the key events of his time, including a major revolt in Cordoba and, five years later, a trip to Marrakesh to advise the amīr on the treachery of the several thousand Mozarabs (or tributary Christians) who joined the attack of Alfonso I el Batallador on several towns and cities of al-Andalus in 519/1125.

Abū al-Walīd Muḥammad b. Aḥmad b. Aḥmad b. Rushd al-Qurṭubī[92] was born in Shawwāl of 450/November-December of 1058. Also known as Ibn Rushd *al-Jadd* (Ibn Rushd the Grandfather), he was the chief judge of Cordoba (*qāḍī al-jamāʿa*, lit. judge of the community)[93] and first member of a line of prominent jurists there. Better known in the Latin West was his grandson, the famous philosopher Averroës – distinguished by the designation *al-Ḥafīd* (grandson).[94] In the Islamic tradition and especially in the Mālikī tradition,

---

90 "Formed part of a generation of *mujtahids* that Ibn Farḥūn thought extinct in his time," and Qāḍī Iyāḍ called him *zaʿīm* of jurists, Delfina Serrano, "Ibn Rušd al-Ŷadd," in *Biblioteca de al-Andalus: de Ibn al-Dabbag a Ibn Kurz*, ed. Jorge Lirola Delgado, and Jose Miguel Puerta Vílchez (Almería: Fundación Ibn Tufayl de Estudios Árabes, 2006). This section follows closely D. Serrano's excellent study of Ibn Rushd's life.

91 An important point borne out in one of the first monographs providing in-depth analysis of a work by Ibn Rushd al-Jadd: Ana Fernández Félix, *Cuestiones Legales del Islam Temprano: La ʿUtbiyya y el Proceso de Formación de la Socidad Islámica Andalusí*, vol. Estudios Árabes e Islamicos: Monografías. 6 (Madrid: Consejo Superior de Investigaciones Científicas, 2003).

92 Serrano provides the extended genealogy: Abū al-Walīd Muḥammad b. Aḥmad b. Aḥmad [b. Muḥammad b. Aḥmad b. ʿAbd Allāh] b. Rushd al-Qurṭubī. See also Delfina Serrano Ruano, "Explicit cruelty, implicit compassion: Judaism, forced conversions and the genealogy of the Banu Rushd," *Journal of Medieval Iberian Studies* 2, no. 2 (2010).

93 A designation particular to the Islamic West.

94 Practically all references to Ibn Rushd in the text below are to the grandfather, Ibn Rushd al-Jadd, unless otherwise noted. A major work by the grandson, Ibn Rushd al-Ḥafīd, however,–his *Bidāyat al-mujtahid wa-nihāyat al-muqtaṣid*–is frequently cited below; as one of the first major works of comparative Islamic law, the *Bidāyat al-mujtahid* provides useful summaries of the schools' different positions regarding particular questions of law.

however, Ibn Rushd al-Jadd was more influential.[95] Ibn Rushd al-Jadd studied law (fiqh) as well as theology[96] in his native Cordoba from a handful of local scholars.[97] He never undertook the *riḥlat al-ṭalab fī al-ʿilm* – a trip to meet, learn, and earn transmission licenses from reputed scholars (in the Islamic West, this trip was traditionally taken to the East). He, nevertheless, acquired deep and extensive knowledge of legal theory and substantive law, of points of agreement and disagreement within the Mālikī tradition, as well as of inheritance law, on which he wrote several treatises (*rasāʾil*).

The Almoravid amīr, ʿAlī b. Yūsuf, appointed him in 511/1117–8 to the chief judgeship of Cordoba, which he held for four years and at the end of which he either resigned to work on his commentary *al-Bayān wa-l-taḥṣīl*[98] or, what is likely, because of his involvement in events that sparked the revolt in Cordoba in I Rabīʿ 515/May-June 1121 in which ʿAlī b. Yūsuf had to intervene and after which Ibn Rushd was replaced by his predecessor, Abū al-Qāsim Aḥmad b. Muḥammad b. Ḥamdīn.[99] The revolt was sparked by the abduction of a Cordo-

---

Written only two generations after Ibn Rushd al-Jadd's lifetime, it is a rich resource, particularly helpful with summarizing the Mālikī tradition.

95 Even though the grandson also excelled as jurist.

96 Delfina Serrano, "Ibn Rušd al-Ŷadd," 618. Serrano writes that none of Ibn Rushd al-Jadd's biographers gives special mention to his excelling in this area. In several passages in his works, however, he skillfully tackles theological issues of the day. One of these is described below; see also Delfina Serrano, "Los almorávides y la teología ash'arí: ¿Contestación o legitimación de una disciplina marginal?," in *Identidades Marginales*, ed. C. de La Puente, Estudios Onomástico-Biográficos de al-Andalus, xiii (Madrid: Consejo Superior de Investigaciones Científicas, 2003). Ibn Rushd attributed his formation in theology, as well as his foundational learning in fiqh to his teacher, Abū Jaʿfar Aḥmad b. Muḥammad b. Rizq al-Umawawī al-Qurṭubī.

97 The above mentioned, Abū Jaʿfar Aḥmad b. Muḥammad b. Rizq al-Umawī al-Qurṭubī, along with Muḥammad b. Faraj b. al-Ṭallāʾ, Abū ʿAlī al-Ghassānī al-Jayyānī, Abū Marwān ʿAbd al-Mālik b. Sirāj, Abū ʿAbd Allāh Muḥammad b. Khayra b. Abī al-ʿĀfiya al-Umawī al-Jawharī, and Abū al-ʿAbbās Aḥmad b. ʿUmar b. Anas al-ʿUdhrī. A brief and surprisingly unremarkable roster of teachers for such an influential and original jurist. Delfina Serrano, "Ibn Rušd al-Ŷadd," 618.

98 Delfina Serrano, "Ibn Rušd al-Ŷadd," 618. Fernández Félix treats *al-Bayān wa-l-taḥṣīl* extensively in her book *Cuestiones Legales del Islam Temprano. Al-Bayān wa-l-taḥṣīl* was Ibn Rushd's commentary of the *ʿUtbiyya*, a key Mālikī work in the Islamic West. Ibn Rushd, *al-Bayān wa-l-taḥṣīl wa-l-sharḥ wa-l-tawjīh wa-l-taʿlīl fī masāʾil al-Mustakhraja*, 2nd ed. (Beirut: Dār al-Gharb al-Islamī, 1988). It superseded previous versions and commentaries of the *ʿUtbiyya*, becoming the standard. Fernández Félix discusses Ibn Rushd's composition of *al-Bayān* in pp. 258–274.

99 Who was his longtime rival. Delfina Serrano, "Ibn Rušd al-Ŷadd," 618. Abū al-Ḥusayn b. Sirāj attributed the ruin of the city and its loss of political preeminence to the rivalry

ban woman by an Almoravid soldier; the population was further upset by the fact that the Almoravid governor, Abū Yaḥyā b. Rawāda, failed to punish the soldier for his crime. The offenses of the soldier and the governor elicited looting by the people of Cordoba – including their jurists and notables – of the Almoravid garrison residences and country homes. ʿAlī b. Yūsuf laid siege to the city. The inhabitants then sought judicial counsel, to which several jurists in Cordoba[100] responded, stating that the inhabitants of the city had been provoked and acted in defense of their families and possessions. The siege continued and a delegation managed to negotiate forgiveness from ʿAlī on the condition of paying reparations for the damaged property.[101] In what may have been a related, but likely subsequent incident,[102] Ibn Rushd became involved in a contentious debate over the validity of the sale of properties usurped in the *Taifa* Period by families including the Banū ʿAbbād, the ruling dynasty of the --of Seville before the Almoravid conquest. According to D. Serrano, Ibn Rushd sided against his predecessor, Abū al-Qāsim Aḥmad b. Muḥammad b. Ḥamdīn, and contemporary muftī Ibn al-Ḥājj, arguing that such sales should be invalidated, eliciting the ire of many Cordobans. Ibn Rushd and those who argued with him had to retract their opinion publicly after being reprimanded by the amīr.[103]

Several of the fatwās analysed below were produced after Ibn Rushd left the qāḍīship in Cordoba. If his own words about becoming more engrossed with the composition of the *Bayān* are correct, the years between 515/1121 and 520/1126 would have been some of the most productive of his life. While remaining active with the *shūra* council, leading prayers at the congregational mosque, and occasionally delivering the sermon, Ibn Rushd became sought after as a teacher, increasing his influence through his students. Moreover, and reprimands such as the above notwithstanding, Ibn Rushd al-Jadd enjoyed great prestige not only in the eyes of the juristic community but also in the estimation of the Almoravid administration, including the Amīr ʿAlī b. Yūsuf. As reported in various sources and as is patent in several of the fatwās below, Ibn Rushd was consulted by ʿAlī on matters of great sensitivity and importance

---

between the Banū Rushd and the Banū Ḥamdīn. Delfina Serrano, "Ibn Rušd al-Ŷadd," 622.

100 Among which Ibn Rushd apparently was not included. Delfina Serrano, "Ibn Rušd al-Ŷadd," 619.

101 Delfina Serrano, "Ibn Rušd al-Ŷadd," 618.

102 In which Ibn Rushd acted as muftī rather than judge. Delfina Serrano, "Ibn Rušd al-Ŷadd," 620.

103 Delfina Serrano, "Ibn Rušd al-Ŷadd," 620.

to the empire.[104] In what was one of the most serious of such episodes, having observed how in the fall of 519/1125 as many as 50,000 Mozarabs (likely an inflated number) joined the forces of Alfonso I el Battallador as he advanced through Daroca, Monreal, Teruel, and Segorbe, sacked the countryside of Valencia, and laid siege to Granada, the Almoravid administrative capital of al-Andalus,[105] Ibn Rushd travelled to Marrakesh to consult with ʿAlī, deeply concerned by the apparent treachery of a sizable portion of this Arabic-speaking community of Christians.[106] Ibn Rushd argued that, through their sedition, the Mozarabs who aided Alfonso I had broken the protection owed them under the law. He recommended expulsion from their lands.[107] On this occasion,ʿAlī b. Yūsuf also consulted Ibn Rushd, in view of the growing threat posed by Ibn Tūmart, on the construction of the Marrakesh ramparts, which began that year as part of a broader urbanization project.[108]

Ibn Rushd returned to Cordoba in Jumāda I 520/23 June 1126. He fell ill as a result of exhaustion brought about by the trip. Five months later, on the night of Sunday, 11 Dhū al-Qaʿada 520/28 November 1126, he died and was buried in the cemetery of al-ʿAbbās, mourned by a great crowd. Several elegies were written in his honor. One, composed by his student and compiler of his fatwās, Abū al-Ḥasan b. Al-Wazzān, is preserved in the colophon of an extant copy of the manuscript.[109]

The number of fatwās produced by Ibn Rushd, their dissemination in Mālikī collections, reverberation in future cases, and percolation into the substantive law of the Mālikī tradition, testify to the great esteem he earned as a legal thinker. D. Serrano has called his fatwās exemplary. Several have elicited de-

104 Which is perhaps why V. Cornell identifies Ibn Rushd as ʿAlī's "vizier." Vincent J. Cornell, *Realm of the Saint*, 44.

105 Granada assumed this role since the first years of ʿAlī's reign. Jacinto Bosch Vilá, *Los Almorávides*, 177.

106 This episode constituted one of a series of internal and external challenges to Almoravid authority that rose with growing force from the end of the first quarter of the twelfth century. While in Marrakesh, Ibn Rushd addressed two of these, one of which resulted in the construction of the city walls, the other in the relocation of many Andalusi Christians to the Maghrib. The *Mafākhir al-barbar* says Ibn Rushd was called to Marrakesh by ʿAlī. Delfina Serrano, "Ibn Rušd al-Ŷadd," 621.

107 An act which, according to the writer of *al-Hulal al-mawshiyya*, was the lightest possible sentence. Delfina Serrano, "Ibn Rušd al-Ŷadd," 620.

108 Or reconstruction with considerable enlargement. Delfina Serrano, "Ibn Rušd al-Ŷadd," 621.

109 Delfina Serrano, "Ibn Rušd al-Ŷadd," 622.

tailed studies.[110] While a comprehensive study of Ibn Rushd's work has not been undertaken to date, estimation of the corpus he produced, both as a historical source and as a major work of Islamic legal thought, has risen considerably in the last two decades. *Law and Urban Transformation under the Almoravids* complements the larger project of understanding Ibn Rushd al-Jadd's work, by focusing specifically on its impact and interaction with the social, legal, and institutional history of the Far Maghrib, during one of its period of greatest socio-historical change.

4 Urban Development of the Far Maghrib

The foundation of Marrakesh in the second half of the fifth/eleventh century and its prodigious growth in the sixth/twelfth was central to the experience and transformation of the southern Far Maghrib under the Almoravids. The urban and institutional development exhibited by the city was not an isolated or aberrant event, but rather reflects a larger process. Marrakesh was certainly the largest urban center of the southern Maghrib – and its emergence had a profound impact on the region – but it was neither the only nor the first city to appear here in Islamic times. Brief reflection on Marrakesh's most illustrious and somewhat mysterious predecessor on the northern edge of the Sahara, Sijilmāsa, will shed light on the nature and scale of this regional transformation.

Without Sijilmāsa there would have been no Almoravid movement to begin with. A look at its development allows us to better identify the continuities and discontinuities entailed in the Almoravid unification of the Far Maghrib, a process which did not take place *ex nihilo*. For the 298 years between its founding in the late second/eighth century and its conquest by the Almoravids in 447/1055–56, Sijilmāsa stood both as direct link to the Islamic past and as prototype for the Berber-Islamic polity the Almoravid state would become. Lying south of the High Atlas Mountains in the Tafīlālt, Sijilmāsa was, until the appearance of Marrakesh, the single most important point of contact and transmission between the Maghrib, the Sahara, and West Africa (or western

110 These have tended to focus on a few of the detailed opinions he wrote on subjects of broad symbolic importance or with theological dimensions, such as his opinion of the permissibility of the study of Ashʿarism. Delfina Serrano, "Ibn Rušd al-Ŷadd," 620. Another kind of example, showcasing the relationship between consultation and the development of substantive law though a single case study, is Wael Hallaq, "Murder in Cordoba: Ijtihād, Iftā' and the Evolution of Substantive Law in Medieval Islam."

Sūdānic Africa).[111] Islam was first introduced into the western Sahara and western Sūdānic Africa through Sijilmāsa, as were the seeds of the Almoravid movement itself, its founder and first spiritual leader having been recruited from its environs.

Known in the Islamic east from the third/ninth century as a city lying in one of the farthest known quarters of the world,[112] Sijilmāsa was characterized by Arab geographers as a Berber city with a Khārijī, religio-politically independent past, which played a pioneering role in the gold trade with West Africa. Al-Bakrī, who wrote in the Almoravid period, described the city and its origins:

> The city of Sijilmāsa was built in the year 140/758–57. Its construction (*ʿimāra*) emptied the city of Targha. Between them is a two-day [journey]. Its construction also emptied [the city of] Zīz. The city of Sijilmāsa is a coastal (*sāhiliya*) city [i.e., on the "coast" of the Sahara], and its soil – of which there is a great extension around it – is saline. In it there are noble houses and generous public buildings (*mabān sarīya*). It has many gardens. And the base of its walls is built of stones and the upper part of baked brick (*ṭūb*); these were built by al-Yasaʿ Abū Manṣūr b. Abī al-Qāsim from his own wealth. No one else shared in the expenditures. He spent one thousands bushels of wheat on it. [The city walls] have twelve gates, eight of which are of iron. Al-Yasaʿ built [them] in the year 199. He embarked on it (*irtaḥala ilayhā*) in the year 200 and divided [the city] among the tribes as it is today…
>
> Between Sijilmāsa and the Wādī Draʿa is a five day journey. The Banū Midrar possessed Sijilmāsa for 160 years, and in it dwelled the aforementioned Abū al-Qāsim b. Yāsūl al-Miknāsī Abū al-Yasaʿ. The grandfather (*jadd*) of Midrār met ʿIkrama Mawlā b. ʿAbbās in Ifrīqiya and heard [hadith] (*samaʿa*) from him. He owned cattle and would often graze [his cattle] in the location of Sijilmāsa. A tribe (*qawm*) of Ṣufrīs gathered there. When they reached forty men they showed preference for (*qadamū ʿalā anfusihim*) ʿIsā b. Mazīd al-Aswad and put him in charge of their affairs. They began to build Sijilmāsa, and that was in the year 140. Others say that Midrār was a smith with an Andalusī caravan (or of an Andalusī silver mine; *min rabḍiyyat al-Andalus*) who was left there when the

---

111 The Tafīlālt is an oasis following the River Zīz, which flows southward from the High Atlas into the Sahara, like the Draʿa and Sūs Valleys to the west. Historically, the southernmost urban centers of Morocco and the Far Maghrib have been located on these three river valleys. James A. Miller, "Trading through Islam," 34.

112 James A. Miller, "Trading through Islam," 35.

> caravan stopped for the night (*kharaja ʿinda waqʿat al-rabḍ*). He resided in the vicinity of Sijilmāsa, and the location of Sijilmāsa was at the time desert plain (*barāḥ*), where the Berbers gathered during a time of year to trade because of its proximity. Midrār would bring the iron tools he prepared. Then he set up a tent there and lived in it. The Berbers lived around him. And that was the origin of its development. As for Midrār, there is no doubt that he was a smith because his children who undertook the affairs (*al-qāʾimīn bi-amr*) of Sijilmāsa were taunted for it.[113]

Ibn Hawqal, who visited the city in the late fourth/tenth century (a full century before the Almoravid conquest), wrote a description, which was later often quoted, of the flourishing city and its wealth:

> Sijilmāsa is a city of beautiful location, venerable people, splendid craftsmanship (*fākhirat al-ʿamal*), on a river that surges in the summer like the increase of the Nile during the time when the sun [rises in the constellations of] Gemini, Cancer, and Leo (*al-jawzāʾ wa-l-saraṭān wa-l-asad*). It is cultivated with its water like the crops of Egypt (*Miṣr*) in tillage. Perhaps once a year they plant grain (*badhr*) and they harvest what thrives (*rāʿa*) of what they sowed. The years with water follow one another (*tawātarat*), so that the soil is copious with [ground] water, one year after another. They harvest up to seven years, with [a kind of] ears of corn that do not resemble those of wheat (*ḥinṭa*) or barley (*shaʿīr*), with a hard seed that when broken makes delightful food, and its nature (*khalq*) is something in between wheat (*qamḥ*) and barely. Sijilmāsa has palmeries and beautiful orchards (*basātīn*) and gardens (*ajinna*), and they have green dates of the vine of utmost sweetness (*ruṭab akhḍar min al-silq fī ghāyat al-ḥalāwa*). And [Sijilmāsa's] people are wealthy [and] magnanimous (*qawm sarāt mayāsīr*), distinct from the people of the Maghrib in appearance and experience, with religious learning, shame, and modesty (*maʿa ʿilm wa-satar wa-ṣiyāna*), and beauty and use for manliness, generosity, and gravity. Its building are like those of Kūfa, including fine gates on its high and lofty palaces …
>
> Qayrawān is similar to Sijilmāsa in the health of its air, and the white streets (*mujāwarat al-bayḍāʾ*) with uninterrupted commerce from it to the Sudān and other lands, abundant profits, droves of travelers, authority

113 Abū ʿUbayd al-Bakrī, *L'Afrique Septentrionale*, trans. Mac Guckin De Slane (Paris: Librairie d'Amérique et d'Orient Adrien-Maisonneuve, 1965), 149. Quoted in ʿAbd al-Aḥad al-Sabtī, and Ḥalīma Farḥāt, *al-Madīna fī al-ʿaṣr al-wasīṭ*, 37–38.

> in action, and complete beauty of character and deed. They stand apart with their customs (*rusūm*) from the meanness (*daqqa*) of the people of the Maghrib in their dealings with others and habits, being up front and famous for advancing good works. They are compassionate with each other on account of their manliness and chivalry. And when there are affections (*al-ḥanāt*) and ancient inheritance among them, they put them aside when in need (*ʿind al-ḥāja*) and dispose of them with leadership and generosity and a natural nobility of character that characterizes them and the politeness they stand on, with the abundance of their travels and the length of their journeys away form their homes, which protracts their absence form their fatherland (*awṭān*). I entered [Sijilmāsa] in the year forty and never saw in the Maghrib elders of finer behavior (*akthar mashāʾikh fī ḥasan samt*) and disposition (*mumāzaja*) for learning and its merits, tending toward capacious and lofty spirits and high and sublime interests. [All the] rest of the lords of the [other] cities are beneath them in [matters of] wealth and resources. Their qualities draw them together in confraternity (*ʿaṣabiyya*) and their circumstances resemble each other. I have seen in Awdaghust a title-deed (*ṣakk*) in which is mentioned that [an individual from Sijilmāsa] is owed (*ḥaqq ʿalā*) 42,000 dīnārs by a merchant of Awdaghust. I have never seen or heard a story similar or equal to this in the Mashriq and I have told it in Iraq and Fāris and Khurasān and it was found novel (*istuṭrifat*). And in the days when al-Muʿtaz was in power as its amīr, he still collected taxes for [Sijilmāsa] (*yajtabīhā*) from the caravans departing for the land of the Sūdān, as well as tithe (*ʿushr*) and poll-tax (*kharāj*) and ancient customs (*qawānīn qadīma*) on what was sold there and what was bought of camels and sheep and cows including what left and entered it from the directions of Ifrīqiya and Fās and al-Andalus and the Sūs.[114]

Sijilmāsa was the first significant urban center conquered by the Almoravids, and what had been the city's principle mercantile activity became the Almoravids' own. It was in Sijilmāsa that the Almoravids first struck gold dīnārs. It was also from Sijilmāsa that they launched their northward campaign. In Sijilmāsa we thus find a precursor to Marrakesh: an urban center whose economic livelihood was based on long-distance trade between West Africa, the Maghrib, and Ifrīqiya, flourishing for almost three centuries before the Al-

114 Ibn Ḥawqal, *Kitāb ṣūrat al-arḍ* (Leiden: 1938), 91–92. Quoted in ʿAbd al-Aḥad al-Sabtī, and Ḥalīma Farḥāt, *al-Madīna fī al-ʿaṣr al-wasīṭ*, 97.

moravid conquest. One could interpret the founding of Marrakesh as a mere continuation or relocation of this trade route.

Such an interpretation, however, would fail to account for the difference in scale between the two cities. The political economy of pre-Almoravid Sijilmāsa was significantly more modest than that of Marrakesh, and, indeed, of Sijilmāsa itself after its conquest by the Almoravids. Most of the major urban features uncovered during the 1988–1998 archeological excavations of Sijilmāsa's site[115] date to the Almoravid period. These include the city walls, an irrigation system, the congregational mosque, and a greatly expanded urban footprint.[116] Arguably the most important population center of the southern Far Maghrib before the Almoravids, and later as the first Almoravid city, Sijilmāsa was one of the first cities to benefit from the unification of the Far Maghrib and the intensification of economic activity. The city thus participated in a significant way in the urban and institutional transformation of the southern Far Maghrib, which is amply supported by archeological and numismatic evidence.

Textual evidence, on the other hand, points to a significant difference between the institutional development of the two cities. Almoravid Sijilmāsa appears not to have been integrated in the Mālikī consultative network in the same way Marrakesh was, and its Islamic judicial institutions appear not to have been as developed. That Sijilmāsa and, in all likelihood, the other, smaller urban centers of the southern Far Maghrib beyond the High Atlas were not integrated into the Mālikī network of learning, transmission, and consultation is apparent from surveying the place names found Ibn Rushd's fatwās.[117] While we find eight fatwās mentioning Marrakesh, there are practically no references to the other known urban centers of the south, including Sijilmāsa – its economic importance notwithstanding.

From this evidence, we may put forward one broad point and make a tentative conclusion about urbanization in the Almoravid Far Maghrib: The point is that several smaller urban centers predated the founding of Marrakesh and these found their support from the same resources and economic activities from which the Almoravid capital did. This should not come as a surprise, since the long-distance trade in gold between West Africa and the Mediterranean is recorded from Byzantine times, when Romans traded with Berbers or Imazighen, whose population was substantial and pre-dated the arrival of

115 Under the direction of Ronald A. Messier.

116 The Almoravid irrigation system transformed the "Wadi Ziz into an engineered irrigation canal which allowed for the expansion of arable land in the Tafilalt oasis and consequent growth in urban population and size." James A. Miller, "Trading through Islam," 46.

117 i.e. the places with which he corresponded as muftī.

Islam. Among the most important of these urban centers were Sijilmāsa and Taroudant, to the south of the High Atlas, and Dāy and Aghmāt, to the north. Before Almoravid unification, the populations and rulers of these towns espoused a variety of forms of Islamic heterodox and syncretistic beliefs, the Khārijīsm of Sijilmāsa being one of the better known.

The tentative conclusion is that urban and Islamic institutional development in the Far Maghrib during the Almoravid period favored a few great cities, chief of which appear to have been Marrakesh, Fez, Ceuta and perhaps Tlemcen. Archeological evidence points to demographic growth at the expense of smaller urban centers, a few of which disappeared altogether.[118] Textual sources illustrate how Mālikī networks of scholars developed predominantly in the large cities. The center of this network in the south, of course, was Marrakesh; and in the 1120s the network appears not to have developed or spread significantly into the countryside.[119]

It is possible that the paucity of references to the smaller cities and towns stems from the fact that only consultations between individuals in the cities and the higher echelons of the network (i.e., individuals of more social and institutional prominence) were recorded. There are reports of jurists active in smaller towns, such as Qāḍī ʿIyāḍ in Dāy.[120] Still, the bulk of the evidence from biographical sources and fatwā collections points to a stronger presence and concentration of Mālikī jurists in the larger cities of the Far Maghrib; in the towns the Mālikī network would develop more gradually. This conclusion is apposite, moreover, for places such as Aghmāt[121] or Dāy. Still, Sijilmāsa, appears to be an anomaly – given its early central status and the sustained growth revealed by the archeological record. This in turn points to a broader, persistent question concerning differences in the nature of the relationship (administrative, religio-political, and cultural) of state and society between the region north of the High Atlas and that south of the High Atlas – closer to the

118 J. L. Boone, et al., "Archeological and Historical Approaches to Complex Societies: The Islamic States of Medieval Morocco," *American Anthropologist New Series* 92, no. 3 (1990), 641.

119 Especially the High Atlas mountains directly to the south where the anti-Mālikī movement was hatching.

120 Admittedly this was during the very beginning of the Almohad period and as a form of exile. Qāḍī ʿIyāḍ nevertheless appears to have been acting as a jurist for a community that presumably had this need or custom.

121 Aghmāt was, nevertheless, an urban center of some importance. Several Mālikī jurists were known to have made their way there in the twelfth century, as attested to by ʿIyāḍ's *al-Ghunya*, where find at least three ʿulamāʾ (contemporary with ʿIyāḍ) associated with the town.

movement's birth place. Sijilmāsa developed considerably during the Almoravid period and presented many of the defining features of Almoravid urbanism: the new city walls, the great mosque, and the irrigation works. It was also the site of the first Almoravid mint. Nonetheless, the Islamic and Mālikī institutions, so closely associated with the Almoravid administration and its other Far Maghribī cities, appear to be relatively absent. This has added to the city's historical mysteriousness: The metropolis survives more in the accounts of travelers and geographers than in the *ṭabaqāt* of scholars.

The cause and nature of the divide between the Almoravid north and south remains unaccounted for in modern historiography. The south must have held social significance for the Almoravids. They originated there. Abū Bakr b. ʿUmar returned to the south after dividing, for all intents and purposes, the empire and while remaining nominal supreme leader, a title that must have been of some importance. Even some eighth/fourteenth-century Catalan maps, recognize Abū Bakr, not Yūsuf, as the leader of the empire, which would suggest that the deep south was central to the movement's identity. Such considerations notwithstanding, the Mālikī and Arabic tradition demonstrates a kind of neglect for the Almoravid homeland and its founding figures, whose writings, whether in the form of treatises or fatwās, were not collected or kept for posterity. Qāḍī ʿIyāḍ tells us in the *Tartīb* that the Almoravids had consulted Ibn Yāsīn during the early period of the movement. None of Ibn Yāsīn's fatwās are preserved, however.[122] This, of course, stands in sharp contrast to those of Andalusī muftīs such as Ibn Rushd.

Why the homeland and symbolic center of the movement was overshadowed by the north in the development of its religio-political institutions is not entirely known. Plausible explanations are not difficult to imagine, however. The gravitation to, and eventual overshadowing of, the south by the north in the textual record supports the understanding of institutional development put forward here as one dominated by north-to-south influence; the discursive practices associated with this development, furthermore, included the cultivation of Arabic historiography, a practice more at home in the north than in the south. Nevertheless, it is important not to forget that Sijilmāsa was the first site and conduit for Islamic institutions (albeit of a more basic, doctrinal sort) into the Almoravid homeland and that the city remained economically vibrant throughout the Almoravid period and beyond. Further study will hopefully

122 Many thanks to Maribel Fierro for an engaging discussion on this issue. She believes that the omission of Ibn Yāsīn's fatwās from the corpus shows how enthralled the Almoravids were with Andalusī learning at the espense of their own.

yield more nuanced information about its development and relationship to the Far Maghrib north of the High Atlas.

•••

None of the fatwās analyzed below explicitly deals with or even mentions Sijilmāsa. Nor do they refer to the other smaller centers alluded to above (such as Dāy and Aghmāt). Nevertheless, it is important that we too imagine as best we can what the development of the urban centers and institutions of the entire Far Maghrib looked like. The disconnect between what is visible in the legal texts, on the one hand, and what is visible from archeology and material culture studies, on the other raises more questions than answers – blind spots in the knowledge and conception of Maghribī history. These blind spots, however, will prove of abiding interest to future inquiry: What did the Berber cities of Sijilmāsa and Aghmāt look like in the sixth/twelfth century? How did customary and Islamic practice intersect and combine here? And how were both changed in the process? What did daily life look like and what roles did Islamic institutions play in these smaller urban spaces as they absorbed newcomers attracted by economic growth? The texts that follow help us imagine that process as well as venture several tentative answers to these questions.

5 Mālikī Law and Custom in the Far Maghrib

My approach to the texts analyzed below is based on asking the questions of what purpose adopting Mālikism served and why was it attractive or effective in the context of the Far Maghrib's move from heterodoxy to orthodoxy. The answer to this relatively simple question is complex. The socio-historical context is key to unpacking the texts' meaning. They don't easily reveal meaning beyond their immediate juridical concern and logic. The analysis below takes an interpretive stance, based on concepts and assumptions, most of which I try to point out in this introduction. One such interpretive stance or assumption is that the diffusion of Mālikī legal discourse occurred by contact (creative, conflictive, synthetic) with the diverse customary practices, both strictly legal and more broadly social, of the Far Maghrib. I believe it would be fair to say that this interpretive stance characterizes much recent scholarship on Islamic law and society, which over past decades has traded assumptions of law as sacred and immutable (and its practitioners as fickle and subjective) for that of an (often rigorously) evolving set of practices but in a system flexible enough to adapt to a great diversity of habitats and cultures. Determining with any degree of certainty, however, whether legal developments are the outcome of the opinions of individual muftīs, or of the local predilections of communities of legal practitioners (including the practices of courts and judges), or of the influences of social practice, turns out to be a difficult endeavor. An important reason for this appears to be a general tendency in Islamic legal discourse (perhaps of legal discourse in general, if such a generalization is possible) to find justification and legitimation through internal logic. Another reason lies in the flexibility, length, and diversity of this historical development, which has multiplied the difficulty of tracing all such permutations diachronically. (Some recent studies, but still rather few, have focused on parsing this development: From the classical formulation to local variegation, through adaptation to local circumstance, and on identifying the language and concepts existing within the legal tradition that allow for this, since they differ according to school and region).[123] In the Mālikī tradition, terms associated with this evolution include *ʿamal* (judicial practice), *ʿurf* (customary law), and *ʿāda* (custom). The exact definition of these is contentious. The shifting boundary between the social and legal uses of each poses one of the difficulties for definition. They are used to refer to local variations in legal practice but have been often confused, especially *ʿamal* and *ʿurf.*

ʿAmal (judicial practice, pl. *aʿmāl*) originated in the concept of the practice of the people of Medina as a source of law but grew to encompass the broader concept of prevailing judicial practice.[124] The concept can be invoked to resolve contradictions between opinions in the legal tradition, sometimes favoring a minority position over a majority one or when justifying a practice that appears to run against the orthodox positions of the school. As a source of law in western Mālikism,[125] it grew in importance after the eleventh century.

---

123 A good example of such work in al-Andalus and the Maghrib is Jean-Pierre Van Staëvel, *Droit malikite et habitat à Tunis au XIVe siècle: conflits de voisinage et normes juridiques d'après le texte du maître maçon Ibn al-Rami* (Cairo: Institut Français d'Archéologie Orientale, 2008).

124 On the concept and evolution see Delfina Serrano, "ʿAmal," EI³, an excellent introduction to the topic, and Jacques Berque, "Essai sur la méthode juridique maghrébine," in *Opera minora* (Paristo: 2001); Yasin Dutton, *The Origins of Islamic Law: The Qur'ān, the Muwaṭṭa' and Madinan ʿAmal* (London: Curzon Press, 1999); Delfina Serrano, "Legal Practice in an Andalusī-Maghribī Source from the Twelfth Century CE: The Madhāhib al-ḥukkām fī nawāzil al-aḥkām."; Henry Toledano, *Judicial Practice and Family Law in Morocco: The Chapter on Marriage from Sijilmāsī's al-ʿAmal al-muṭlaq* (Boulder: 1981).

125 There is a tradition of eastern Mālikism (as the chart of jurists below indicates); presumably it is not as institutionalized as the western form. It also has not been as well studied. For an introduction, see Ahmed Bekir, *Histoire de l'école malikite en Orient jusqu'a la fin du Moyen Age* (Tunis: Imprimerie de l.U.G.T.T., 1962).

(Compilations of court practices appeared in the fifteenth century, and a systematic method of applying *ʿamal* was developed by the eighteenth century.) *ʿAmal* can be defined as the practices of the courts or as the legal practices accepted by a majority of qāḍīs and muftīs of a particular time and place.

In early Islamic jurisprudence, *ʿamal* consisted of the Qurʾān and the Prophetic Sunna as enacted by the companions and early successors of Muḥammad. The *Muwaṭṭaʾ* of Mālik b. Anas (d. 795), the foundational text of Mālikism and one of the earliest compendia of Islamic law, records ḥadīth, the interpretation of Medinan jurists, including those of Mālik, and the practice of the people of Medina (referred to as *al-ʿamal ʿindana* or *al-sunna ʿindana*). In its simplest form, *ʿamal* can be said to be the implementation of the sharīʿa by the inheritors of Muḥammad's foundational community in Medina.[126] With the consolidation of the Sunni schools of law and the post-Shāfiʿī articulation of a more textually-rigorous legal methodology based on ḥadīth, Mālikī jurists defended the concept of Medinan *ʿamal* as epistemologically superior to interpretation based on ḥadīth limited to single transmitters (*khabar al-āḥād*) Qāḍī ʿIyāḍ argues, therefore, for the superiority of the Mālikī tradition, and Mālikī *ʿamal* specifically, because it enjoys of a consistency of wide transmission, passed down by the Medinan community as a whole from Muḥammad and from the practice of his time. *ʿAmal ahl al-Madina* can thus be understood as a less "textual" interpretation of the sharīʿa but which enjoys the highest epistemological value afforded to knowledge in Islam (characterizing the Qurʾān itself): *tawātur*, or wide and consecutive transmission within a community as a whole. Since ḥadīth can be transmitted by single individuals at far remove from the original community of interpretation, when conflicting with the *ʿamal* of the people of Medina, the latter is preferred by Mālikī jurists for its greater epistemological certainty. Also by the time of ʿIyāḍ, a distinction between two forms of *ʿamal* had been formulated by Mālikī jurists: *ʿAmal naqlī*, or transmitted *ʿamal*, which enjoys *tawātur*, comes from the time of Muḥammad and includes those Medinan practices he tacitly thought lawful by not censoring them, and *ʿAmal ijtihādī*, which originates from a subsequent time, is the product of interpretation, and is thus a kind of acknowledgement of diverse communities of practice and interpretation.

---

126 A definition close to that endorsed by Mālikī jurists themselves. A more nuanced definition would account for the difference between the jurists' apologetic definition of the term and the real content covered by it, which included pre-Islamic local practices whose normative value was legitimized *a posteriori*. With thanks to the reviewer who pointed this out.

From the fifth/eleventh century in al-Andalus and the sixth/twelfth century in the Maghrib, a variety of sources refer to authoritative judicial practice. When a practice became established, qāḍīs and muftīs were expected to abide by it, whether or not it followed the majority opinion of the school. These sources include notarial formularies (*shurūṭ*), manuals for judges (*adab al-qāḍī*), and compilations of opinions (*fatwās*) and cases (*aḥkām* and *nawāzil*). Regional centers that became identified with specific traditions of *ʿamal* included Toledo, Cordoba, and Fez. The *ʿamal* of al-Andalus was influential in the Maghrib. And the *ʿamal* of Cordoba was preeminent in the former, that of Fez in the latter. By the sixteenth century, specialized *ʿamal* compilations began to appear in the Maghrib.[127] These are composed as elliptic mnemonic poems with extensive commentaries by their authors or others. A concomitant development to these compendia was the formulation of a set of rules to apply *ʿamal*. In public interest cases, *ʿamal* favoring minority opinions could only be adjudicated by qualified judges (not so in simple cases of observance of custom); changes in *ʿamal* favoring minority opinions must be justified by current circumstances, including but not restricted to public welfare; practices based on minority opinions must not contravene scriptural principles; and *ʿamal* deemed lawful by minority opinions must be widespread and attested to by trustworthy witnesses.

As the above description of *ʿamal* indicates. The relationship between sharīʿa and practice is a complex one, especially since the avenues for their interaction and interpenetration varied over the long evolution of sharīʿa. *ʿUrf* is a term, perhaps the most common today, used to designate customary law. It can be understood as customary law, broadly, concerning the diversity in practices such as the giving of dowries, but it is most closely associated with the conflict resolution and negotiating practices existing across the Middle East and North Africa, especially in places with little central government representation, in which figures other than qāḍīs[128] were elected by the community to act as arbitrators and mediators (and whose designations vary: *ḥākim*,

127 Some of the best known of these include *al-Lamiyya* by ʿAlī b. al- Zaqqāq (d. 1507), the *ʿAmal al-Fāsī* by ʿAbd al-Raḥmān b. ʿAbd al-Qādir al-Fāsī (d. 1695), and *al-ʿAmal al-muṭlaq* by al-Sijilmāsī al-Ribāṭī (d. 1800). Delfina Serrano, "ʿAmal," EI³.

128 i.e., judges presiding over Islamic courts. This is not meant to imply that *ʿurf* is alien to the qāḍī's field of activity or that it is limited to rural areas. My approach, in fact, is based on the notion that qāḍīs and muftīs were in constant creative interaction with customary practices and that these formed a much greater part of the picture than Islamic legal theory allows.

ʿārif, marādī, and sometimes even qāḍī).[129] The rules by which such arbitrators act and the parties interact and accept arbitration is understood to fall under the category of *ʿurf*; it is also a term more associated with Arab tribal customary practice than with non-Arab custom, but it is also associated with the practice of specialized subgroups and professions, such as fishermen and mariners. On the whole, modern sharīʿa is accepting of *ʿurf*, based on the idea that normative social practice, when not in contravention of the sharīʿa, should be respected and serves a complementary the role for the functioning of sharīʿa itself.

ʿĀda is a term for social practice or custom more broadly construed.[130] At times, jurists explicitly cite local custom as the guiding parameter to follow on issues about which the sharīʿa is silent. Moreover, even in the most "Islamic" of societies, certain jurisdictions have historically fallen outside of that of the sharīʿa and the qāḍīs, notably the courts and decisions of military rulers, which were often conducted according to the customary practice of a specific group. In many other cases, perhaps more easily visible on the borders of the Islamic world, Islamic law has been in constant and creative interaction with local practice; jurists at times have found means to incorporate or justify through legal reasoning practices that would appear to contradict or go against the letter of the law. In the very wide world of Islamic and Islamicate societies the examples of the interaction of Islamic law and custom are endless. Islamic law's flexibility, I believe, made its diffusion possible and fomented its diversity.

I describe these three terms, *ʿamal*, *ʿurf*, and *ʿāda* (by no means singularly used to denote local practice and custom), to make a few points: While it is safe to say that many and perhaps most western scholars assume there to have been a creative interaction between custom and Islamic law, the details, identification, and development of such practices and processes are poorly understood. Local judicial practice (*ʿamal*) which often resulted from evolution

---

129 On *ʿurf* and custom, see F. H. Stewart, "ʿUrf," EI[3]. Also, Maribel Fierro, *Ill-Treated Women Seeking Divorce: The Qurʾānic Two Arbiters and Judicial Practice Among the Malikis in al-Andalus and North Africa* (Leiden: Brill, 2006); Aharon Layish, *Sharīʿa and Custom in Libyan Tribal Society: An Annotated Translation of Decisions from the Sharīʿa Courts of Adjābiya and Kufra*, Studies in Islamic law and society, v. 24 (Leiden ; Boston, Mass.: Brill, 2005); Frank H. Stewart, "Tribal Law in the Arab World: A Review of the Literature," *International Journal of Middle Eastern Studies* 19, no. 4 (1987): 473–90; A. Shabana, *Custom in Islamic Law and Legal Theory: The Development of the Concepts of ʿurf and ʿādah in the Islamic Legal Tradition* (New York: Palgrave Mcmillan, 2010).

130 EI[2], s.v. ʿĀda. For an analysis of the theological relationship between the two terms see A. Shabana, *Custom in Islamic Law and Legal Theory: The Development of the Concepts of ʿurf and ʿādah in the Islamic Legal Tradition*, chap. 3.

within a particular community (e.g., through interpretation) has often been confused with practices associated more with customary law, i.e., non-Islamic practices and jurisdictions that survive and work in parallel with sharīʿa jurisdictions. The evolution of such diversity through interpretation or interaction is difficult to trace textually. How did the Mālikī judicial practice of Toledo, Cordoba, Fez, and Qayrawān come to be differentiated and what part of this differentiation is a result of local interpretation or interaction with local circumstances or with existing local custom? This process is just beginning to be decribed and understood. Additional difficulty is due to the fact that while Muslim jurists have been accepting of custom and its interaction with the law, they have been reticent to describe it as an authoritative source or to define it in much detail. On the contrary, there would seem to be a strong tendency to either argue for the legitimacy of such practices by Islamic legal means and terms, the result of which is difficult to excavate.

•••

The texts analyzed here form part of the rich corpus for the study of local practice (*ʿamal*) and the interaction of custom (*ʿurf*) and law. But while I have taken this interpretive approach to good effect, I believe, it is also true that most of the texts and cases here cannot be said to describe either unequivocally. The one clear case in which we see Islamic law and custom plainly interacting is in Chap. 2, in the "Case of the Plundered Cattle," which I have bundled with a case on the privatization of communal property. These two instances appear to describe the process whereby property known to have been acquired in a non-Mālikī or non-Islamic[131] framework is exchanged or acquired in one. The cases illustrate the creative processes and possibilities through which practices or statuses could be "Islamized." The other cases analyzed below, on the other hand, do not make explicit mention of custom. However, they illustrate this interaction on a broader level. And taken together, these texts provide a glimpse into how Mālikī legal discourse became rooted in the Far Maghrib, interacting with what was there before by regulating new practices, spaces, and jurisdictions and bolstering the burgeoning establishment and legitimating the rulers who patronized its cultivation and implementation. That is, many of these texts may not directly describe the interaction between law and custom, but they do describe the requisite development of an insitutional context that allows this to happen.

131 Or at least non-orthodox.

6 The Development of the Network and Its Activity as seen through al-Wansharīsī's *Mi'yār* and Qāḍī Iyāḍ's *Tartīb al-Madārik*

The Almoravid period was a pivotal moment for the development of the Mālikī legal and learning establishment in the Far Maghrib. The following brief analysis of two representative works of the western Mālikī tradition amply supports this impression and allows us to better contextualize the fatwās of Ibn Rushd al-Jadd to the Far Maghrib. It is first of all noteworthy, in and of itself, that these two works – a famous compilation of fatwās and a biographical dictionary – are two of the most authoritative of their sort in the tradition and that they were produced in the Far Maghrib (originally not the center of the tradition). As can be gleaned from the numbers presented in the figures below, the Far Maghrib went from being a marginal region of little Mālikī activity and representation to one that produced some of the school's greatest exponents and works.

Completed between 901–914/1496–1508 in Fez, the monumental compilation of fatwās by Aḥmad al-Wansharīsī, *al-Mi'yār al-mu'rib wa-l-jāmi' al-mughrib 'an fatāwī ahl Ifrīqiya wa-l-Andalus wa-l-Maghrib* is perhaps the most important compilation of its sort in the school.[132] It has a great number of recensions. Of the major collections it has been longest in print and has been the best studied. It is thus perhaps the best known Mālikī fatwā compilation both inside and outside North Africa. (The cases analyzed in this book, do not come directly from the *Mi'yār* but are referenced or compiled in it in briefer from.) The *Tartīb al-Madārik*, likewise, compiled in the first half of the sixth/twelfth century in Ceuta by al-Qāḍī 'Iyāḍ, is one of the founding biographical dictionaries of the Mālikī school – it lists thirteen generations of scholars beginning with the school's founder, Mālik b. Anas.[133] Again, we find a region historically

132 The title can be rendered as: "The Clear Standard and Extraordinary Collection of the Legal Opinions of the Scholars of Ifrīqiya, al-Andalus, and the Maghrib." On al-Wansharīsī and the *Mi'yār* see Fransisco Vidal Castro, "Aḥmad al-Wansharīsī (m. 914/1508). Principales Aspectos de su Vida.," *al-Qanṭara* XII (1991): 315–52; Fransisco Vidal Castro, "Las obras de Aḥmad al-Wanšarīsī (m. 914/1508) Inventario analítico," *Anaquel de Estudios Árabes* III (1992): 73–112; Fransisco Vidal Castro, "El *Mi'yār* de al-Wanšarīsī (m. 914/1508). I: Fuentes, manuscritos, ediciones, traducciones," *Miscelánea de Estudios Árabes y Hebraicos* 42–43 (1993): 317–61; Fransisco Vidal Castro, "El *Mi'yār* de al-Wanšarīsī (m. 914/1508). II. Contenido," *Miscelánea de Estudios Árabes y Hebraicos* 44 (1995): 213–46; David S. Powers, *Law, Society, and Culture in the Maghrib, 1300–1500*, 4–9; Jocelyn Hendrickson, "The Islamic Obligation to Emigrate: Al-Wansharīsī's *Asnā al-Matājir* Reconsidered" (PhD diss., Emory University, 2009), 11–21.

133 Qāḍī 'Iyāḍ, a key link in the transmission of Mālikism from north to south, figures prominently in Chapter Three. Biographical and bibliographical information are supplied there.

peripheral to the school (even if Ceuta entered the Andalusī orbit before the rest of the Far Maghrib) producing, in the Almoravid period, what became a foundational text by one of the school's best known scholars.

A breakdown of the identifable or ascribable fatwās in the *Mi'yar* shows that between the third/ninth and fifth/eleventh centuries, Ifrīqī scholars wrote 434 fatwās, Andalusīs 342, whereas scholars of the Far Maghrib wrote only four. The central Maghrib likewise produced a meagre twenty-one fatwās. In the post-Almoravid period, by contrast – from sixth/twelfth to ninth/fifteenth centuries – the Far Maghrib witnesses a seventy-two fold increase (4 to 286); the central Maghrib witnesses a similarly significant increase (from 21 to 111) while production in Ifrīqiya and al-Andalus remains relatively stable with an 18% drop in the former and a 22% rise in the latter (that is, relatively stable numbers). When al-Wansharīsī was writing the *Miʿyār* at the turn of the ninth-tenth/fifteenth-sixteenth centuries, al-Andalus was disappearing as a political and cultural entity and Ifrīqiya was soon to be absorbed by the Ottoman empire (under whom the Hanafi School would receive state support). The Far Maghrib, on the other hand, had caught up in its juridical and scholarly production. In many ways, it would assume the centrality once held by al-Andalus and Ifrīqiya.

TABLE 1 *Fatwās of identifiable origin in al-Wansharīsī's* Miʿyār.[134]

	Procedural, Ritual, Family IXth-XIth c.	**Procedural, Ritual, Family XIIth-XVth c.**	**Economy, Endowments IXth-XIth c.**	**Economy, Endowments XIIth-XVth c.**
Far Maghrib	1	106	3	180
Central Maghrib	9	43	12	68
Ifrīqiya	256	180	178	136
al-Andalus	160	179	182	260

134 For a more detailed breakdown, see Appendix A: the Fatwās of al-Wansharīsī's *Miʿyār* by subject and region, based on Vincent Lagardère's descriptive index, Vincent Lagardère, *Histoire et société en occident musulman au Moyen Age: analyse du Miʿyār d'al-Wanšarīsī.* Lagardère's index is immensely useful. In it, he classifies and briefly describes some 2,100 containing historical information (or details that allow identification and dating) of the roughly 6,000 fatwās contained in the *Miʿyār*. There are two minor discprepancies with the numbers presented here: Lagardère counts a total of 2,144 fatwās. Based on his own numbering system, I count a total of 2,096. This may be the result of two typos: on p. 73 the numbering jumps from 301 to 320, adding 18 fatwās; it appears likely that 2,144 is a result of a typographical error, substituting a four for a one (2,096 + 18 = 2,114). The fore-

Also significant for our broad understanding of this legal activity and its development is the proportions of the fields of consultation, insofar as they can be separated into discrete categories. Of the 2,096 of the *Miʿyār's* fatwās indexed by V. Lagardère, 1,101 can be categorized as dealing with economic matters (such as sales, exchange, transactions, service and rental contracts, as well as property and the management of endowments), in contrast to the 995 that deal with religious, ritual, procedural, personal status, and other diverse issues not directly economy related. While such numbers and ascriptions are rough, the fact that 53% of the questions were on economic issues, does give a sense of how substantive Mālikī law developed over seven centuries. And when considering the Far Maghrib alone, this proportion is even higher. Of a total of 294 fatwās, 187 deal with economic issues. That is, 64% of the Far Maghribi questions and opinions compiled by al-Wansharisi – a full 184 of which date to after the rise of the Almoravids – dealt with economic, commercial, and property questions.

TABLE 2 *Jurists recorded in Qāḍī ʿIyāḍ's biographical dictionary by region and generation* (ṭabaqa).[135]

Gen.	Medina	Mecca	Yemen	Iraq	Syria	Egypt	Ifrīqiya	Andalus	F. Maghrib
I	17		1		1	10	11	8	
II	30	1	2	7	6	24	10	10	
III	5	1			1	11		1	
IV	4			4		16	14	23	

word by P. Guichard and M. Marín state, however, that Lagardère based his study on 2,144 "fiches." So there may be another explanation for the difference (a few of the fatwās have multiple questions and answers, for example). For the Almoravid period, I included jurists active between 1090 and 1147. Unlike Lagardère, I count Qāḍī ʿIyāḍ's fatwās as originating in the Far Maghrib. He counts him as Andalusi, which is reasonable, given that he was active for a time in Granada. The classification is, therefore, not 100% precise; the numbers do, however, present a useful and broad picture of juristic activity in the Islamic West. The urban centers where most of this activity occurred are the following: in Ifrīqiya: Qayrawān, Mahdia, and Tunis; in the Central Maghrib: Tlemcen, Bougie, Alger, Tourat, and Bône; In the Far Maghrib: Fez, Taza, Marrakesh, and Meknes; and in al-Andalus: Cordoba, Zaragoza, Seville, Granada, Málaga, Játiva, and Murcia.

135 Based on the indeces of Muḥammad b. Tāwīt al-Ṭanjī, ed. *Tartīb al-madārik wa-taqrīb al-masālik li-maʿrifat aʿlām madhhab Mālik* (Rabat: Wizārat al-Awqāf wa-l-Shuʾūn al-Islamīyah, 1981). Ifrīqiya, generation IV, includes some jurists from the Far Maghrib. Iraq, generation VII, includes some jurists from Syria.

TABLE 2 *Jurists recorded in Qāḍī ʿIyāḍ's biographical dictionary (cont.).*

Gen.	Medina	Mecca	Yemen	Iraq	Syria	Egypt	Ifrīqiya	Andalus	F. Maghrib
V	1			2		41	27	71	
VI	2			5		21	79	118	
VII	1			22		26	51	174	3
VIII	1	1		13	1	15	59	108	2
IX		2		23		13	21	82	5
X		2		25	2	9	11	56	6
XI				8		2	29	64	6
XII				5	3	3	24	21	15
XIII	3					3	20	43	
Total	64	7	3	114	14	194	356	779	37

A break down of the regional identities of ʿIyāḍ's biographical dictionary yields similar numbers.[136] Al-Andalus produced the preponderance of Mālikī ʿulamāʾ before the sixth/twelfth century, according to Qāḍī ʿIyāḍ. This is almost twice as many as its closest regional competitor, Ifrīqiya, and a full 50% of the totality of the jurists recorded (779 of a total 1,568). By contrast, he records only thirty-seven in total for the Far Maghrib. In the first six generations, ʿIyāḍ records almost no jurists in the Far Maghrib (compared to 231 for al-Andalus and 123 in Egypt). It is only after the seventh generation that the small numbers of Far Maghribi Mālikī ʿulamāʾ begin to grow: 3, 2, 5, 6, and 6 (as compared to 174, 108, 82, 56, and 64 for the corresponding generations of Andalusī scholars). And it is only in the last generation recorded by ʿIyāḍ that there is a bump in the numbers for the Far Maghrib, doubling to fifteen. This is the generation that included ʿAbd Allāh b. Yāsīn, the founder of the Almoravid movement.

7 Book Structure

The basic structure of the book is grounded in a geographical classification of the fatwās, each chapter focussing on a specific area of the Far Maghrib

136 On biographical literature and its relationship to reproducing the social order and institutionalization, see Fernando Rodriguez Mediano, "El Género Biográfico Árabe: Apuntes Teóricos," in *Biografías y Género Biográfico en el Occidente Islámico*, ed. María Luisa Ávila, and Manuela Marín, Estudios Onomástico Biográficos de al-Andalus, VIII (Madrid: CSIC, 1997).

(Marrakesh, the general Far Maghrib, and Ceuta).[137] The chapters themselves

137 The fatwās analyzed in Chapters One and Two were selected by scanning Ibn Rushd, *Fatāwā Ibn Rushd: li-Abī al-Walīd Muḥammad b. Aḥmad b. Aḥmad b. Rushd al-Qurṭubī al-Mālikī*, 3 vols. (Beirut: Dār al-Gharb al-Islāmī, 1987). The indices compiled by the editor were particularly useful. The basic criteria for inclusion was the presence of a geographical link to the Far Maghrib. This includes the known residence of the person posing the question (the *mustaftī* or *sāʾil*) as well as a questioner's identification of the question as one being relevant to the Far Maghrib (often referred to as *al-ʿIdwa*). Only questions dealing with issues pertinent to the Far Maghrib have been included. Those dealing with individuals from the Far Maghrib residing in al-Andalus were not. The texts of the first two chapters are based on al-Talīlī's edition (compiled primarily from three manuscripts of Ibn Rushd's fatwās as originally compiled by Abū al-Ḥasan Muḥammad b. al-Wazzān and, secondarily, from a variety of other sources, including Ibn Rushd's works and later collections of fatwās and *nawāzil*), primarily because of the quality and transparency of his method of selection and critical edition. An alternate compilation of comparable quality, even if its indexing and editorial criteria are less clear, is Ibn Rushd, *Masāʾil Abī al-Walīd b. Rushd al-Jadd*, 2 vols. (Casablanca: Dār al-Afāq al-Jadīda, 1992). Both editions were based on the editors' doctoral theses. For a comparison of the comparative merits of the editions, see Delfina Serrano, "Ibn Rušd al-Qurṭubī al-Māliki, Abū l-Walīd Muḥammad b. Aḥmad b. Aḥmad, *Fatāwī Ibn Rušd*, taqdīm wa-taḥqīq wa-ŷamʿ wa-taʿlīq al-Duktūr al-Mukhtar al-Ṭāhir al-Talīlī. *Masāʾil Abī l-Walīd Ibn Rušd* (*al-ŷadd*); taḥqīq ʿan sitt nusaj jaṭṭiyya maʿa dirasāt ʿan l-muʿtallif wa-l-kitāb Muḥammad al-Ḥabīb al-Tiŷānī.," *al-Qanṭara* xv (1994): 531–34. The text analyzed in Chapter Three is based on a different source altogether: Muḥammad b. ʿIyāḍ and ʿIyāḍ b. Mūsā, *Madhāhib al-ḥukkām fī nawāzil al-aḥkām*, 2nd ed. (Beirut: Dār al-Gharb al-Islāmī, 1997). These are the *nawāzil* of Qāḍī ʿIyāḍ as compiled by his son. Because of the nature of the production and compilation of the text, it includes opinions from a number of jurisconsults over several stages of a single case. It therefore affords deeper insight into the process of a particular case and the role of jurisconsultation in its development. The text is significant, furthermore, as an example of the consultative correspondence between Ibn Rushd and one of his most important students and correspondents in the Far Maghrib, Qāḍī ʿIyāḍ, who, by far, petitioned the greatest number of recorded opinions from Ibn Rushd to the Far Maghrib: of 41 questions arising from the Far Maghrib (tallied from al-Talīlī's edition – several of the opinions Ibn Rushd wrote for Qāḍī ʿIyāḍ appear in both the edition of Qāḍī ʿIyāḍ's *nawāzil* and Ibn Rushd fatwās), 23 were destined for Ceuta, where Qāḍī ʿIyāḍ was in most cases the *mustaftī*. I have chosen to include only one case in which Qāḍī ʿIyāḍ sought an opinion from Ibn Rushd, however, because Ceuta had been within the sphere of Andalusī cultural and institutional influence for much longer than the rest of the Far Maghrib, and also because Qāḍī ʿIyāḍ's *nawāzil* have received a fair degree of treatment in the translation and an introductory study found in Muḥammad b. ʿIyāḍ, *Madhāhib al-ḥukkām fī nawāzil al-aḥkām* (*La actuación de los jueces en los procesos judiciales*). To avoid replicating D. Serrano's work, I have opted to focus most of my attention on questions relevant to the region south of ʿIyāḍ's sphere of activity. I have deemed it important to include at least

consist of thematic groupings, the arrangement of which responds to the nature of the material.

Chapter One examines a group of questions directed to Ibn Rushd from Marrakesh, the Almoravid capital and center of institutional change in the south Far Maghrib. The fatwās analyzed highlight the interaction between commercial activity with the development of a Mālikī network and jurisdiction in the urban markets. They also point to the cultivation of Mālikī learning, specifically in the resolution of disputes over ritual questions, that bolstered the development of this network. The chapter concludes with an examination of the impact these developments had on Almoravid and religio-political authority.

Chapter Two examines Ibn Rushd's responses to questions arising from regions of the Far Maghrib other than Marrakesh and the urban centers of the Mediterranean coast (Ceuta and Tangier).[138] The analysis presents a sketch of the state of development and impact of the Andalusī-Maghribī Mālikī consultative network in the Far Maghrib outside of the capital and the region where the relationship with al-Andalus had been longest established. Moving from center to periphery, the first section of the chapter analyzes questions from the highest echelons of Almoravid authority on issues of widespread importance to the Far Maghrib. These fatwās shed light on the nature of the relationship, in its most direct form, between Andalusī Mālkīsm – as represented by Ibn Rushd al-Jadd – and the Almoravid political center. The remaining fatwās suggests how Mālikī learning developed over discussions of specific points of law and highlight the social context in which these developments occurred, as well as the nature of the interaction between a growing Mālikī jurisdiction and existing customary practices.

Chapter Three analyzes a case that took place in Ceuta – through the correspondence between Qāḍī ʿIyāḍ, chief judge of Ceuta, and a group of Andalusī muftīs – for which Ibn Rushd wrote the leading opinion. Unlike the previous ones, this text consists of a correspondence over several weeks involving a single case. It therefore uniquely illustrates the role of consultation (*futyā*) in a developing legal case and juxtaposes Ibn Rushd's opinions with those of other important muftīs of the period. Written to the most active of Ibn Rushd's correspondents and most important transmitter of his opinions into the Far

one of his *nawāzil* here, however, because of his unique role as student and major transmitter of Ibn Rushd's opinions into the legal tradition of the Far Maghrib.

138 When they are explicitly identified as coming from one of these places; this chapter thus includes fatwās generically described as directed to the Far Maghrib, without stating a specific urban center or location.

Maghrib, the text provides an illustration of how Qāḍī ʿIyād of Ceuta acted as a conduit for Andalusī Mālikism into the Far Maghrib.

The Epilogue considers the question of continuities and discontinuities between the Almoravid and Almohad periods, in the context of the sociohistorical developments highlighted here.

CHAPTER 1

Fatwās to Marrakesh: Regulation of the City Market and the Symbolic Authority of Mālikī Learning

1 Introduction

If one had to chose a single object to illustrate the complex relationship between al-Andalus and the Far Maghrib under the Almoravids, one could do worse than step into the side-room of the Badīʿ Palace (today a museum in the old city of Marrakesh) where the original "Kutubiyya Minbar"[1] is on display. This stepped pulpit, standing 3.86 meters tall, 3.46 meters deep, and 87 cm wide, and consisting of some 1.3 million pieces of wood, is one of the oldest and most exquisite objects of its kind in the Islamic world. It is one of the most significant surviving objects of Almoravid material culture and, arguably, was a symbol of power and prestige for the empire; the Amīr ʿAlī b. Yūsuf himself commissioned it for the Great Mosque of Marrakesh he built. As the mosque neared completion, he had turned to Cordoba for the crafting of this masterpiece woodwork, which took five years to make.[2]

The minbar was the focal element of religio-political authority in the traditional congregational mosque – the miḥrāb provided the spiritual one. The minbar developed from the "raised seats" used by judges in pre-Islamic Arabia and is "the only common feature of the modern mosque that was used by the Prophet Muhammad himself."[3] This seat or pulpit from which the Prophet spoke in the earliest mosque of Islam in Medina was reproduced by the Prophet's successors. It became a symbol of caliphal authority and eventually appeared in the congregational mosque of practically every city of the Islamic world. From the minbar, the caliph, his deputy, and later imāms addressed the believers and invoked the name of the community's leader. It was a powerful symbol of continuity with Islamic traditions and of the religious and politi-

1 The name, Kutubiyya Minbar, is something of a misnomer, since it was originally built for the Almoravid Great Mosque of Marrakesh, not the Almohad Great Mosque, known as the Kutubiyya.

2 Jonathan Bloom, *The Minbar from the Kutubiyya Mosque* (New York, Madrid [Rabat]: Metropolitan Museum of Art, Ediciones el Viso, Ministry of Cultural Affairs, Kingdom of Morocco, 1998), 3.

3 Jonathan Bloom, "The Masterpiece Minbar," *Saudi Aramco World* (1998), 2–11.

 | DOI 10.1163/9789004279841_003

cal authority that stemmed from this continuity. So when ʿAlī b. Yūsuf commissioned, on 24 Rabīʿ I 531/19 September 1137, this centerpiece for the great mosque of his capital city, it would have been lost on no one that by turning to the recognized, master craftsmen of the region,[4] the Almoravid amīr was physically appropriating the prestige of Cordoba and invoking its Umayyad past. Likewise, it would have been lost on no one that the successor dynasty of the Almoravids (the Almohads, who invoked their caliphal right more deliberately and conspicuously) spoliated the minbar commissioned by ʿAlī and placed it in the symbolic center of their own empire (the new great mosque of the capital).

The Almoravids were not to enjoy the view of this beautiful minbar for long. In the same year it was delivered (after some delay) from Cordoba to Marrakesh, the Almohads took the city and, characteristically, sought to erase the Almoravid legacy, remaking elements of the urban and political landscape into their own. They razed ʿAlī b. Yūsuf's mosque on the grounds of correcting an aberration in its orientation, and replaced it with the first Kutubiyya Mosque, located on the site of what had been the Almoravid amīr's palace. They kept the minbar. In the opinion of a fourteenth-century North African traditionist, preacher, and statesman, Shams al-Dīn Muḥammad b. Marzūq, the minbar was long recognized as a masterwork. Comparing it to a mosque built by his patron in Tlemcen he wrote:

> As for the minbar, all craftsmen at the time declare that nowhere in the world was the equivalent ever made. They agree that the minbar of [the Great Mosque of] Cordoba and the minbar of the Booksellers' [i.e., the Kutubiyya mosque] in Marrakesh are the most remarkable in craftsmanship, because it is not customary for Easterners to have fine woodwork in their buildings. A number of fragments from the Cordoba minbar have appeared [in the Maghrib] and these have been compared with those from the Tlemcen minbar. The [latter] minbar does not suffer in comparison. It has carved pieces of wood the size of a hazelnut or a chickpea and incrustations of the size of a grain of wheat or almost: to see it, one is amazed. God will demand an account of he who causes the ruin of his masterpieces and chastise him because he destroyed monuments in

4 Whose predecessors in the tenth century were behind the famous minbar of the great mosque of Cordoba, commissioned by al-Ḥakam II, for the then greatest mosque of the greatest state of the Islamic West.

which all the people of Islam took glory and which would have illustrated religion for eternity.[5]

•••

While not as dazzling as the Kutubiyya Minbar, the texts analyzed here provide an equally vivid illustration of this complex cultural relationship, as well as of the role of al-Andalus in the poorly understood process by which society in the the Far Maghrib was transformed in the Almoravid period. Unified for the first time under a single indigenous Muslim power, the population centers grew along with the economic engine spurring this development.[6] It is no mere coincidence that "orthodox" Sunnī Islam, in the form of Mālikism, became firmly established in this period in regions where it had only a tenuous presence before the fifth/eleventh century (such as the Atlantic coastal plain where the Barghawāta lived, and the region south of Fez and Meknes). At the center of this process stood the great caravan city of Marrakesh. It's founding *c.* 463/1070 marked the Almoravids' arrival at a threshold of regional leadership and imperial aspiration. It would be the capital city throughout their imperial experience and, as mentioned above, would be usurped as capital by the Berber-Islamic empire that followed.

The texts analyzed in this chapter describe a series of questions posed from this new city some fifty years after its founding, by jurists and judges active there, to the muftī Ibn Rushd al-Jadd of Cordoba. They are the only such texts originating from the Almoravid capital out of more than the 660 fatwās by Ibn Rushd that have reached us.[7] They thus present important and rare glimpses into what remains an obscure period in the city's early development. While these brief and sometimes difficult texts do not provide what one would call a panoramic view – they are rather more like snapshots from interesting angles – combined with other data, they afford us deep insight into the city's socio-economic and institutional evolution during its first half-century of existence.

Analysis of the fatwās below, I argue, bears out the following critical points: They reinforce the notion that an Almoravid commercial revolution was accompanied by an elaboration of the body of Mālikī fiqh or positive law in the

---

5 Quoted in Jonathan Bloom, *The Minbar from the Kutubiyya Mosque*, 4. Brackets in original. I reproduce the quote in its entirety because it is significant on several levels, including the clear appreciation it demonstrates for the symbolic value of the minbar and of Andalusī craftsmanship in the Maghrib.

6 J. L. Boone, et al., "Archeological and Historical Approaches to Complex Societies: The Islamic States of Medieval Morocco," 635.

7 According to al-Talīlī's count.

Far Maghrib, that long distance trade and gold and its exchange was at the heart of this process, and that a developing network of Mālikī jurists there played a key role in facilitating this commercial growth. Half of the questions analyzed in this chapter involve some element of commercial transaction. They inquire into the legality of selling raw bullion for dīnārs, settling a debt with dīnārs of a different denomination from that in which it was incurred, trading different qualities of gold, as well as into a judge's supervisory role and jurisdiction over such activity and the settling of disputes over claims of defective merchandise and fraud or shortchanging.

Concomitant with the elaboration of both the body of substantive law (commercial or otherwise) and the development of a network of jurists who supported and implemented it, was a process of adoption of Andalusī Mālikī religious and ritual knowledge, with a resulting evolution of its influence and prestige. In other words, the "technical" authority enjoyed by Andalusī Mālikī jurists in areas such as the mediation and administration of urban commercial exchange (activities that were central to Almoravid success), extended to the areas of ritual, religious, and, ultimately, political authority; the significance of this influence was felt, moreover, across the full range of religio-political issues affecting the every-day lives of Marrakeshīs (from technical matters to those of high public profile), extending even to matters that touched at the core of Almoravid ideology and its reformist mission.

The remaining questions inquire into a broad range of such matters, including legal procedure, personal status, ritual law, and an accusation of apostasy. The examination of this last case, of the Muslim convert accused of apostasy, considered alongside the more mundane cases, allows us to develop our understanding of Almoravid authority, of the spread of Mālikī law and its interaction with local custom, and of the broad topic of religious change in the Far Maghrib in this period.

2 The Founding and Development of Marrakesh

Founded on a sparsely populated marsh *c.* 463/1070, Marrakesh became a major gateway for the commercial and urban development of the southern Far Maghrib. The city's development from military camp to metropolis in only a few decades typifies the transformation undergone by the Far Maghrib with Almoravid unification and the attendant influx of wealth. The texts described in this chapter concern events that occurred during what has been called the "third phase" of the city's earliest history (marked by the accession to power of ʿAlī b. Yūsuf), a period characterized by the first organized effort to develop the city's layout and produce structures befitting an imperial capital.[8] This initiative, sponsored by the Almoravid amīr, coincided with a great influx of Andalusī learning and skill in a variety of areas, of which the architectural, secretarial, and legal are only the most visible in the historical and archeological record. On a first level of appreciation, then, these texts, as objects, are evidence of this influx of Andalusī learning, marshaled for the development of the Almoravid capital.[9]

The Almoravids had first moved into the plain north of the High Atlas Mountains (which constitutes the most significant north-south geographical barrier in the Far Maghrib) in the late 440s/1050s. They began by taking two towns, Nafīs and Aghmāt, each of which lie at the heads of valleys that feed into the plain north of the High Atlas. Chronicles report that after taking these towns, the Almoravid leader, Abū Bakr b. ʿUmar, set out to determine an appropriate site for a new city to claim as his movement's own. This new city would be strategically placed further into the plain than either Nafīs or Aghmāt (away from the population of the foothills) where Abū Bakr b. ʿUmar could control a greater area.[10] Ibn ʿIdhārī writes that Abū Bakr was compelled to stake out a new location on the plain when conditions became too cramped in Aghmāt, to which immigrants had been drawn by the Almoravid success of raiding and trade. The local Masmūda tribes wanted to play a part in founding the new city, Ibn ʿIdhārī relates that in the year (461/1068–1069):

---

8 This periodization coincides, perhaps too conveniently, with changes in the Almoravid leadership, Hamid Triki, "Marrakech: Retrato Historico de una Metropolis Medieval. Siglos XI-XII," in *La Architectura del Islam Occidental* (Granada: 1995).

9 For such a significant city (and UNESCO world patrimony site), surprisingly little work has been carried out toward unravelling its early history. The classic and to some extent singular study of the urban history of Marrakesh, based on excavations during the 1950s, is Gaston Deverdun, *Marrakech, des origines à 1912* (Rabat: Éditions techniques nord-africaines, 1959). More recent reevaluations include Hamid Triki, "Marrakech," in *Le Prix Aga Khan d'Architecture: Cèrèmonie de remise des prix 1986, Maroc* (1986); Hamid Triki, "Marrakech: Retrato Historico de una Metropolis Medieval. Siglos XI-XII." And Quentin Wilbaux, *La médina de Marrakech: formation des espaces urbains d'une ancienne capitale du Maroc* (Paris: L'Harmattan, 2002). Both are valuable but have not had the benefit of further archeological surveys. Later periods are better served by works such as Emily Gottreich, *The Mellah of Marrakesh: Jewish and Muslim Space in Morocco's Red City* (Bloomington: Indiana University Press, 2007). It argues for the agency of Jewish communities in the Maghrib, through the example of Marrakesh, in shaping urban spaces and institutions, reassessing the concept of the "Islamic city" as one in which institutions are not shaped merely by the perceived necessities of Islamic faith and ritual.

10 Quentin Wilbaux, *La médina de Marrakech*, 208; Hamid Triki, "Marrakech: Retrato Historico de una Metropolis Medieval. Siglos XI-XII."

> The place of assembly in the town of Aghmāt Warīka grew too narrow for the people in it. The Shaykhs of Warīka and Haylāna complained of this to the Amīr Abū Bakr b. 'Umar time and again until he said: "Determine for us a place in which I will build a city – if God, may He be exalted, so wills." His dwellings with his brothers was in tents ... until he married Zaynab al-Nafzāwiyya in this year and the people in Aghmāt multiplied as a result ... The Haylāna and Hazmīra were still determining a place where the city would be built. A dispute between them broke out over this, as each demanded that the city be built in their own land, so that its children could trace their lineage to them. It was on account of this that strife and the alternation of chieftainship (*mudāwalat al-imāra*) ensued between them until the shaykhs of the fighting tribes and others came together [to find a solution].
>
> The final consensus was that the city be located between the land of Haylāna and the land of Hazmīra. They [the representatives of the tribes] then informed their amīr, Abū Bakr b. 'Umar, and said to him: "We have thought of a desert spot where there is nothing tame but gazelles and ostriches, and nothing grows but the Christ's thorn (*sidr*) and the colocynth." Then some [others] of them [the representatives of the tribes] wanted the city to be on the Tānsīft valley. This became impossible for them, however, when [Abū Bakr b. 'Umar] said: "We are people of the dessert and our livestock [travels] with us. Dwellings on the valley don't befit us." So they settled on the [first] place [proposed], where the valley of Nafīs would serve as its gardens, Dukkāla its fields, while the reigns of the Daran Mountains would be in the hand of its amīr for the duration of [the new city's] days. The Amīr Abū Bakr rode in [with] his troops with the shaykhs of the tribes. They walked with him to examine Marrakesh, in which was open country with nothing tame in it. They said to him: "Build here a city that will be an intermediary between Haylāna and Hazmīra."[11]

This description comprises the earliest news of the city: Its founding resulted from the selection of a site by Abū Bakr b. 'Umar with the assistance of representatives of local parties who negotiated over the neutrality of the location. This was presumably followed by the encampment of Almoravid forces at the site and the sprouting of an informal market that served the needs of the settlement. Little is known of this time, as no significant contemporary archeological remains have been discovered. The next major event reported in the

---

11 Ibn 'Idhārī, *al-Bayān al-mughrib* (Leiden: 1948), vol. 4, 19.

chronicles is that which ushered in what is understood to have been the "second stage" in the city's development (and of the empire as a whole): the peaceful transfer of command from Abū Bakr to his cousin, Yūsuf b. Tāshufīn, one of the Maghrib's most successful and charismatic leaders.

Before the accession, Abū Bakr b. ʿUmar had ordered the construction of the city's earliest structure, the Qaṣr al-Ḥajar (Stone Fortress). This was begun on 23 Rajab 463/8 May 1070. The fortress became a pole on the north-south axis upon which the city developed.[12] Abū Bakr would not see the fortress completed. It was at this time that he was called south to put down a rebellion in the Sahara. Abū Bakr repudiated his wife Zaynab so that his cousin, Yūsuf b. Tāshufīn, could marry her while he assumed temporary command of the northern operations of the Almoravid principality. And when Abū Bakr returned from the south, as noted in the introduction, Yūsuf met with him outside the city and let him know that he would not be ceding power. Whether or not this transferral happened peaceably, as recorded, Yūsuf b. Tāshufīn's assumption of command of the Almoravids would neither divide nor weaken the movement. Rather, it marked the point when the movement was transformed from a desert tribal confederation that exercised power over a sparsely inhabited area, albeit considerable, into a state with great urban centers.[13]

While Yūsuf b. Tāshufīn's contribution to the older, northern city of Fez (conquered by the Almoravids in 455/1063) was significant and indelible – he united the two cities on opposite banks of the river that had comprised it, Fez and al-ʿĀliya, and renovated the congregational mosque –[14] his role in the development of Marrakesh was foundational. Here, Yūsuf oversaw the construction of its first mosque – the spiritual center of the empire – which he reportedly helped build with his own hands.[15] The Masjid al-Tūb was made of packed dirt or adobe.[16] It was a rustic structure as likely was most everything else in the city. The Marrakesh of Yūsuf b. Tāshufīn is described as a burgeoning

---

12 Quentin Wilbaux, *La médina de Marrakech*, 213.

13 Sheryl L. Burkhalter, "Listening for Silences in Almoravid History: Another Reading of "The Conquest That Never Was.""

14 Quentin Wilbaux, *La médina de Marrakech*, 209. On the early history of Fez, see H. Terrasse, "Fās," EI², and Roger Le Tourneau, *Fez in the Age of the Marinides* (Norman: University of Oklahoma Press, 1961). More recently, S. O'Meara has used a variety of sources to focus on the social construction of space and the use of walls in a Maghribī context. Simon O'Meara, *Space and Muslim Urban Life: At the Limits of the Labyrinth of Fez* (New York: Routledge, 2007).

15 Quentin Wilbaux, *La médina de Marrakech*, 219; Gaston Deverdun, *Marrakech, des origines à 1912*, 73.

16 ʿAbd al-Aḥad al-Sabtī, and Ḥalīma Farḥāt, *al-Madīna fī al-ʿaṣr al-wasīṭ*, 32.

and colorful encampment: a fortress with a market growing around it and an adobe mosque for the faithful to pray.[17] This mosque of packed dirt became the second, and southern, pole on the city's axis (with the citadel, or Qaṣr al-Ḥajar, on the northern one). To this day, this axis functions as the principal artery of commerce (the area of the *sūq al-sammārīn*) in the old city of Marrakesh.[18] Another development under the aegis of Yūsuf b. Tāshufīn was the expansion of the citadel, which added significantly to the city's layout. Speculating on the origin of the unique features of the Marrakesh citadel, Q. Wilbaux attributes its irregular (roughly a parallelogram) structure, to the (at least partial) use of the Abbasid cubit as a standard measure, and its double wall technique rarely seen in the Maghrib (with roots, or at least similarities to a technique used in Ancient Egypt) to Yūsuf's employment of builders and stone workers who were much more skilled than those previously employed.[19]

These developments notwithstanding, on balance, the scarce information on Yūsuf b. Tāshufīn's Marrakesh suggests that his capital was still little more than a camp, albeit a booming one, evolving in a haphazard way into a rudimentary city. Growth resulted from the fact that, under Yūsuf b. Tāshufīn, Marrakesh became the headquarters of the movement as it entered its greatest period of expansion. But while Marrakesh under Yūsuf b. Tāshufīn was the capital of an empire that conquered Cordoba, Seville, and Granada, the city appears to have retained some of the stark simplicity of the early Almoravid movement,[20] a spirit personified by the character of its charismatic leader, said to have worn simple desert garb and lived in rustic dwellings, eating and drinking camel meat and milk until the end of his days.[21] It was not until the reign of Yūsuf's son, ʿAlī b. Yūsuf (who came to power in 500/1106), that a concerted initiative to urbanize the capital began. The most salient characteristics of this process during the city's "third phase" – gleaned from archeological and textual evidence – included the building (or massive enlarging) of city ramparts, along with construction of a larger and more permanent congregational mosque, as well as the establishment of basic urban layout.

---

17 ʿAbd al-Aḥad al-Sabtī, and Ḥalīma Farḥāt, *al-Madīna fī al-ʿaṣr al-wasīṭ*, 32–33.

18 Quentin Wilbaux, *La médina de Marrakech*, 213.

19 Quentin Wilbaux, *La médina de Marrakech*, 213.

20 This is more of an imaginative speculation than proof-driven conclusion.

21 Fransisco Vidal Castro, "La Expansión en el Magreb y al-Andalus," in *Mauritania y España: Una Historia Común: Los Almorávides, Unificadores del Magreb y al-Andalus* (s. XI-XII), ed. Amor Ben Hamadi (Seville: Fundación el Legado Andalusí, 2003), 84.

Some of these differences between the second and third phases in the city's history, it is important to note, can be overstated.[22] The fact that descriptions of these phases conform so closely with the idealized type embodied by each of the two leaders (readily perceived in Maghribī historiography) should give one pause: Yūsuf is the warrior and ʿAlī the aesthete. In the traditional accounts, Yūsuf b. Tāshufīn epitomizes the pious desert warrior and leader, mimicking Islamic prototypes, such as that of ʿUmar b. al-Khaṭṭāb, second caliph of Islam, who, like him, is credited with bringing pastoral purity and spiritual intensity to a successful imperial project. ʿAlī b. Yūsuf, on the other hand, is described as a kind of Maghribī Louis the Pious, a leader dangerously respectful of religious authority and one in whom the signs of declining natural leadership are foreboding. In a Khaldūnian vision of political development (for which Almoravid history served, after all, as a model), ʿAlī would appear one degree removed from the fountain of charismatic leadership and solidarity that is the tribal group, and one degree closer to civilization: cultivated but critically weakened.[23]

There is an element of truth, to be sure, in the reified images of each of these leaders as presented in the literature: Yūsuf was a Ṣanhājī tribal leader from the Sahara who, while a successful conqueror, remained at heart a man of the desert. ʿAlī, by contrast, was born and educated in a cosmopolitan city (Ceuta) with long ties to al-Andalus. As amīr, ʿAlī commissioned the greatest works of architecture and art of the Almoravid period: the Barudiyyīn dome, the Kutubiyya Minbar, the Great Mosque of Tlemcen.[24] Although easy to depict one as warrior and the other as aesthete, several significant continuities between these two leaders can be readily perceived. After all, it was Yūsuf who was responsible for the foundational gestures of urban development in the Almoravid period.[25] Like ʿAlī, he professed deep respect and personal commitment to the Mālikī ʿulamāʾ, actively recruiting them into the Almoravid imperial project. This gesture was not a mere nod to religious authorities but an alliance and a strategic investment in the structural organization and success of the new state.[26]

22 As with the difference between the reigns of the two most successful leaders of the Almoravid dynasty, Yūsuf b. Tāshufīn and his son ʿAlī.

23 It is surprising how uncritically much twentieth-century historiography adopted the Khaldūnian meta-narrative, accountable perhaps to the investment of some historians in identifying al-Andalus with civilization and Berbers with tribalism and religious fervor (situating the loci of opposing values in different continents, Europe and Africa).

24 Jamil M. Abun-Nasr, *A History of the Maghrib in the Islamic Period*, 85.

25 The building of Marrakesh and unification of Fez.

26 Yūsuf b. Tāshufīn's investment in Mālikism and the Mālikī ʿulamāʾ was visible and influential at key moments of his political career. One illustrative example occurred when, in

Like his father, ʿAlī was an effective leader and second in terms of tenure (lasting thirty-six years) only to his father. He was a capable and determined military leader. This kind of leadership was sorely missed after his death in 537/1143. In more ways than one, ʿAlī modeled himself after and continued the legacy of his father. His iteration of the model was a wealthier and more developed one. The difference between the two reigns is not as stark as suggested by the stock descriptions of the two leaders. Development, in Marrakesh as elsewhere, proceeded gradually and under the influence of events and forces at work throughout the empire.

Textual and material evidence does suggest, however, that it was not until ʿAlī assumed power in 500/1106 that the urbanization of Marrakesh began in earnest. Not only does the Kutubiyya Minbar (the oldest surviving work commissioned for a city building) bear proof of ʿAlī's sponsorship (in an engraving at the back)[27] but the city's oldest surviving structure, the Qubbat al-Barudiyyīn, also bears evidence of his patronage. Evidence suggests that the mosque for which the minbar was commissioned was associated with this *qubba* (or dome), which is believed to have stood in its ablutions court.[28] The excavation and restoration of the *qubba*, with the "rediscovery" of its surprisingly sophisticated Andalusī decorative style, has led to a reconsideration of Maghribī architectural history. The introduction of elements regarded as Almohad innovations has been back-dated to the Almoravid period.[29] These elements signaled the appearance of a cosmopolitan artistic, decorative, and architectural style across the Maghrib and al-Andalus, lending the region a unity of style that is still visible today. The earliest Maghrībī structures displaying elements of this new style – the *qubba* in Marrakesh and the great mosque of Tlemcen – were built under the aegis of ʿAlī.

Reports of ʿAlī's urbanization projects in Marrakesh describe the making of ramparts: eight meter high walls spanning nine kilometers.[30] Moreover, the layout of the mosque and ramparts (while not necessarily built at the same time), were aligned to a single orientation. This was both an innovation and

---

1090, he convened a group of eminent *fuqahāʾ* before making his move to conquer the *taifa* states of al-Andalus. Jacinto Bosch Vilá, *Los Almorávides*, 147–50.

27 Jonathan Bloom, *The Minbar from the Kutubiyya Mosque*, 19.

28 The *qubba* appears to have been either the ablution court of ʿAlī's mosque or part of a monumental structure covering the city's first well. Quentin Wilbaux, *La médina de Marrakech*, 222.

29 Which is not to say that the process was absent or insignificant in the Almohad period, as attested by buildings such as the Kutubiyya mosque of Marrakesh, the Ḥasan Mosque of Rabat, and the Giralda of Seville.

30 Quentin Wilbaux, *La médina de Marrakech*, 224.

part of a plan for future development. Deliberate re-orientation of the city was undertaken in response to developments in astronomical observation and to their application in determining the qibla. ʿAlī appears to have wished to incorporate these developments through the re-definition of the city's shape (in so far as a city's walls determine its shape).[31] Previously, historians (classical and modern) attributed ʿAlī's overhaul of Marrakesh (along with his extensive use of astronomical and astrological calculations and juristic consultations) to excessive religious observance, and/or his seduction (and thus weakening) by the civilization of al-Andalus.[32] More recent scholarship, with good reason, has argued that ʿAlī's gestures were characteristic of his employment of the ʿulamāʾ to legitimate his rule and actions,[33] a strategy very much in the tradition of his father.

•••

The fatwās sent by Ibn Ruhsd to Marrakesh convey an image of a period in the city's history when, having reached a certain level of demographic density and economic activity, typically Islamic institutions began to develop. The texts here bear out how the introduction of the Mālikī institutions of learning, regulation, and mediation played a (if not *the*) key role in this process.[34] The increase in the flow of Mālikī learning into Marrakesh under ʿAlī provided a basis for the burgeoning urban mechanisms of commerce and mediation that emerged as the city was transformed from Almoravid military headquarters to capital of the Far Maghrib and first Ṣanhāja city urbanized on an Andalusī model.

It is in Marrakesh also that we encounter the first well-known Ṣanhāja jurist of the southern Far Maghrib (and one of the first belonging to the Almoravids'

31 Quentin Wilbaux, *La médina de Marrakech*, 223–24. Such overall orientation of the city to the qibla of the congregational mosque is rare. Focus on the orientation of the congregational mosque, however, was common and had specific political import, as demonstrated by the Almohads' razing of the Great Mosque of Marrakesh precisely on these grounds. For a survey on the orientation of mosque and city streets in Morocco, see J. L. Boone, et al., "Archeological and Historical Approaches to Complex Societies: The Islamic States of Medieval Morocco."

32 Quentin Wilbaux, *La médina de Marrakech*, 226–27.

33 For more on this point, see Kenneth Garden, "Al-Ghazālī's Contested Revival," 149.

34 Corroborating in some way the traditional characterization of ʿAlī's obsequiousness to the *fuqahāʾ*.

tribal group):[35] Mūsā b. Ḥammād, chief judge of the city.[36] Although information on him is sparse, in the biographical literature of the Mālikī school he is referred to as "one of the first famous Ṣanhājī jurists."[37] In the emergence of Mūsā b. Ḥammād and in his correspondence with Ibn Rushd, we catch a glimpse of a budding network of Mālikī jurists, sponsored by the Almoravid leadership, under the tutelage of Andalusī jurists. The well-documented life of Qāḍī ʿIyāḍ (the chief judge of Ceuta, featured in Chapter Three), while himself not of the Ṣanhāja, provides an excellent example of such sponsorship and tutelage: His educational travels to al-Andalus were sponsored by ʿAlī b. Yūsuf, who later appointed him chief judge of Ceuta. In Chapter Three, we will encounter Mūsā b. Ḥammād once again, not as a *mustaftī*, as he appears here, but as muftī. This may come as a surprise – the emphasis here being squarely on the influence of Andalusī muftīs on Maghribī jurists. But the fact that Mūsā b. Ḥammād acted as both *mustaftī* and muftī does not undermine the point. The development of the Mālikī judicial network in the Far Maghrib was an interactive and participatory process. Mūsā b. Ḥammād's fatwā to Qāḍī ʿIyāḍ in Chapter Three is brief and one among multiple and more elaborate opinions from mostly Andalusī counterparts. Although this brevity may have been characteristic of a more simple and straightforward legal culture in Marrakesh, Mūsā b. Ḥammād's participation in a correspondence between judges and jurisconsults tying Marrakesh, Cordoba, and Ceuta into a single network, illustrates how the consultative process was instrumental to the integration of the south into the institutional culture of the north. The appearance of a network of "local" Ṣanhāja jurists in the south (embodied here by Mūsā b. Ḥammād) was significant to the development of the Almoravid state, and, in the long term, to the spread of Islamic institutions and learning further south, to the Tafilalt, the Draʿa, the Sūs, and into and across the Sahara.

The burgeoning institution served – perhaps first and foremost – to regulate commerce in the city markets. Furthermore, it regulated (and transformed) family relations and inheritance practices, and eventually suffused the multiple levels of Marrakeshī society. Mālikism itself was changed in this process,

---

35 In the cities of the northern Maghrib and al-Andalus, jurists from local scholarly families were most often employed. Maribel Fierro, "The Qāḍī as Ruler" (Paper presented at the Saber religioso y poder político en el Islam. Actas del Simposio Internacional: (Granada, 15–16 October, 1991), Madrid, 1994), 108; Rachid El Hour, "The Andalusian Qadi in the Almoravid Period: Political and Judicial Authority," *Studia Islamica* 90 (2000), 77.

36 Mūsā b. Ḥammād is one of the few Maghribī jurists mentioned by name in the fatwās analyzed here.

37 al-Ḍabbī, *Bughyat al-multamis fī taʾrīkh rijāl ahl al-Andalus* (Beirut, Cairo: 1989), 398. See also the editor's note in Ibn Rushd, *Fatāwā Ibn Rushd*, 1462.

resulting in the creation of a uniquely Marrakeshī and Far Maghribī set of institutional practices and traditions of learning. It was the successful creation of these institutions, with their unique social powers of mediation and religious knowledge, that lent the ʿulamāʾ their social prestige (much more effectively than the amīr's indulgence). The resulting growth of their influence in Maghribī (and Andalusī)[38] society as a result of Almoravid support, and the challenges to their influence as a class arising from other parts of society, accounts for much of the dynamic surrounding the religious and intellectual debates of the time, including the infamous and much-discussed episode of the public burning of al-Ghazālī's *Iḥyāʾ ʿulūm al-dīn* in 503/1109.[39]

One of the principal reasons for the hostile reception of the *Iḥyāʾ* in the Maghrib was its "anti-ʿulamāʾ" message. Al-Ghazālī's *Iḥyāʾ* was read (at least in the Islamic West) as an intellectual attempt to subordinate Mālikī learning or *ʿilm* to a "higher" kind of knowledge, to make it secondary to an alternative, "purer" locus of spiritual authority (the *ʿilm al-ākhira*).[40] This was interpreted by the ʿulamāʾ as a direct challenge to the establishment for social supremacy. That this peculiar episode became emblematic for the period (even in the earliest historiography) is testimony to the power gained by this particular social group under Almoravid unification.[41] It also highlights the powerful emotions raised by the challenge to the Mālikī ʿulamāʾ and their social standing. The multiplicity of issues addressed by the fatwās of Ibn Rushd serves to underscore the important fact that the social prestige of the ʿulamāʾ was far from being merely "religious." This social power was accompanied by real skills of patent value to the growing needs of Marrakesh (and, arguably, to any such developing urban center within the Islamic world). It is thus that we find in the texts discussed here Marrakeshī jurists asking Ibn Rushd about the scope of their role and authority in widening fields of activity, such as the regulation of the sale of gold and the settlement of claims over defects in merchandise.

Together, these questions represent a key period of institutional formation in the city of Marrakesh, in which the network of juridical authority, along with the urban institutions they served, had reached a certain critical mass of

---

38 On the importance of judges in local leadership from the *Taifa* Period, see Maribel Fierro, "The Qāḍī as Ruler."

39 This was the first of two official campaigns that led to the public burning of al-Ghazālī's work. The second occurred during the reign of Tashfīn b. ʿAlī (538–540/1143–1145). Delfina Serrano, "Why did the scholars of al-Andalus distrust al-Ghazāli? Ibn Rushd al-Jadd's fatwā on Awliyāʾ Allāh," *Der Islam* 83, no. 1 (2006), 137.

40 Kenneth Garden, "Al-Ghazālī's Contested Revival," 17–31.

41 The episode also points to a new, perhaps even unwanted visibility, as the Mālikī ʿulamāʾ became the targets of serious contenders for dominance.

development that in turn encouraged a more formal means of consultation using more authoritative sources.[42] The success of these institutions was such that, even in cases that touched at the heart of Almoravid religious identity – which could have been exploited as opportunities for political posturing – the city's authorities chose to consult (if not necessarily defer entirely to) an Andalusī authority such as Ibn Rushd.

3 The Motor of Gold: Two Questions Involving Gold Exchange

Two short fatwās deal with the commodity at the heart of the transformation of the Far Maghrib in the late fifth/eleventh and early sixth/twelfth centuries. The consolidation of the trans-Saharan gold trade by the Almoravids, followed by the minting of their own dīnārs from 450/1058 at Sijilmāsa, was part of a broader regional increase in trade throughout North Africa and the Mediterranean. It was in itself a revolution in the quality, but mostly in the abundance and dependability, of the region's gold currency.[43] Such was the Murābiṭī dīnār's success that it quickly became the standard unit of currency in western Mediterranean trade. The coin was traded widely and its name was adopted into other languages as the apellation for various currencies, some of which survived until the nineteenth century.[44]

While it would appear that the Almoravid military administration had, at least from the 440s/1050s, devised an organized system for trading, minting,

42 Christian Müller, *Gerichtspraxis im Stadtstaat Córdoba: zum Recht der Gesellschaft in einer mālikitisch-islamischen Rechtstradition des 5./11. Jahrhunderts* (Leiden: Brill, 1999). Müller describes the nature of legal institutions and administration in *Taifa*-period al-Andalus. On the development of legal administration in the Almoravid period, in which legal officials, principally judges but also members of the *shūrā* council, became more integrated into the state administration, see Vincent Lagardère, "La Haute Judicature à l'Époque Almoraivde en al-Andalus," *Al-Qantara* 7 (1986): 135–228. and Rachid El Hour, "The Andalusian Qadi in the Almoravid Period: Political and Judicial Authority." The focus of these studies lies primarily in al-Andalus, where the transition from Umayyad to *taifa* to Almorvid state and the role that judges played therein has proven particularly compelling. See also Maribel Fierro, "The Qāḍī as Ruler." These were not absent, furthermore, from the Far Maghrib, where the case of Qāḍī 'Iyāḍ is particularly relevant.

43 What this currency revolution entailed has been debated. It appears that the Almoravid dīnārs were not of purer gold than Fāṭimid ones, as analysis of the coins reveals, but that the Ghanian ore they tapped needed very little refining. Ronald A. Messier, "The Almoravids: West African Gold and the Gold Currency of the Mediterranean Basin," *Journal of Economic and Social History of the Orient* 17, no. 1 (1974), 35.

44 The Iberian *maravedí* being the prime example.

and taxing the flow and exchange of west African gold, in these two texts we detect the growing role of Mālikī judges in the commercial life of the city markets in assisting, or bridging the gap between the fiscal system (about which, unfortunately, we know very little) and the daily commercial needs of an urbanizing community.

To the extent that we can perceive anything from a single instance, the first text reflects the relative abundance of gold for trade in the Marrakesh market, the growing trade with al-Andalus, and the specific problems that arose from this exchange. The second concerns the nature and scope of a judge's role in the regulation of the market gold trade, and, to some extent, it bears witness to the appearance of this function and jurisdiction. On a legal level, both fatwās deal directly with the problem of the permissibility of certain kinds of transactions involving gold, a commodity that was subject to *ribā* restrictions, or Islamic prohibitions against unlawful enrichment.

A Question on Gold for Dīnārs and Murābiṭīs for ʿAbbādīs[45]

The question was written in 515/1121–2 by "a group of jurists from Marrakesh,"[46] at least one of whom is identified as a certain Abū ʿAbd Allāh al-Tuṭīlī. The question is straightforward. As with many of our texts, a scenario (or in this case, perhaps a recurrent problem) presented itself in one case or several cases that came before a local judge, leading a group of local jurists (perhaps after discussing or consulting at the local level) to formulate the question in a sense that was generally applicable or appreciable. A few associated questions were then appended. The unidentified jurists summarized the problem as follows: What should be done, they asked, when one man owes another man a quantity of dīnārs (the gold coinage)[47] and this man settles the debt not in dīnārs, but in pieces of gold jewelry (*ḥuliyy*). The pieces of gold were described as being of the same or of lesser weight. The debt was fulfilled "without repetition (*ʿāda*), condition, or specified number."[48]

The crux of the question, it appears, revolved around the issue of whether the settlement of this debt, because it involved gold, was subject to the restrictions of *ribā*, specifically *ribā al-fadl* or the *ribā* of "excess," i.e., the sale or

45 Ibn Rushd, *Fatāwā Ibn Rushd*, 1030.

46 Ibn Rushd, *Fatāwā Ibn Rushd*, 1027.

47 For a survey of Almoravid numismatics, including the religio-political meaning of their Qurʾānic phrases, invocation of sovereign titles, and location of principal mints, see Hanna E. Kassis, "La Moneda, Pesos y Medidas," in *El retroceso territorial del al-Andalus: almorávides y almohades. Siglos XI al XIII*, ed. María Jesús Vigerua Molíns, Historia de España fundada por Ramon Menéndez Pidal (Madrid: Espasa Calpe, 1987), 303–21.

48 Meaning that the settlement or transaction was done with an unspecified consideration. Ibn Rushd, *Fatāwā Ibn Rushd*, 1030.

exchange of specific commodities of the same kind for quantities that not are strictly equivalent.[49] Concerning this prohibition in the Mālikī school, we find in the book of *ṣarf* (exchange) in the *Bidāyat al-Mujtahid*: "The jurists agreed that the sale of gold for gold and silver for silver is not allowed, except from hand to hand and like for like (in similar quantity and quality)."[50] This view was supported by the prophetic tradition: "Do not sell gold for gold except like for like and do not devour some of it with the rest, do not sell silver for silver except like for like and do not devour some of it with the rest and do not sell a thing absent for one that is present."[51]

The first point of the inquiry was to ask whether a debt incurred or defined in terms of the official, minted gold currency may be settled with a commodity of the same type, species, or genus (here gold), especially since, because not minted, the exchange was characterized by indefiniteness. This indefiniteness stemmed from the fact that it was not possible to ascertain by measuring weight whether or not the pieces of gold represented an amount equivalent to the debt incurred in dīnārs (the gold was not necessarily of the same quality, and dīnārs on average were irregular). The indefiniteness was expressed by the *mustaftī*'s statement that if the dīnārs (presumably not the ones owed since they were not present, but rather a selection of 100 Murābiṭī dīnārs) were to be examined one by one, they would prove to be of unequal weight and quality. A random selection of dīnārs would therefore weigh more or less than the gold tendered by the debtor. The fact, moreover, that raw bullion had a potentially different purpose or use (*gharaḍ*) was a second source of uncertainty.[52]

For the sake of obtaining a comprehensive answer, the jurists of Marrakesh appended a short, related question concerning what should be done in a similar situation in which a debt incurred in ʿAbbādī dīnārs[53] is settled with Murābiṭī ones. In other words, what effect (or uncertainty) is entailed in the settling of a debt incurred in one gold currency with another? The broader question was how lawful exchange (*ṣarf*)[54] of gold of discrepant quality,

49 Mohammad Fadel, "Riba, Efficiency, and Prudential Regulation: Preliminary Thoughts," *Wisconsin International Law Journal* (2008), 661.

50 Ibn Rushd al-Ḥafīd, *Bidāyat al-Mujtahid* (*The Distinguished Jurist's Primer*), trans. Imran Ahsan Khan Nyazee, vol. I & II (Reading, UK: Garnet, 1994), II: 233.

51 Ibn Rushd, *Fatāwā Ibn Rushd*, 233.

52 This was so at least for the *mustaftī*, and it was a factor Ibn Rushd addressed in his response. Thanks to Mohammad Fadel for his comments on this section.

53 The gold coin of al-Andalus's most powerful state before the Almoravid conquest.

54 Settlement of a debt, according to the Mālikī tradition, being understood as a currency transaction. Mohammad Fadel, "Riba, Efficiency, and Prudential Regulation: Preliminary Thoughts," 658.

weight, and formal or official denomination can or should be defined in order to adhere to *ribā* restrictions.

Ibn Rushd's response to these questions was succinct. Any inconsistency in quantity or weight, he wrote, whether exceeding or falling short of the amount (defined in number of dīnārs) on the part of the debtor is impermissible because of the resulting lack of equivalence (*mumāthala*) between payment and debt (or aim of the deed: *qaṣd al-mubāyaʿa*) and because of what Ibn Rushd termed the "difference of uses" (*ikhtilāf al-aghrāḍ*), since raw gold can have a completely different use from that of minted gold currency. This perceived indefiniteness in what was in effect treated as a sale of gold for gold presented an intolerable level of uncertainty for Ibn Rushd.

To the related question regarding the settlement of a debt incurred in one gold currency (the ʿAbbādī dīnār) with another gold currency (the Murābiṭī dīnār) Ibn Rushd responded positively. This kind of settlement is permissible because, he wrote, if the ʿAbbādī dīnārs fall short of the Murābiṭī in terms of quality or weight, the excess (*faḍl*) in the exchange (or payment) is "one-sided" (*min jiha wāḥida*). This is the extent of his response.[55]

A Question on the Exchange of Different Qualities of Gold and a Judge's Role Therein[56]

An undated question from an unidentified jurist of Marrakesh poses a question similar to the one above, but of much wider scope and with greater emphasis on determining the judge's jurisdiction in supervising and regulating the exchange and production of gold. The fact that participants enter an exchange for different reasons and with varying levels of expertise and knowledge of the commodity was of particular concern to the *mustaftī* here. Again, however, the driving preoccupation appears to be the issue of the legality or permissibility of the exchange of different qualities of gold in light of *ribā* restrictions. The *mustaftī* set up the question by reminding the muftī that – as doubtless was occurring in Marrakesh in the first two decades of the sixth/twelfth century – people participated in the exchange of gold for different reasons and with vastly differing abilities for determining its quality:

> People's objectives in acquiring gold [he wrote] are various. There is he who wants the noble kind as treasure for savings (*li-zamānihi*) and as

55 I am inclined to say that the exchange of ʿAbbādī for Murābiṭī dīnārs was found permissible by Ibn Rushd because, since the Murābiṭī dīnārs set the standard, any deficiency in the average ʿAbbādī value can be made up for or calculated in the transaction.

56 Ibn Rushd, *Fatāwā Ibn Rushd*, 1095–97.

> ornament for his women. Others desire the kind widely available, which is bought and sold according to people's wealth or lack of means. Then there is he who goes for the lowest standard. His objective is slightness of weight at maximum size and insignificant price.[57]

Given that people have different uses for gold, and that it can be of varying quality ("the pure, noble metal (*ṭīb khāliṣ*) with no impurities, the kind that is partial or half gold, and that which is of an eighth, two-thirds, three-fourth, seven-eighths gold and the like"),[58] the *mustaftī* asked whether its exchange is lawful to begin with. To this he added the question of whether it is lawful to exchange the various types of gold, spanning the gamut of qualities, "for dirhams" (the silver coinage). The crux of the first part of the *istiftā'* was twofold: Can gold of varying qualities be sold for dirhams, and can different qualities of gold be weighed (as a basis for exchange) against each other (*murāṭala*).

This inquiry into the exchange of varying qualities of gold among people with dissimilar knowledge of those qualities led the *mustaftī* to ask about the scope of the judge's duty of oversight in this exchange. He asked whether the judge should allow people to purchase gold that is lesser than "the noble kind," and whether he should oversee the exchange or have any supervision over production. Does the judge have jurisdiction or the right to keep goldsmiths from plying their trade when they are found to be using substandard materials? Does he have the right to keep smiths from working and selling for others and for themselves? Lastly, contemplating a further consequence of a judge's oversight or control of the production and exchange of gold, is the judge, when the gold has been found to be under a certain standard, obligated to destroy or remove it from circulation and from the possession of individuals? Should he destroy the "non-noble" variety he finds in people's possession in order to "devalue it and compel people to acquire gold exclusively of the noble kind?"[59]

Ibn Rushd's concise answer stated a clear position regarding the lawful commerce of gold and the limits of a judge's responsibility over its trade and production. Working and selling gold of all varieties is lawful, he wrote. "The smithing of jewelry from pure and impure gold, alloyed with (*mashbūh bi*) silver, brass, and copper is permissible (*jā'iz*) and its use is allowed." He substantiated this statement with a citation attesting to its permissibility (if not laudability) through its mention in Qur'an 43:17. Procuring gold of all qualities for savings is likewise permissible, he added, as long as the *zakāt* is paid on it,

57 Ibn Rushd, *Fatāwā Ibn Rushd*, 1095–96.

58 Ibn Rushd, *Fatāwā Ibn Rushd*, 1095.

59 Ibn Rushd, *Fatāwā Ibn Rushd*, 1096.

when appropriate. The same holds for the sale of gold as merchandise for specie or credit, as well as for silver or dirhams, when performed hand to hand (*yad bi-yad*).[60] *Al-murāṭala*, however, Ibn Rushd wrote – addressing the technical term for weighing one quantity of gold against another, using a specified unit of weight – is lawful only when restricted to gold "of the pure kind, excluding the lesser."[61]

As for the judge's jurisdiction regarding these practices, Ibn Rushd told the *mustaftī* that it is inappropriate for a judge (or for anyone else) to prohibit or prevent a goldsmith from plying his trade or selling his wares to others or for his own use, "because all of this activity is lawful and permissible." It is, furthermore, unlawful to destroy gold that is in people's possession, because this is their private property, and because worked gold is counted among merchandise that individuals "who circulate it for commerce provide in payment of the *zakāt*" (and is therefore lawful). The exception, however, is gold that is counterfeit, which Ibn Rushd described as the kind that is made of an outer layer of gold over an interior of brass or copper. Such a counterfeit product, Ibn Rushd wrote, "must be destroyed" and removed from circulation.

Ibn Rushd's opinion is again succinct and to the point, leaving room for interpretation. Implicit in his opinion is that the buying and selling of all other qualities of gold is lawful and that the control or supervision of the trade can take a variety of forms.

•••

Several questions linger concerning these two fatwās, especially the first one. One wonders why the debtor would want to pay his debt in raw bullion, whether this came about because of a shortage of minted dīnārs, or because the fee for procuring or minting coins made trading in bullion attractive. One is also left curious about what interests, public or otherwise, were served by Ibn Rushd's interpretation of *ribā* restrictions, if any. The answers to these questions may not be forthcoming. That they deal with the commodity central to the formation of the Almoravid state, however, is indisputable. We may conclude that the discussion of the exchange of gold in the legal literature (of which these two questions form part) is important. More significant, and more germane to these specific texts, is that they bear witness to the appearance of a mechanism of exchange and mediation in the urban space of Marrakesh (where Mālikī jurisdiction was first based), complementing and intermeshing with customary practices about which we know little. From these texts we can

60 In a spot transaction.

61 Ibn Rushd, *Fatāwā Ibn Rushd*, 1096.

speculate that the developing institution of Mālikism in Marrakesh was especially useful or applicable in mediating commercial disputes, by presenting a respected, legitimate, and (significantly) a kind of self-imposed mechanism for maintaining standards and peacefully and 'fairly' resolving differences. That these Mālikī legal practices and institutions became a part of the city fabric can be seen in the other cases to which Ibn Rushd responded, as is evident in the following section.

4 Mediating Exchange: Two Questions over Commercial Disputes

The two cases presented in this section also deal with questions arising from the application of Mālikī law to the commercial activity of the markets of Marrakesh. These do not deal with the production of gold and its use in commerce, but with more mundane commercial exchange. They prominently feature Mālikī law as a force in commercial mediation. The focus in these questions shifts from an effort to determine what kinds of exchange are lawful and what jurisdiction a judge exercises vis-a-vis this exchange to an effort to determine the mechanisms for resolving disputes arising from such transactions. Settling commercial disputes, presumably, was one of the most appealing functions of Mālikism as it developed in Marrakesh. The social value of such a mechanism would have been evident to contemporaries, supplying the means for resolving, in a way that was regular and predictable, disputes of varying degrees of gravity, including the most quotidian.

The two questions deal with such minor issues. Technically, they involve two different kinds of legal transactions. The first is an exchange (*ṣarf*), the second a sale (*bayʿ*). The *mustaftī*s were particularly interested in determining the procedure to be followed for resolving disputes, including how to determine the precise limit at which disputes or complaints pass from one level of seriousness to another (impacting their methods of resolution). The relative insignificance of the amounts involved in the disputes points to the fact, far from trivial, that the extension of these mechanisms to disputes involving small sums assisted the fluid functioning of city markets.

A Question on a Currency Exchange Dispute[62]

Ibn Rushd received a letter from Marrakesh in which a judge asked him about a dispute which arose after a man exchanged an amount of money in one coinage for its equivalent in a smaller denomination. The question centered on

62 Ibn Rushd, *Fatāwā Ibn Rushd*, 160–70.

whether oath-taking to resolve the dispute should take place at the congregational mosque (an index for the gravity of the dispute). The manner in which the dispute came about was described by the judge in narrative dialogue form (a common style in the genre). A man, he wrote, exchanged dīnārs for dirhams (a larger denomination for a smaller one) from another man.[63] He took the dirhams and left the site of the exchange but returned (presumably shortly afterwards, although the judge omitted mention of the time elapsed), claiming that the dirhams he had received fell short of the amount agreed upon at the time of the exchange. The man making the complaint then said,

> "I returned the dirhams and there was a dirham missing." To which the individual who bought the dīnārs from him replied: "On the contrary, I paid you the full amount." The individual who took the dirhams said: "The dirhams did not leave my hands. You have paid me a lesser amount."[64]

Taking oaths (*al-aymān*) in Islamic law is an essential performative utterance for the establishment of individual legal liability. In the various Islamic legal schools the precise definition of what constitutes an oath received a good deal of attention, much of which centered on the intention of the individual taking the oath (in contrast, for example, to how the words of the oath are construed) as well as on determining what utterances, though in form identical to oaths, are not deemed to produce liability.[65] More relevant to this particular case/question is the discussion of what procedures, individuals, and situations must be present for delivering a judgment (*ḥukm*). Oath-taking by litigants is recognized as a means of asserting a claim, although the option of oath-taking differs between plaintiff and defendant. Specification of a solemn place for taking such an oath has long been part of the tradition (although there is disagreement among the schools on this being a necessity). Mālik relied on the criterion of the amount over which there is a dispute to determine whether the oath should be taken at a solemn place: If the plaintiff makes a claim equal to three dirhams or more, the oath must be sworn at the congregational mosque.[66] Of equal importance, however, is the effect of a party claiming that there has been a "short-coming" or "defect" in a currency exchange. When dīnārs were exchanged for dirhams and one of the parties found that some of the currency

63 That is, exchanging gold coins (dīnārs, the larger denomination) for silver coins (dirhams, the smaller).

64 Ibn Rushd, *Fatāwā Ibn Rushd*, 1070.

65 Ibn Rushd al-Ḥafīd, *Bidāyat al-Mujtahid*, I: 488–490.

66 Ibn Rushd al-Ḥafīd, *Bidāyat al-Mujtahid*, II: 560–563.

was counterfeit or of less value than agreed, that individual had a few options (the results of which varied according to school). For some jurists, substitution or correction of the deficiency is lawful; disagreement over this method stemmed from the delay, as a result of the substitution, and the perceived *ribā* restrictions concerning such a delay. Alternately, the individual can simply accept the transaction, which was generally understood to be lawful. But a predominant opinion in Mālikism (coming from Mālik himself) maintains that if an individual puts forth such a claim, the entire exchange is to be rendered void.[67] This was the point Ibn Rushd stressed in his opinion.

The judge in this case thus wanted to know whether, in Ibn Rushd's opinion, an oath should be sworn at the congregational mosque. With characteristic brevity, Ibn Rushd answered that oath-taking is required, and that it should take place at the congregational mosque specifically (*tataʿayyana fī al-masjid al-jāmiʿ*). This was the case, he explained, because the man's claim that the dirhams fell short could result in "the eventual invalidation of the exchange of the full amount of dīnārs."[68] The claim, even if over a small amount, might lead to the reversal or invalidation of the entire exchange which, according to standard Mālikī practice, had to be substantiated by an oath at the congregational mosque. In Ibn Rushd's opinion, it was the invalidation and not the amount of the dispute that was operative in necessitating the oath at the congregational mosque.

A Question over a Claim of Less than a Quarter Dīnār[69]

This question concerns the requirement of oath-taking. The questioner sought to determine the minimum value required for there to be oath-taking (by either party) to resolve a claim over a defect in a sale. As with similar consultations, the *mustaftī* used the opportunity of the *istiftāʾ* to address a set of questions. These involved two situations that posed similar problems.[70] Whatever the specific set of circumstances, it appears from this *istiftāʾ* that two men in Marrakesh rescinded a sale of a value of a quarter dīnār or more, but then disagreed over whether the amount had been paid in full. The *mustaftī* wrote

67 Ibn Rushd al-Ḥafīd, *Bidāyat al-Mujtahid*, II: 235–236.

68 Ibn Rushd, *Fatāwā Ibn Rushd*, 1070.

69 Ibn Rushd, *Fatāwā Ibn Rushd*, 1031–32.

70 It is uncertain whether one case raised a set of associated hypothetical questions (in the mind of the *mustaftī*), or he was presented with two similar cases which he chose to bundle into one consultation, or whether, perhaps even more plausibly, several cases coming before the court raised a persistent set of questions (as well as local disagreement over the correct answer) driving the jurist(s) to compose a summary and set of questions for the muftī of Cordoba.

that the seller told the buyer that he still owed an eighth of a dīnār. To this the buyer responded that the disputed amount had been included in the money he had paid. Does the settlement of these contradictory claims, the jurist of Marrakesh asked Ibn Rushd, require oath-taking at the congregational mosque?

Similarly, what should be done when the buyer sues the seller for a defect he claims to have found in the merchandise, and the seller presents a counter-claim that the nature and existence of the defect had been disclosed to the buyer at the time of the transaction (which the buyer then denies)? What unites these two questions is the fact that the value involved in the claim was less than a quarter dīnār. The specific question posed to Ibn Rushd then was whether and where oath-taking to resolve the disputes should take place. Finally (and given the fact that much of what was bought and sold was agricultural produce), the *mustaftī* inquired into the impact that the passing or perishing of the merchandise in question would have on the judge's ruling.

As with disagreements over currency exchanges, disagreements over price paid and over defects found in merchandise after a sale, often involve oath-taking as a means to a resolution.[71] Juristic discussion over defects in sales and their consequences are extensive in the legal literature and center on what was known by the seller and disclosed to the buyer at the time of sale, the definition of what constitutes a defect in different kinds of goods, and the time-frame within which a claim over a defect can be raised. The Mālikis generally stipulated that a sale is followed by a period of three days (*ʿuhda*) during which claims over defects can be made for which the seller can be held responsible.[72] When a defect in what was bought (*mabīʿ*) is found, the buyer has the option of accepting its existence without compensation, of voiding the sale, or of receiving compensation (depending on the quality and value of the defect and the nature of the goods). For immovables, Mālik distinguished between minor and major defects. A minor defect does not necessitate the return of the property but does necessitate compensation for the value of the defect (known as *arsh*). A claim over a major defect requires the return of the property and invalidation of the sale.[73] The school's position over movable goods is more varied (Mālik having not specified it), but several jurists, including Ibn Rushd's teacher, Abū Bakr b. Rizq,[74] extended the principle on immovables to movables, which appears to have become the majority opinion.[75]

---

71 Currency exchange is treated as a sales transaction.

72 In general, one can say that Muslim jurists favored defending the rights of the buyer.

73 Legally tantamount to the sale having never occurred.

74 Likely Abū Jaʿfar Aḥmad b. Muḥammad b. Rizq al-Umawī al-Qurṭubī, Ibn Rushd's principal teacher.

75 Ibn Rushd al-Ḥafīd, *Bidāyat al-Mujtahid*, II, 208–219.

In his answer (and as in the opinion above), Ibn Rushd made the important distinction that what makes oath-taking in the congregational mosque necessary is not the amount per se, but the consequence of a successful claim: if the merchandise is extant and the plaintiff vindicated, the exchange would be cancelled *in toto*, resulting in the return of all of the merchandise. In the opinion, Ibn Rushd thus stated that settling the first case (involving the individual who claimed to have been underpaid by an amount that was less than a quarter of a dīnār) does not require oath-taking at the congregational mosque. Only in the second case (the buyer who sues over a defect of less than a quarter of a dīnār), and only if the merchandise is extant, is this required, since the successful claim would result in the plaintiff's returning the entirety of the merchandise.

> This is similar to the case in which two parties to a contract of sale (*mutabāyiʿān*) disagree over the price of the merchandise by a margin of less than a quarter dīnār and the merchandise is extant. They are mutually bound to take oaths at the congregational mosque, as opposed to the case in which the merchandise has expired. This and none other is what is correct.[76]

This last phrase (and the paragraph that follows it in Ibn Rushd's fatwā) provides a clue to another possible genesis for the *istiftāʾ*. In the closing lines of his fatwā, Ibn Rushd points out that the chapter on defects in Ibn al-Mawwāz's version/commentary of the *ʿUtbiyya*,[77] "concerning the summoning of buyer and seller when there is a defect of outer appearance in merchandise," contradicts the position put forth by Ibn Rushd in the fatwā. Ibn Rushd was therefore rectifying (or changing) a previous interpretation of a legal question in the *ʿUtbiyya*: "The only correct stance is that which I have explained above."[78] His mastery of this particular work of reference, one of the most important of his

76 Ibn Rushd, *Fatāwā Ibn Rushd*, 1032.

77 Ibn Rushd, *al-Bayān wa-l-taḥṣīl wa-l-sharḥ wa-l-tawjīh wa-l-taʿlīl fī masāʾil al-Mustakhraja*, 8: 264. According to the audition of Ibn al-Qāsim (d. 191–193/807–808), one of the most important early transmitters and contributers to the *ʿUtbiyya*, who transmitted (listened, *samaʿ*; a technical term used to designate a form of transmission of Islamic learning, particularly when early in the chain) from Mālik and transmitted to multiple students, including Saḥnūn. These auditions and transmissions, often in the form of question and answer, were compiled by al-ʿUtbī (d. 255/869). Ana Fernández Félix, *Cuestiones Legales del Islam Temprano*, 115–38.

78 Ibn Rushd, *Fatāwā Ibn Rushd*, 1032.

time, gave Ibn Rushd particular authority.[79] This settling of juristic debates or confusion caused by contradictory opinions within Mālikism – within the various recensions, commentaries, and transmissions of Mālikī texts – was a key function performed by the muftīs of al-Andalus for the jurists of the Far Maghrib. Ibn Rushd al-Jadd was particularly influential in this role, during the foundational period in the development of the Mālikī legal network in Marrakesh. This role is conspicuous in the four cases that follow.

5 Transmitting and Developing Juristic Knowledge: Two Questions Resolving Contradictions within the School

In the following cases, Ibn Rushd disentangled contradictions on subtle points of law found in the corpus of the Mālikī school. The first question, while straightforward, elicited a complicated answer, which went well beyond the identification of one correct choice among several options. The second, likewise, resulting from a textual contradiction (or from the existence of alternate opinions within the school as transmitted to the jurists of Marrakesh) posed a complicated set of considerations. Coincidentally, both questions dealt with divorce. The guidance provided by Ibn Rushd to the two Marrakeshī jurists posing the questions illustrates the importance of his tutelage (and the scholarly Cordoban establishment) for the developing Mālikī practice of Marrakesh. This point is underscored by the fact that the two *mustaftīs* here, Abū ʿAbd Allāh al-Tuṭīlī and Mūsā b. Ḥammād, are identified in the *ṭabaqāt* literature as two of the first important jurists of the southern Far Maghrib. The opinions are prime examples of an important kind of legal development within the school: the revision of unsettled, ambiguous, or problematic points.[80] A final issue

---

79 On assessing the importance of this work before and after Ibn Rushd's commentary, see Ana Fernández Félix, *Cuestiones Legales del Islam Temprano*, 282–94.

80 Ibn Rushd performed this function in his work as a whole, as well as in his opinions, largely through the application of the methods derived from *uṣūl al-fiqh*. Ana Fernández Félix, *Cuestiones Legales del Islam Temprano*, 285. On Ibn Rushd's role as reformer of the Mālikī tradition, M. Fierro writes: 'The scholar who is to be credited with that reform is Averroes's grandfather, Ibn Rushd al-Jadd. Like ʿUmar b. ʿAbd al-Barr and Ibn Ḥazm (and contrary to al-Bājī and Abū Bakr b. al-ʿArabī), he did not travel to the East. He was able to cater to his interest in legal theory with the teachers and books he found in al-Andalus. Under Almoravid rule he was named *qāḍī al-jamāʿa* of Cordoba in 511/1117. It was after leaving this position in 515/1121 that he managed to complete the two works with which he achieved the "modernization" of two crucial early Mālikī texts. By "modernization," as A. Férnandez Félix has shown, is meant what appears to be a "Traditionalization" of

that deserves mention is that the specialized knowledge possessed by the individual who is the subject of the second fatwā afforded him special consideration by the judge and muftī. The consideration of an individual's cognizance of the law was characteristic of Mālikī practice as whole, but was particularly significant in the fifth/twelfth-century Far Maghrib, where such knowledge, in practitioners and laymen alike, was more variable than elsewhere and, because rarer, highly valued. The range in legal literacy in the south Far Maghrib affected in no small manner the application of Islamic law (or at least the approach to cases).[81]

A Question on Contradictory Testimony Relating to Repudiation[82]

This question[83] sought to determine the correct version between variants of a Prophetic *hadīth* and its conflicting interpretations. The *ḥadīth* addresses the problem that arises when witnesses to the number of repudiations uttered by a husband to his wife contradict each other. Transmitted on the authority of Abū al-Zinād and Ibn Shihāb, it reports that three witnesses gave various or contradictory testimony concerning the number of times a man repudiated (*ṭallaqa*) his wife: one witness testified that the man had repudiated his wife once, another that it had been twice, and a third that it had been three times. The *mustaftī*'s reading of the *Mudawwana*, regarding this same *ḥadīth*, led to the understanding that there is a distinction to be made between when witnesses testify together or separately, with a concomitant impact on the decision.[84] The *mustaftī* inquired about a further distinction, which may have been relevant to the local case (if there was one): What happens when the wit-

Mālikism, as his effort was directed at connecting the legal doctrine found in these two early texts with the Qur'ān, the prophetic Tradition, the consensus, and analogical reasoning (*qiyās*). In other words, Ibn Rushd al-Jadd was able to insert early Māliki *ra'y* within the context of *uṣūl* methodology, without such substantial change being introduced in traditional Andalusī Malikī practice. Maribel Fierro, "Proto-Malikis, Malikis, and Reformed Malikis in al-Andalus," 74. It was, likewise and significantly, after the year of 511/1117, when Ibn Rushd was engaged in the project outlined above, that he produced most of the opinions analyzed here (or at least those which can be dated).

81 This question is illustrative of what life may have been like in the 1120s in a city that attracted people possessing a range of skills and coming from varying economic statuses and tribal/ethnic groups (including individuals with valuable skills hoping to flee their past, which, in this case, while not exactly scandalous, may have been gladly left behind).

82 Ibn Rushd, *Fatāwā Ibn Rushd*, 1027–29.

83 One of a group of three, identified as being either composed by a group of jurists from Marrakesh or, specifically, by Abū 'Abd Allāh al-Tuṭīlī.

84 I. e. how many repudiations the couple has accumulated. Saḥnūn b. Sa'īd al-Tanūkhī, *al-Mudawwana al-kubrā li-l-imām Mālik b. Anas al-Aṣbaḥī. Riwāyat al-imām Saḥnūn b. Sa'īd*

nesses provide different dates for when each repudiation occurred? This distinction figures prominently in Ibn Rushd's response.

The question that emerges (from what appears to be a somewhat truncated text) is whether the fact that each witness testifies separately and provides a different date for the repudiations affects the judge's ruling, which in turn will determine the number of repudiations that apply to the couple's status.

In a complex opinion, Ibn Rushd identifies what he understood to be the operative criterion in the situation. It is not the fact that the testimonies are contradictory (resolution depending on the reconciliation of disparate evidence) that matters, but rather, that one witness alleged that the testimony of another witness was false. Ibn Rushd thus approached the problem as an allegation of fabrication of testimony. He attributed the misidentification of the key element of this ḥadīth by the Marrakeshī jurists to al-Lakhmī al-Qayrawānī (d. 478/1085) who, in his *Tabṣira*, focuses on distinguishing between situations in which one witness dates his or her testimony to after or before the time given by two witnesses whose dating concurs. This distinction between one witness dating the repudiation to "before both, or one of the two," in Ibn Rushd's opinion "is not sound."

> Likewise, [he wrote,] his stating that there is a difference when dates are absent, and his asking whether this enjoins two or three repudiations, is also not sound. This is because it is wrong to exceed a determination of two repudiations on doubtful grounds. This is furthermore unsound because there is no disagreement in the school over a judge (*ḥākim*) not deciding against one who rejects an accusation when there is doubt (*bi-shakk*).[85]

The correct approach to such a problem is to conceive of it as involving one testimony that alleges that another is false, which is how the question is interpreted by Ibn al-Qāsim in his transmission of the *Mudawwana*, in which the issue of the date provided by each witness is disregarded.

> This is because, [Ibn Rushd wrote,] were it obligatory to accept the testimony of the one single witness concerning the specification of the day in which he witnessed the divorce, then it would be necessary to accept his testimony, by itself. When the testimony of the divorce's date by the

---

al-Tanūkhī ʿan al-imām ʿAbd al-Raḥmān b. Qāsim. Wa-yalīhā muqaddimat Ibn Rushd (Beirut: Dar al-Kutub al-ʿIlmiya, 2005), 2: 91–94.

85 Ibn Rushd, *Fatāwā Ibn Rushd*, 1028–29.

> single witness is not accepted, it follows that no single testimony should be permitted to stand alone in the assignment of a date (*fī-mā infarada bihi min al-taʾrīkh*), and the date should not be considered, having no effect, and not being an established requirement for divorce.[86]

In a case presenting a situation similar to that found in the ḥadīth of Ibn Shihāb al-Zuhrī, Ibn Rushd concluded, it would be unlawful for the judge to determine that the man – about whom only one witness has stated that he divorced his wife three times – has repudiated his wife more than twice, given the doubt cast by the contradictory testimony of the other two witnesses. The judge can only do so if the man corroborates the evidence himself (that he had repudiated his wife three times and thus definitively). Even if this were the case (that the man corroborated the testimony of three repudiations), Ibn Rushd suggested that the judge may still use his discretion in determining the legally effective number of repudiations, since this is a point about which there is clear disagreement within the school (offering distinct but defensible opinions).

A Question on the Recusal of a Regular Witness[87]

The status of decisions passed by the principal court of Marrakesh was put in jeopardy when there emerged evidence that cast doubt on the reliability of a witness regularly employed by the court. This evidence, which was presented to Mūsā b. Ḥammād, chief judge of Marrakesh, consisted of a document, "in the hand" of this regularly employed or "professional" witness. It attested to the fact that the man was unlawfully married to his wife, having divorced her three times in the past. Alarmed that this would mean the invalidation of all of the documents and decisions enacted by the court to which this man had served as witness, Mūsā b. Ḥammād wrote to Ibn Rushd for counsel.[88]

Eighteen years earlier, the professional or regular witness in question resided in a town (*balda*) where he married a woman to whom he remained married for three years before moving to Marrakesh. During the fourteen years following the move to Marrakesh, the man was considered an upstanding member of the community, of unimpeachable character in the eyes of his neighbors. During the five years immediately preceding the present case he served as a regular witness in court. It is unclear whether he had served as witness only for Mūsā b. Ḥammād, or also for the chief judge who preceded him.

---

86 Ibn Rushd, *Fatāwā Ibn Rushd*, 1029.

87 Ibn Rushd, *Fatāwā Ibn Rushd*, 1475–79.

88 This is the second of the two recorded questions Ibn Rushd received from Mūsā, who appears again as a muftī in Chapter Three.

Whatever the case, this man had served as a witness for countless judgments and contracts.[89] During the five years that Mūsā b. Ḥammād had known the man, he had learned of nothing that would compromise his integrity as a witness. That is, until the surfacing of this document (*ʿaqd*) – how exactly this happened is not clear. The document stated that the man, presumably before moving to Marrakesh, although this is also left unsaid, had three-times repudiated the woman to whom he was currently married, thereby making their marriage and current state of cohabitation unlawful, as well as casting doubt on his integrity as a witness.

In response to the appearance of the document, judge Mūsā b. Ḥammād summoned the man and questioned him. The latter disavowed authorship of the document and denied the truth of its content. This satisfied the judge, but witnesses then testified that the document's handwriting was indeed that of the man in question,[90] which prompted a second summons. In response to this new evidence the man claimed that he could produce evidence to absolve himself, for which the judge granted a deferral. It was at this juncture that Mūsā b. Ḥammād wrote to Ibn Rushd asking for guidance. He asked what should be done if the man was unable to substantiate evidence in his defense and whether the man's resulting loss of trustworthiness or *ʿadl* would lead to the invalidation of the marriages and other contracts to which he had served as witness. Echoing the previous question,[91] Mūsā b. Ḥammād asked whether disagreements in the Mālikī tradition over this particular point of law countervailed the invalidation. Lastly, he asked whether the man could continue to serve as a court witness during the period prior to the date set by the judge to produce evidence in his defense, something the man appears to have requested.

In his opinion, Ibn Rushd eschewed legalism and favored a flexible approach. He admitted that if the man were unable to produce exculpatory evidence and the document were authenticated, the divorce would be enforced and the couple separated. However, he set a very low bar for the admissibility of evidence in defense. This was because, he reasoned, outside of its ostensible purpose, there were any number of possible justifications for the existence of the document. The testimony given by the man for the court, therefore, should not be invalidated unless he himself confirmed his authorship of the document with intent: that he composed it with the unambiguous purpose of repudiating his wife for a third time, under oath of irrevocable divorce (*al-ṭalāq*

89 Including marriages.

90 A document's authenticity was often ascertained by identifying an individual's handwriting, which served as a kind signature.

91 Ibn Rushd, *Fatāwā Ibn Rushd*, 1027–29.

al-batta), and that he then remarried her, knowing and believing it to be unlawful, "an insolence against God."[92] If, on the other hand, the man believed that he could lawfully remarry her after a third repudiation because of the disagreement in the Mālikī school over the finality of such a divorce, then he should be forgiven for his mistake and his testimony remained valid. This approach was especially justifiable, in Ibn Rushd's opinion, if it were known that the man had studied the Islamic sciences (*naẓara fī al-ʿilm*) or had "heard" ḥadīth.[93]

Ibn Rushd provided additional means for resolving the problem. Even if, he wrote, in light of the evidence, the judge considered it likely (*iḥtamala*) that the man had remarried his wife after an irrevocable divorce and that he had perjured himself (by denying that the divorce had taken place), still, the man's marriage should not be dissolved and his testimony in court should not be invalidated if he can argue convincingly that he only lied in fear for his marriage. The man's testimony should not be invalidated on a mere likelihood. Furthermore, Ibn Rushd believed that he should not be forcefully divorced from his wife, either, if the single piece of evidence against him was this document which he disavowed. This holds even if the man were unable to provide evidence to the contrary. This is because of the principle that identification of handwriting is not admissible as evidence, Ibn Rushd wrote, "in cases of divorce, manumission, marriage, or in any *ḥadd* case, according to what is stated by Ibn Ḥabīb in the *Wāḍiḥa*, among others."[94]

Ibn Rushd concluded by suggesting that the man may have written the document as a notarial exercise: as a document for consultation or study and not for implementation. If the man were to claim that he had never implemented or had the intention of implementing the document, nor did he bring witnesses to testify to its execution (after all, had he intended its execution why not carry it out?), he should be believed, following established Mālikī tradition as found in the *Mudawwana*.

• • •

Ibn Rushd's eschewal of legal literalism together with his commitment to a sophisticated understanding of the law, underscores the point that the Almoravid investment in Mālikism went far beyond simplistic pietism and often

92 Ibn Rushd, *Fatāwā Ibn Rushd*, 1478.

93 One is inclined to believe that Ibn Rushd wished to avoid blind adherence to the letter of the law, which in this case would harm many individuals unrelated to the case.

94 Ibn Rushd, *Fatāwā Ibn Rushd*, 1479.

avoided overt strict adherence to the law in favor of a more subtle understanding. The Mālikism sponsored and cultivated by the Almoravids, as evinced by these cases, was capable of incorporating the sophistication of a jurist such as Ibn Rushd. In fact, one may ask whether Ibn Rushd would have been nearly as prolific without the support of the Almoravid state. I think it unlikely. The territorial expansion of the Almoravid empire, the influx of Andalusi traditions into the southern Far Maghrib, and Ibn Rushd's own significant contribution to the Mālikī tradition are integrally related and interdependent processes. That the cultivation of this institution comprised not only the strictly technical (as in the cases above) but also the political and symbolic, becomes evident in the cases below, in which powerful cultural and religio-political forces were at play.

6 The Symbolic Religious Authority of Cordoba: the Case of the Man who Wouldn't Remove his Turban and the Case of the Apostate

The last two Marrakeshī cases for which Ibn Rushd wrote opinions present vivid illustrations of religious developments in the Almoravid capital. They also support one of the central arguments in this book, which is that the Almoravid investment in Mālikism transcended a preoccupation with religious purity. They understood Mālikism to be the glue that held together a civilization such as that to which Marrakesh aspired, a capital of an empire encompassing both African and European shores of the western Mediterranean (*al-ʿidwatayn*, or "the two banks"). More than a banner of religious identity for holy warriors,[95] the Mālikism cultivated by the Almoravids in the Far Maghrib embodied their aspirations for a great civilization. Just as the Umayyads had adopted and transformed Roman building techniques, the Almoravids adopted the tradition of law and learning of al-Andalus. It is therefore not surprising that in cases that struck at the heart of the movement's reformist mission and identity, Almoravid authorities not only deferred to the religious and legal tradition of a city with more established Islamic institutions, but also demonstrated their regard for the complexity of the social functions of these institutions.

That in a case easily exploited for symbolic or political effect,[96] the authorities of Marrakesh would choose to defer to an Andalusī muftī, as well as to a kind of "due process," underscores that Almoravid ideology was more complex than is usually acknowledged, and, more broadly and significantly, that the legitimating force of a complex religio-legal system such as Mālikism was not

95 Although not entirely without such effect.

96 The second case of this section, below.

well-served by summary observance and execution. To the contrary, it was the system's ability to provide predictable and stable means of mediation and resolution in different and evolving social contexts that made it attractive, and indeed essential, for an urban center such as Marrakesh.[97]

In the following two cases we find the administrative and religio-legal authorities of the city fully committed to this system, consulting with the Cordoban muftī, Ibn Rushd, in cases in which they need not have done so. These cases involved ritual law and religious identity. Fortunately for the historian (and quite possibly for the accused) they did.

A Question on Dispensations for an Ill Man[98]

The opening line from the compiler of the text informs the reader that the muftī Ibn Rushd received a letter from a jurist in Marrakesh, conveying a lengthy question concerning a man who requested permission to perform his ablutions without removing his "turban" and without using water. The man who was reportedly "weak of body and brain" claimed that his illness (the nature of which is unspecified) became aggravated by washing with water, making him catch "the worst cold he'd ever caught." The man complained of being afflicted by paroxysms, which prevented him from washing with water – hot or cold – for months at a time. He also feared catching cold from exposure to wind or drafts. At the time the jurist wrote the *istiftā'*, three to four months had passed since the man's last bath.

The *mustaftī* in Marrakesh wanted to know, firstly, whether a man in such a condition could attain ritual purity for prayer by means of *tayammum* (wiping with sand). The *mustaftī* also asked what this man should do when he has had sexual relations with his wife, while suffering from the aforementioned affliction.

> Should he cleanse his major ritual impurity with sand, so long as the condition persists? Does this suffice?... Is it his obligation, in this situation, to wash with water (*ghusl*) or, rather, to wipe (*masḥ*) his head without water and wash his body with water?[99]

---

97 The language of Mālikism that was being adopted by the Almoravid ruling class and the growing institution of practitioners and transmitters (who clearly shared an interest in its success, at least in Marrakesh, as a major political and economic arbitrator) was not, therefore, just one of ritualistic and legalistic detail, but one that suffused the broadest and highest ideas of the proper functioning of a just society, the ethics of its leaders, and the morals of its inhabitants.

98 Ibn Rushd, *Fatāwā Ibn Rushd*, 1065–68.

99 Ibn Rushd, *Fatāwā Ibn Rushd*, 1066–67.

The Marrakeshī jurist had consulted with local jurists before writing to Ibn Rushd. They disagreed over the approach to the question. Initially, they formulated the problem as that of an individual who has incurred a major ritual impurity through unlawful design or sin (*maʿṣiyya*). Should such an individual be given dispensation (*rukhṣa*) from incurring (and therefore from cleansing) this major ritual impurity (*janāba*)? They proposed to answer this question by comparing the situation (*qāsūhā*) to a well-known scenario in the case literature of the Mālikī school: that of the traveler who has traveled with unlawful design. Unlike lawfully traveling individuals who encounter difficulties in observing ritual and dietary obligations, this kind of traveler, Mālikī jurists had established, is not allowed to shorten his prayers, break the *Ramaḍān* fast, or eat carrion even when necessity obliges him to do so.

Following this logic, some of the local jurists said that the ill man should not be given permission to perform his ablutions with sand or without removing his turban, because he had incurred the major ritual impurity deliberately (if not exactly by "unlawful design"). Others disagreed. They said that the purpose of not granting the traveler license for doing certain things (shortening prayers, breaking the fast, eating carrion, etc.) was only so that he may not be "heartened" in the pursuit of his "unlawful design" (i.e. in order not to assist him in his unlawful intent). Since the behavior of the ill man that had caused the major ritual impurity was past and not ongoing, they argued, he should be allowed to perform his ablutions with sand and without removing his turban, so long as he does not persist in his unlawful behavior.

This was the complicated question posed to Ibn Rushd by the Marrakeshī jurist, who closed his query with of the traditional formula:

> Clarify for us, by your favor, this last question as well – may you be rewarded – what is correct regarding it and explain that to us clearly – May God reward and bring you success, by His omnipotence and compassion. There is no lord but Him.[100]

In spite of the forbearance manifested by the second group (and in spite of the longwindedness of the question, or, one senses, perhaps because of it), Ibn Rushd showed little patience for the man's predicament and answered summarily in the negative. No special consent to perform ablutions by wiping over his turban should be granted to this man. "This is the case under almost any circumstance," he wrote, "unless there is a wound on his head that prevents him from wiping in any way whatsoever." Ibn Rushd justified his answer by

100 Ibn Rushd, *Fatāwā Ibn Rushd*, 1067.

stating that "the fears you described of what will afflict him are farfetched."[101] Indeed they were, in Ibn Rushd's opinion, "a temptation from Satan who should not be heeded." Anyone who has acted in such a manner has the obligation to perform ablutions and resume prayer, in support of which Ibn Rushd cited Qur'ān 22: 78, "And laid on you no burdens of the faith," to drive home the point that ritual purity and ablutions before prayer are not among the difficulties of which God had chosen to "unburden his servants in faith." The man's ability to have carnal relations with his wife, furthermore, provided ample proof, in Ibn Rushd's opinion, that his illness had not incapacitated him in such a manner that he was unable to wash with water. If, Ibn Rushd conceded, the man has had relations with his wife and, at a later date, is afflicted by paroxysms, which exacerbated an existing weakness, then and only then would cleansing with sand be permissible. Whether the obligation has been incurred lawfully or unlawfully has absolutely no impact on the requirement to wash (*ḥukm al-ghusl*), he concluded, in terse acknowledgment of the jurists' debate.[102]

Rumors of an Apostate[103]

Some years before 520/1126, an inhabitant of the city of Marrakesh called unwanted attention to himself after rumors spread that questioned the sincerity of his conversion to Islam from Christianity. Suspicion was cast on this man's religious conviction after stories about his peculiar behavior reached individuals important or powerful enough to call the matter to the attention of the city's ruler (*al-sulṭān*). Acknowledging the gravity of the accusations implicit in the rumors (and involving neither military nor tribal affairs), the sulṭān remitted the matter to the capital's chief judge (*qāḍī ḥaḍrat Marrākush*), Mūsā b. Ḥammād, who ordered an investigation. As a result, the residence of the man suspected of apostasy was searched. To his misfortune, a collection of incriminating objects was discovered; on the surface they substantiated the rumors.[104]

To begin with, inspectors found a room that, at least to them, was suspiciously lacking a bed and was decorated like a chapel, with a hanging lamp and what were described as numerous religious objects (*āthār*) to which candles were affixed. Further inspection yielded books written in the "script of the

---

101 Ibn Rushd, *Fatāwā Ibn Rushd*, 1067.

102 A debate which in retrospect appears somewhat pedantic.

103 Ibn Rushd, *Fatāwā Ibn Rushd*, 1462–64.

104 This fatwā, as compiled in the *Mi'yār*, is analyzed in brief in Vincent Lagardère, "La Haute Judicature à l'Époque Almoraivde en al-Andalus," 209.

Christians,"[105] more candles, a lectern (described as a board on four legs), a staff or pole with a small, hand-length crosspiece at the top, and a number of disk-shaped pieces of dried bread, each bearing an embossed shape at its center. Two witnesses with knowledge of "the conditions and laws of the Christians"[106] were summoned before the judge, to whom they provided expert testimony regarding the nature of the objects.[107] The candles, they said, were of the kind used by Christians in their services; the lectern, one used by priests to read the Gospel (*al-Injīl*); and the staff of a type used by priests to support themselves while reading the Gospel. They also identified the disk-shaped, dried pieces of bread, as the oblations eaten by Christians after fasting. At this point, with this testimony and evidence, judge Mūsā b. Ḥammād became unsure as to how to proceed. He wrote a succinct description of the case, followed by two simple questions: May these objects be used as evidence in trying the said man for apostasy? And should this man be tried for apostasy to begin with? (His behavior having been aggravated by the fact that he had, at some point, publicly professed Islam). Mūsā b. Ḥammād sent this description and questions to Ibn Rushd.

Why, one may ask, were there Christians in Marrakesh, a town founded by a Muslim dynasty on a sparsely-inhabited, swampy plain, in a region, as far as we know, lacking a recent historical Christian presence.[108] Although the *istiftāʾ* does not provide much detail regarding the origin of the accused, it does afford the opportunity to discuss another illuminating contradiction of Almoravid history. As it happens, some of the most effective soldiers of this dynasty were Romance speaking Christians (albeit soldiers of fortune). The most famous of these was Reverter, the Catalan lieutenant of Tāshufīn b. ʿAlī, son of ʿAlī b. Yusūf, and last able military leader of the Almoravids. Together, Tāshufīn b. ʿAlī and Reverter, supported by a Christian militia, led the doomed defense of the Almoravid state against the Almohads. How a Christian militia played such a

105 Most probably Latin.

106 Ibn Rushd, *Fatāwā Ibn Rushd*, 1462.

107 On expert-witnesses, see Delfina Serrano, "Legal Practice in an Andalusī-Maghribī Source from the Twelfth Century CE: The Madhāhib al-ḥukkām fī nawāzil al-aḥkām," 193–94.

108 The growing Christian presence from the Almoravid and into the Almohad period, the most significant segment of which appears to have developed from the employment of Christian mercenaries, led to the establishment of a bishopric in Marrakesh, a surprising fact that should lead to a reappraisal of Muslim-Christian relations under the first two Maghribī Berber empires (traditionally believed to have been implacably hostile to non-believers). On the establishment of the bishopric of Marrakesh, see A. Fromherz, "North Africa and the Twelfth-century Renaissance: Christian Europe and the Almohad Islamic Empire," *Islam & Christian-Muslim Relations* 20, no. 1 (2009), 49–50.

prominent role defending a dynasty whose legitimacy was based on defending Islam against the infidels has not been well accounted for (it provides yet another example of Almoravid borrowing of Andalusī institutions and practices).

We do not know the identity of the Christian convert to Islam in our case. Did he belong to an existing Christian community about which we have no record? Perhaps he was one of the Mozarab (or Andalusī Arabized) Christians who were relocated to the Maghrib after aiding Alfonso the I, el Batallador, of Aragon during the attack deep into al-Andalus in 519/1125. Maybe he was involved with the Almoravid state in an official capacity or as member of the Christian militia described above (this might explain the reticence in dealing with his case on the part of the Marrakesh authorities). Christian converts to Islam may have been so rare in Marrakesh that Mūsā b. Ḥammād, having no experience with such cases, thought it best to consult with Ibn Rushd, who lived in a city that had experience with religious diversity. All of these scenarios are possible, although some more likely. The relocation of Mozarabs occurred (in and after 520/1126) slightly after this case took place, so it is unlikely that the subject was a relocated Mozarab. It also seems unlikely that a "local" or Arabized Christian would have had books in Latin. What seems most plausible is that the man was a foreign merchant or mercenary soldier of some kind. His status as a servant to the Almoravid state may very well have played a role in how the case was dealt with.

Ibn Rushd's answer to Mūsā b. Ḥammād's question about the Christian convert to Islam reveals concern for protecting the rights of the individual shared by many Muslim legal thinkers, most often, in the face of a government and military administration that, for natural reasons, was keen to co-opt the right to make law, a right which, with varying degrees of success, belonged to the jurists across pre-modern Muslim societies.[109] The individual Muslim enjoyed a series of rights as well as obligations. Ibn Rushd, like a number of other Mus-

109 This is a system of law with nothing like a bill of rights, nor definitions of individuals separate from their religious affiliation. Which does not mean, however, that Muslim jurists were not concerned with the protection of individual rights, a view that only a very superficial understanding of Islamic law would support (i.e., that a sacred law responds only to the unchanging rights of "God"). I (and many others) would argue, rather, that the protection of individual rights (albeit limitedly) was integral to the constitutional framework developed in various pre-modern Islamic societies, in which the defense of a legal discourse independent and protected from direct state, administrative, or executive pressure, was a central feature. On the constitutional structure of pre-modern Islamic societies, see Noah Feldman, *The Fall and Rise of the Islamic State* (Princeton, New Jersey: Princeton University Press, 2008).

lim legal thinkers, endeavored to define and defend these in the face of summarily executed justice.

Ibn Rushd's answer to Mūsā b. Ḥammād was concise and called for caution; above all, it demanded the highest standard of evidentiary probity. As long as it remained unproven by just proof (*bi-bayyina ʿādila*) that this man, Ibn Rushd wrote, who publicly and voluntarily converted to Islam, secretly practiced Christianity, then a sentence of execution could not be passed on him before calling on him to repent for his apostasy. This was because the objects themselves do not constitute convincing evidence, since their ownership remains in question. They may have belonged to Christians living with the accused or to others who frequented him. Ibn Rushd emphasized the fact that this lack of just proof was especially relevant to this case in which rumors were responsible for initiating the investigation. The evidence provided by these rumors, along with the discovery of the objects – even if it were highly likely (technically, "preponderantly likely," *bi-ghalabat al-ẓunūn*) that these objects belonged to the accused – does not constitute "just" proof in a case of apostasy. This is because such accusations, which warrant the most severe punishments meted out by Islamic law, known as *ḥudūd* punishments, are not to be substantiated by hearsay. *Ḥudūd* crimes, which include blasphemy, drunkenness, theft, and adultery – each carrying different punishments and demanding various levels of evidentiary probity – are conceived as direct infringements by man on his obligations to God, there being clear Quranic prohibitions of these actions. Dispensation of *ḥudūd* punishments, therefore, also bears the highest level of evidentiary requirements.[110]

This was the point that Ibn Rushd stressed in his opinion to Mūsā b. Hammād. *Ḥudūd* punishments, he explained, are not to be applied on the basis of hearsay (*bi-samāʿ*) or preponderant likelihood. They are to be applied only on the basis of just proof. He elaborated by providing an example: if it were said that a Muslim man had committed adultery with a woman who is a known adulterer (*fājira maʿlūma bi-l-fujūr*) and that she was seen entering into his house where they were together, alone, for some time, the *ḥadd* punishment would still not be applied to him, even if it is most likely that adultery was committed. In such a case, a punishment, and even a painful one (*al-ʿuqūba al-mūjiʿa*), may and should be applied. Likewise, Ibn Rushd wrote, the man accused of apostasy in this case must not be executed. He may be repri-

110 Probity of evidence varied according to the offense. Adultery, for example, requires four just eyewitness. Theft requires two and/or a confession. On *ḥadd* offenses see EI², s.v. Ḥadd. For a discussion of *ḥadd* punishments being averted in cases of doubt, see David S. Powers, *Law, Society, and Culture in the Maghrib, 1300–1500*, 72–73.

manded, and harshly, but that is all.[111] Ibn Rushd's defense of this man is significant because there was precedent, in the *Muwaṭṭa'*,[112] for executing a covert apostate. Ibn Rushd does not defend the man's right to be an apostate. But he does demand that the bar for leveling such an accusation be very high, minimizing its incidence.

This case does not illustrate the tolerance between the different Abrahamic faiths of Iberia and North Africa in our period. Indeed, it took place during what was a sharp worsening of relations, as members of minorities fell under suspicion of fifth-column activity. Ibn Rushd's opinion regarding this Muslim accused of apostasy (or of "backsliding") would appear to point, rather, to the intensity with which the boundaries of the religious communities were guarded in the multi-confessional society that was the Almoravid state. These communities were defined not just religiously, but politically and legally. The distinct sense of these boundaries was an integral component to living together in a state in which law and religious allegiance were so closely intertwined. The anxiety raised by such "boundary crossing" was considerable, conversion being a clear example of an action provoking "judicial violence" of the severest kind.[113] Here this violence was at the ready, to be employed against transgression. This readiness may also point to the anxiety over religious identity felt in the young capital of Marrakesh. Perhaps just having Christians in the Muslim capital was enough to spark anxiety and rumor. We cannot be sure. What is certain, however, is that Ibn Rushd called for restraint, defending the right of this Muslim man not to be rashly convicted. In a way perhaps closer to what Ibn Rushd actually thought, he called for the right of God's law to be applied as it should be, observing its exacting requirements, so that, in so far as it was possible for men, His will could become known to them, fulfilling the ultimate goal of the Sharīʿa.

• • •

These two cases – that of the ill man's ablutions and of the Muslim accused of crypto-Christianity – underscore the key fact that Almoravid regard for Andalusī learning extended beyond an interest in technical expertise in the commercial, secretarial, and architectural fields. Even when the administrative and judicial authorities of Marrakesh were confronted with issues that were not technical but also religio-political – questions striking at the root of Al-

111 Ibn Rushd, *Fatāwā Ibn Rushd*, 1464.

112 Mālik b. Anas, *al-Muwatta'*, 2 vols. (Cairo: Dar Iḥyā' al-Kutub al-ʿArabiyya, 1955), 736.

113 For a discussion of inter-confessional boundary crossing and the role of violence in an Iberian context, see David Nirenberg, *Communities of Violence: Persecution of Minorities in the Middle Ages* (Princeton, N.J.: Princeton University Press, 1996).

moravid identity – they found it beneficial to seek counsel from a Cordoban, instead of exploiting the situation to prove a public point.

Through the consultations analyzed in this chapter, Almoravid authorities demonstrated their commitment to a social institution which did not depended on literalist adherence or summary application, but rather on cultivating the full system of learning to which Ibn Rushd himself was so committed. It was the belief in – as well as the practical benefit derived from – this system that bound together someone like Ibn Rushd al-Jadd and the Ṣanhāja jurists and administrators of the southern Far Maghrib. It was most likely precisely because of the new-found importance and success of this system, which developed from this relationship and investment – that it became the principal object to be overcome or opposed by political competitors. In the sixth/twelfth century, these competitors were turning to (and greatly stimulating) the development of Ṣūfism (and other popular religious practices) as an alternate locus of religious, spiritual, and political authority.[114] The Messianic Almohadism of the Mahdī Ibn Tūmart partook of this energy and development and, especially in its formative stages, made the institution of Mālikism a prime object of denunciation.[115]

The history of the rise of these alternate forces and loci of religio-political legitimation, which had profound and lasting impact on the history of the Far Maghrib, falls outside the scope of this book. Suffice it to say that while these currents or tendencies were at times (perhaps especially in the beginning) deeply and outspokenly opposed to each other, over the long run they combined in novel and *sui generis* ways. In spite of the Almohad campaign against it, Mālikism survives to this day as the living legal tradition of the region. And the Sūfī and the Mālikī jurist would not for long remain distinct figures on the Far Maghribī landscape, but would mesh into one. The following chapter explores the development of Mālikī institutions in the Far Maghrib as a whole, where it took root and ultimately flourished by adapting to and melding with the forces which challenged and opposed it.

---

114 To which, for example, the judge of Cordoba, Ibn Ḥamdīn, was reacting when he ordered the public burning of al-Ghazālī's *Iḥyā'* in 1109. Kenneth Garden, "Al-Ghazālī's Contested Revival," 8. On the rise of oppositional Ṣūfī movements in al-Andalus, see Maribel Fierro, "Opposition to Sufism in al-Andalus," in *Islamic Mysticism Contested: Thirteen Centuries of Contrversies and Polemics*, ed. Frederick De Jong, and Bernd Radtke (Leiden: Brill, 1999)..

115 Maribel Fierro, "The Legal Policies of the Almohad Caliphs and Ibn Rushd's *Bidayat al-Mujtahid*."; Mercedes Garcia-Arenal, *Messianism and Puritanical Reform: Mahdis of the Muslim West* (Leiden: Brill, 2006).

CHAPTER 2

Fatwās to the Far Maghrib: Ibn Rushd's Consultations for the Amīr and Cases of Murder and Stolen Cattle

1 Introduction

In addition to jurists in Marrakesh, Ibn Rushd wrote opinions in response to questions originating from jurists and officials active in other regions of the Far Maghrib. A majority of the opinions were solicited by the chief judge of Ceuta, Qāḍī ʿIyāḍ (who will be discussed in Chapter Three). The remaining opinions were directed at a variety of locations – many unidentified in the text. While disparate and elliptical, taken together, these fatwās complement the picture of legal activity, institutional development, and social change sketched out in the Introduction and Chapter One. They corroborate several points while raising a host of other issues, some involving rural and tribal life and others impacting the intellectual and religio-political life of the Far Maghrib as a whole. Keeping with the theme of religiously sensitive subjects for the Almoravid administration before progressing to more rural matters, the first set of questions results (at least purportedly) from direct correspondence between the Almoravid commander and the muftī Ibn Rushd. In the analysis of these texts, I focus on elucidating the context for questions warranting such high-level correspondence and their relationship to social change in the sixth/twelfth-century Far Maghrib. The questions posed by the Almoravid commander serve to situate these changes in a broader pan-Islamic framework. They illustrate how the Almoravid leadership saw itself within the wider Islamic and Mediterranean worlds.

The fatwās in this chapter include a question of ritual law, comparable to that of the man who refused to remove his turban (even if with a bit less flare). Reading this text reinforces the impression of authorities who were more concerned with defining basic ritual practices and the implementation of orthopraxy than with identifying or combating unorthopraxy or "heretical" variations, perceived or real.[1] A second question seeks elucidation on a

1 As encountered in other regions and periods of the Maghrib, as for example in Qayrawān under Fāṭimid and Zirid rule where ritual law and practice was one of the central areas of contestation and articulation of Fāṭimid and Mālikī identity. For a discussion of this, in the

 | DOI 10.1163/9789004279841_004

particular point of law, but in a criminal framework. The clarification the jurist sought from Ibn Rushd was, again, not unlike that encountered in Chapter One (contradictory testimony relating to divorce), although in a substantially more interesting scenario.

Analysis of a last set of questions provides glimpses of the widespread demographic and structural change that was taking place in the countryside of the Far Maghrib under the Almoravids. Both questions deal directly with legitimating or sanctioning ownership and the transmission of ownership of specific forms of property. As with ritual observance, customary practice conflicted with Mālikī practice, raising difficult questions over the lawful course of action. The cases also reveal the impact of the socio-economic changes ushered in by the new regional order, the advent of which is thought to have coincided with significant redistribution of land and redefinition of land-ownership.

2 Questions from the Almoravid Leadership: On the Permissibility of Ashʿarism and the Exceptionalism of the Islamic Maghrib

The first two fatwās to be discussed in this chapter have been discussed at some lengh by scholars previously, for the topics they deal with are of clear political and theological significance and because the prominence of the *mustaftī* suggests that the questions were of importance to the fortunes of the state. I will not go into detail over the more theoretical aspects of either question, but rather address their significance within the framework of the present inquiry. These texts, first of all, add to our understanding of the relationship between the Far Maghrib and al-Andalus. In a way more perspicuous than with the fatwās on ritual law and apostasy in Chapter One, they shed light on the relationship between Andalusī politico-religious learning and the Almoravid leadership: When ʿAlī b. Yūsuf asked Ibn Rushd about the permissibility of *uṣūlī* theology and the virtue and obligation of jihād, he was asking the Andalusī muftī for counsel on religio-legal issues at the heart of Almoravid identity and of the greatest political importance for the legitimacy of the state.

Perhaps even more compelling, the two questions posed here by the Amīr al-Muslimīn betray an emerging Far Maghribī political identity and thus provide a valuable perspective from which to understand the Far Maghrib's solidification as a political entity with regard to the rest of the Islamic world. The

---

framework of a study of the life and work if Ibn Abī Zayd al-Qayrawānī (d. 382/996), see Sayeed Sajjadur Rahman, "The Legal and Theological Thought of Ibn Abī Zayd al-Qayrawānī (310–386/922–996)" (Yale, 2009), 8–9, 58–69.

texts display a deepening connection with trends sweeping in from the Islamic East as well as a stronger sense of independence. Both of these forces were prevalent as Almoravid unification was followed by a more forceful articulation of Berber Islamic identity.

On the Permissibility of Studying the Works of Abū al-Ḥasan al-Ashʿarī[2]

Ibn Rushd answered a query, identified once as coming from the city of Fez and a second time as coming from the amīr himself, on the permissibility of studying Ashʿarī works. What we have is the text of two fatwās that are practically identical, except for the introductory lines, identifying the *mustaftī*.[3] The style of the *istiftā'*, with rhymed prose and parallel constructions, betrays a deft secretarial hand and is markedly unlike the other fatwās discussed here.[4] It is plausible that the question was first formulated by scholars in Fez and that ʿAlī b. Yūsuf seconded the question because of its topical relevance, or, alternatively, that it had originally been directed to ʿAlī's own scholars and court before being redirected to Ibn Rushd.

Irrespective of whether the question originated from the amīr or was later taken up by him, his presence as *mustaftī* lent undeniable consequence to the symbolic and political nature of the question. The questioner, addressing Ibn Rushd as "jurist, great judge, one and only *imām*, Abū al-Walīd," asked whether six theologians (*mutakallimūn*), identified by name, may be read and studied without moral endangerment. These theologians were the shaykh Abū al-Ḥasan al-Ashʿarī (d. 330/942), Abū Isḥāq al-Isfaraynī (418/1027), Abū Bakr al-Bāqilānī (403/1013), Abū Bakr b. Fawrak (d. 406/1015), Abū al-Maʿālī (d. 473/1085), and Abū al-Walīd al-Bājī (d. 474/1081). The *mustaftī* asked what should be said to those who "insult and disparage them and revile anyone associated with the school of Ashʿarism, accuse them of unbelief, disclaim any association with them, turn away from them in [holy] righteousness, and believe them to be in error and rushing into ignorance?"[5]

2 Ibn Rushd, *Fatāwā Ibn Rushd*, 802–05.

3 The first text identifies the *mustaftī* as the Amīr al-Muslimīn, ʿAlī b.Yūsuf. Ibn Rushd, *Fatāwā Ibn Rushd*, 802–05. The second question is identified as "coming from the city of Fez." Ibn Rushd, *Fatāwā Ibn Rushd*, 943–45.

4 Except for a question which is identified as coming from a group of "outstanding students of [Islamic] science from Tangier." Ibn Rushd, *Fatāwā Ibn Rushd*, 1494–505. To be sure, this doesn't mean that our question here necessarily originated with a group of scholars in Fez, but the belletristic formulation and the thoroughly political and prominent nature of the subject matter makes it likely.

5 Ibn Rushd, *Fatāwā Ibn Rushd*, 804.

The tone of the *istiftāʾ* reveals sympathy with the practitioners of *kalām* and adherents of Ashʿarīsm. The *mustaftī*'s central preoccupation was determining the appropriate response to what appears to have been the vehement reaction against Ashʿarism and *kalām* in the Far Maghrib. Indirectly, he describes the character of this reaction:

> What should be said, done, and believed about them [those who practice *kalām* or adhere to Ashʿarism]? Are they to be left to their own convenience or shall they forbear their excesses? Does this constitute an invalidation in their religion and defect in their faith? Is prayer behind them permissible or not? Clarify for us the value of the aforementioned imāms, their place in the faith, and inform us about the position of those who disparage and turn away from them, as well as the position of those who entrust and befriend them generally.[6]

The opponents of Ashʿarism had thus apparently taken to accusing those associated with Ashʿarīsm of being beyond the pale of acceptable religious practice. However, the *mustaftī*, as mentioned, described them simply as practitioners of dialectical theology (*ʿIlm al-kalām*), people who "speak of the origins of religious beliefs (*uṣūl al-diyānāt*), and write in answer to the people of whim (*ahl al-hawāʾ*)." This last formulation plainly establishes a link of fellowship between the *mustaftī* – most probably a learned scholar himself – and the *mutakallimūn* against the people of whim. Are these *mutakallimūn*, he asked, "leaders of good sense and divine guidance, or are they leaders (*qāda*) of confusion and blindness?"

In contrast to fiqh (law), *kalām* applied rational interpretation to the foundational religious texts of Islam. One of the predominant ways in which *kalām* came to be conceived of in the East, over the first three centuries of Islam, was as a practice that defended the faith against hostile ideological attack and heresy. Its practice was thus defined as a way of deepening understanding to strengthen knowledge of the truth.[7] Ashʿarism itself is a broad term that came to comprise the traditions of mainstream Sunnī *kalām*. It consisted of the Sunnī interpretive practices that applied rationalist and Muʿtazilite tools and concepts to the epistemology and ontology of Islam while keeping conceptual restraint on certain proscribed questions. It is also seen to constitute a kind of compromise toward the construction of faith, using tools once employed by parties later seen as beyond the pale. Among other things, our ques-

6 Ibn Rushd, *Fatāwā Ibn Rushd*, 804.

7 Gerhard Endress, *An Introduction to Islam* (New York: Columbia University Press, 1988), 47.

tion points to, if not the introduction, definitely a greater dissemination in the Far Maghrib of theological discourse that was current in the greater Islamic world.

The historiography of this particular issue has been inordinately influenced by a report by the Almohad chronicler, al-Marrākushī – resulting in a dramatic skewing of the narrative of the reception of Ashʿarīsm under the Almoravids. It is to al-Marrākushī's chronicle that we owe the long-held notion that the Almoravid amīr, ʿAlī b. Yūsuf, condemned the practice of *kalām*. According to al-Marrākushī's chronicle, ʿAlī fell under the sway of the *fuqahāʾ*, consultation with whom he was said to be "addicted" to for the making of each and every decision. Under the Almoravids, the *fuqahāʾ* gained prominence they had not enjoyed in the early period of the conquest of al-Andalus. As a result of this influence, they reaped considerable material gains and sequestered the amīr from outside influence; only those who knew the science of *furūʿ* (substantive law) according to the school of Mālik were said to have been allowed any access. So pervasive was their influence, al-Marrākushī famously said, that knowledge of the Mālikī rite and its substantive law were favored to the exclusion of "the book of God and the traditions of His messenger." Al-Marrākushī wrote that the insistence of the *fuqahāʾ* that *kalām* was repugnant won over ʿAlī's heart.[8] This led him to order that instructions be sent to all provinces of the empire prohibiting the study of *kalām* and threatening those found with books on the subject (the nature of the threat was left unspecified).

In the same breath, al-Marrākushī discussed the introduction of al-Ghazālī's famous work, *Iḥyāʾ ʿulūm al-dīn*, in the Islamic West, the public burning of which (said to have been ordered by the amīr) he conflated with this opposition to *kalām*: "And when the books of al-Ghazālī penetrated in the West, the amīr ordered that they be burned and threatened those whom were found with some of those [books] even more severely with death and the confiscation of goods. This order was rigorously enforced."[9]

The complex of social currents perceived to be colliding in this passage have, for understandable reasons, produced a rich historiography, one of the unfortunate results of which has been a simplistic understanding of the Almoravid movement as fanatically adherent to Mālikism. The accusation that they cultivated Mālikism to the exclusion of the Qurʾān should raise red flags, however. Few charges in Islamic social discourse could be more charged politi-

8 Implying he was not so inclined by nature.

9 Delfina Serrano, "Los almorávides y la teología ash'arí: ¿Contestación o legitimación de una disciplina marginal?," 465.

cally. Understanding the bias in al-Marrakushī's description has been a first crucial step toward a better understanding of Almoravid history.

A second step is reading the fatwā in question with an awareness of the effect this bias has had on the long historiography of the issue.[10] While a full treatment of the development of *kalām*, Ashʿarism, and the reception of al-Ghazālī in the Far Maghrib falls outside the scope of this study, a few important points about their relevance to the present inquiry can be made here. Firstly, as D. Serrano notes, the fact that Ibn Rushd – himself an *uṣūlī* and sympathizer with *kalām* (as evident in the opinion) – had a privileged relationship with the Almoravid intellectual and political elite indicates that neither ʿAlī nor his *fuqahāʾ* were anti-*kalām*. Texts such as this one, and scrutiny of other sources, suggest that the narrative of an enthusiastic reception and cultivation of *kalām* in the *Taifa* Period followed by its suppression under the Almoravids (for which reason they are so often referred to as fanatical Mālikīs) does not stand up under scrutiny. The debate over *kalām* in this fatwā points to the significant level of intellectual ferment and anxiety over the appearance of multiple new loci of authority – principally the movement of Ibn Tūmart, whose overt hostility to Mālikism, an institution closely associated with the urban revolution and the regime, is strongly suggestive of the dynamic opposition to these new loci. Likewise, the dispute over *kalām* was not merely a matter of entrenched conservatives rejecting rationalism in favor of blind obedience to Mālikī *furūʿ*, as previously understood, but rather a more complex competition between multiple voices within the emerging and interlinking Islamic discursive traditions that characterized the sixth/twelfth-century urban transformation of the Far Maghrib.

The burning of the *Iḥyāʾ* is the embodiment of one such competition. Scholars have shown that, contrary to later characterizations, Almoravid reaction to al-Ghazālī fell on both sides of the debate.[11] Al-Ghazālī (notably absent from

10 These have been analyzed in Vincent Lagardère, "Une théologie dogmatique de la frontière en al-Andalus aux XIe et XIIe siècles: l'ašʿarisme," *Anaquel de estudios árabes* 5 (1994): 71–98. And Delfina Serrano, "Los almorávides y la teología ash'arí: ¿Contestación o legitimación de una disciplina marginal?" The latter's work and reading on these particlar fatwās has been particularly influential on my own reading. Other works on the diffusion of Ashʿarism in al-Andalus include J. M. Fórneas, "De la transmisión de algunas obras de tendencia ašʿarī en al-Andalus," *Awrāq* 1 (1978): 4–11; ʿIsmat Dandash, "Mawqif al-murābiṭīn min ʿilm al-kalām wa-l-falsafa," in *Aḍwāʾ jadīda ʿalā al-murābiṭīn* (Beirut: 1991); Maribel Fierro, "La Religión," 437–546. For a full list see Delfina Serrano, "Los almorávides y la teología ash'arí: ¿Contestación o legitimación de una disciplina marginal?," 462.

11 Dominique Urvoy, *Pensers d'al-Andalus: la vie intellectuelle à Cordoue et Séville au temps des empires berbères (fin XIe siècle-début XIIIe siècle)* (Paris [Toulouse]: Editions du CNRS

the list of thinkers above)[12] and his book, for a variety of reasons, assumed symbolic power that would develop gradually but unswervingly. While the Almoravids attempted to co-opt this symbolic force it eventually and retrospectively came to symbolize opposition to the Almoravids. The *kalām* of al-Marrākushī along with a host of other ideas and figures – notably those associated with the appearance of Ṣūfism in the region – took on symbolic power in the Almohad and post-Almohad telling of the past. Almohad deployment of these symbols closely associated with the success of their movement, along with the foundational role of Almohad historians, such as al-Marrākushī, in the historiography of the Far Maghrib, has led to a very limited understanding of such figures in Almoravid history. The limitations and distortions inherent in this narrative led, in the modern period, to placing excessive emphasis on the questions of why the Almoravids burned the *Iḥyā'*, why they were against *kalām*, and by extension why the were so legalistic and anti-rationalist, instead of to entertaining the more germane and interesting questions of why these issues, symbols, and figures became so urgent and forceful in this period and what was their social significance.[13]

In his opinion on the permissibility of Ashʿarism, Ibn Rushd lent unequivocal support to the *mutakallimūn*. His reason for this was simple: the *mutakallimūn*, he wrote, were cogniscent of the sources of the religion. Ibn Rushd (a Mālikī *faqīh*) defended the practitioners of *kalām* for precisely the reason al-Marrākushī said he should have condemned them: for addressing and knowing the sources. What legitimated the practice was precisely the rootedness of the sources (not the "branches") that al-Marrākushī claims they neglected.

Presses Universitaires du Mirail, 1990), 161–71; Maribel Fierro, "La Religión," 483–95; Kenneth Garden, "Al-Ghazālī's Contested Revival," 144–88; Delfina Serrano, "Why did the scholars of al-Andalus distrust al-Ghazāli? Ibn Rushd al-Jadd's fatwā on Awliyā' Allāh."

12 Serrano speculates that this is because al-Ghazālī was still alive.

13 Al-Marrākushī's description of the *fuqahā'*s success under the Almoravids does, after all, bear some resemblance to the picture of historical development argued for here. Their network and institution developed very significantly during this period. The development of Mālikī institutions in the transforming cities of the Far Maghrib, however, witnessed the rise of religio-political (intellectual/religious) opposition that used the same language as that cultivated by the developing discursive tradition. This opposition in the Far Maghrib – these alternate loci of authority – would be identified with the Ṣūfī movement and, to a lesser extent perhaps, with the *mutakallimūn* (both of which Almoravids and Almohads worked to rally to their cause); Mahdism and anti-Mālikism were, of course, what set the Almohads apart; both elements they eventually suppressed.

> These ʿulamāʾ [Ibn Rushd wrote] are leaders of good and right guidance (*khayr wa-hudan*), and are among those who must be emulated (*mi-man yajib bihim al-iqtidāʾ*), because they advocate the supremacy of the Sharīʿa (*qāmū bi-naṣr al-sharīʿa*) and thwarted the likes of those who sow distortion and error. They clarified ambiguities and made clear to us what beliefs (*muʿtaqidāt*) must be professed. For, with their knowledge of the origins of faiths (*dīyānāt*), they are learned in the Truth, by virtue of their knowledge in God (*li-ʿilmihim bi-llāh*) – lofty and sublime – what is owed Him, what is permissible to Him, and what concerning Him is [to be] refuted (*wa-mā yantafī ʿanhu*). This is because the branches of knowledge become known with knowledge of the origins. It is incumbent, then, that their virtues be acknowledged and their eminence recognized (*sawābiq yuqarru lahum*).[14]

For Ibn Rushd the practice of *kalām* as performed by these *mutakallimūn* was necessary for the defense of the faith or "orthodoxy." He was explicit in his epistemological understanding of the practice. "Right guidance" in religion and knowledge of Truth "becomes known with knowledge of the origins." He supported his position by citing the prophetic hadith: "This knowledge is borne from every back, this honesty is repudiated by the distortion of the extremists, and the arrogation of the liars, and the interpretation." For only an ignorant person, he glossed, or a heretic deviating from the truth would believe them (the *mutakallimūn*) to be in error and ignorance, and only the "wicked (*fāsiq*) reviles and ascribes controversy" to what the *mutakalimūn* believe. He marshaled the Qurʾānic phrase, "Those who traduce believing men and believing women undeservedly shall bear the guilt and slander of grievous sin," to his argument. The ignorant must be enlightened by these *mutakallimūn*, he said, the "unrighteous" disciplined, and the heretic, called to repent from *bidʿa*.

> If he does not repent, he should be beaten relentlessly until he repents [he cited in closing], as ʿUmar al-Khattāb – God be pleased with him – did with Ṣabīgh, whose belief was under suspicion. ʿUmar beat him until Ṣabīgh said to him: "Oh Amīr al-Muʾminīn, if you intend to cure me, you have brought me to illness, and if you intend to kill me, finish me off." Then ʿUmar released him.[15]

---

14 Ibn Rushd, *Fatāwā Ibn Rushd*, 804–05.

15 Ibn Rushd, *Fatāwā Ibn Rushd*, 805.

Kalām, as described by Ibn Rushd, is the protector of the true knowledge of God from heresy, the hand that safeguards from deviation, and the tools of reason mobilized to defend the religion. His opinion articulates a position that is the polar opposite of that attributed to the Almoravids by al-Marrākushī (and by much modern historiography). Even if in this particular instance ʿAlī b. Yūsuf decided not to heed Ibn Rushd's opinion (of which we have no evidence, other than al-Marrakushī's version of events), preserved in this consultation is his willingness to listen, his high regard for a muftī sympathetic to Ashʿarism and Andalusī *mutakallimūn*, and the muftī's staunch defense of these against their critics.

Concerning the Virtue of Jihād over the Performance of the Ḥajj[16]

This question also features ʿAlī b. Yūsuf as *mustaftī*. It bears an addendum, which consists of a second, related question, and which may have been asked in person. The fatwā thus consists of two questions and two opinions on one important issue: The relative virtue of jihād compared to that of the ḥajj and the attendant obligations incumbent upon Muslims. In the first question, the *mustaftī*, ʿAlī, was concerned with knowing how this issue bore upon the people of al-Andalus, and in the second, how it bore upon the people of al-ʿIdwa ("the bank," referring to the Maghrib, often the Far Maghrib specifically). The text (other than being a communication from the highest authority in the empire on what was, after all, an epoch-defining matter) illustrates the prominent role played by jihād and the Muslim-Christian frontier in the development and identity of the Islamic West in the Almoravid period. While this issue is multifaceted and of profound importance to the region in this period,[17] there is one particular point upon which I will focus here: Contrary to the long-established notion that jihādism arrived in the peninsula with the "Almoravid hordes," it was the presence of the Christian-Muslim frontier that was most influential in shaping regional attitudes (among other things) over jihād; this frontier's movement and militarization affected Iberians and Maghribīs, and even Christians and Muslims, in profoundly similar ways.[18] The centrality of jihād to regional identity should be seen, therefore, not as something that grew in the peninsula with the arrival of Almoravids and Almohads but as a phenomenon

16 Ibn Rushd, *Fatāwā Ibn Rushd*, 1021–27.

17 This fatwā is treated briefly in Vincent Lagardère, "La Haute Judicature à l'Époque Almoraivde en al-Andalus," 154.

18 For further discussion on the effect of the Muslim-Christian frontier on both societies, see Amira K. Bennison, "Liminal States: Morocco and the Iberian Frontier between the Twelfth and Nineteenth Centuries."

arriving in the Maghrib *from* the Iberian peninsula; the escalation of the Muslim-Christian conflict from 478/1085 unified the experience of Iberian and Maghribī Muslims and impacted their cultures in analogous ways.

An introductory passage of the text reports that the Amīr al-Muslimīn, Nāṣir al-Dīn ʿAlī b. Yūsuf, "may God perpetuate his rule and raise his victory," wrote to Ibn Rushd with the following question: "Is the ḥajj more virtuous for the people of al-Andalus or is jihād?" The question was succinct:

> Concerning those of the people of al-Andalus who have not performed the pilgrimage in this, our time: Is the ḥajj or jihād more virtuous? How [does it affect your opinion if the individual] has already performed the obligatory pilgrimage (*qad ḥajja ḥajjat al-farīḍ*)? Go over what you think about this for us – may you be rewarded and granted success, if God so wills.[19]

The main import of the question was to identify the "virtue" derived from waging jihād and determine the nature of the associated obligation incumbent on Muslims (generally understood to be a communal and not individual one). More specifically, ʿAlī wanted to know the effect of performance or non-performance of the ḥajj (an individual duty) upon the obligation of jihād. The subtext of the *istiftāʾ* is the question of whether a communal duty could trump, or be given priority over, an individual one. More generally, the *mustaftī* sought to resolve the conflict resulting when obligations to God and the community appeared mutually obstructing. It is interesting to note, furthermore, that these two obligations, possibly more than any other in Islam, were most affected by geographical location and by the political status of the community. In his response, Ibn Rushd produced one of the defining formulations these obligations would take in the Islamic West.

The ḥajj is the performance of the pilgrimage to Mecca, incumbent upon all Muslims who are able, as defined by the jurists. Mālikī jurists defined "ability" as having minimal means. A person who is able to walk and eke out an existence by working en route is deemed "able" and thus obligated. Ḥanafī and Shafiʿī jurists, on the other hand, imposed a higher standard and defined "ability" as having means of transport and livelihood, based on the prophetic tradition: "He was asked, 'What is the ability (to perform the pilgrimage)?' He said, 'Food provisions and a riding animal.'"[20] Security, moreover, was widely understood to be a pre-requisite for the ḥajj. There were several opinions concerning

19 Ibn Rushd, *Fatāwā Ibn Rushd*, 1022.

20 Ibn Rushd al-Ḥafīd, *Bidāyat al-Mujtahid*, I: 375.

the concept of delegating the ḥajj. If an individual is physically unable to perform the ḥajj but has the financial resources, might he or she make it possible for someone else to go on ḥajj? In Mālikism this delegation was not obligatory; the performance of the ḥajj by the individual was prioritized. Taking wages (to perform the ḥajj on someone's behalf) was frowned upon.[21]

The question of when the obligation became effective posed a more intractable conceptual problem. Is it obligatory the moment the individual becomes capable (and when the specific time of year arrives)? Or may its performance be postponed to a time that better suits the particular individual? In the *uṣūl* literature, this question was associated with discussions over time, fulfillment, and obligation,[22] which center on the problem of how certain obligations occur in time and must occasionally be deferred, even when the obligation itself is understood to be eternal and ever present and thus immediate (i.e., not deferrable). Some jurists argued that postponement is entirely lawful, based on the example of the prophet, who delayed the performance of his own ḥajj. Others argued (in the vein of the debate in fiqh literature) that the obligation was more akin to prayer. It was thus understood to be an obligation that becomes incumbent during specific and limited periods of time. This made it an unqualified command from God. However, others argued that the fact that a relatively long period elapses between ḥajj seasons, makes the obligation distinctly different from prayer.[23] The fact that each passing year increases the possibility of an individual's death is a further complicating consideration.[24]

The nature and conditions of obligations associated with jihād are both simpler and less defined. Jihād is understood to be a communal and not an individual or universal obligation. This means that so long as a sufficient number of people in the community fulfill the obligation, others may abstain. This concept is based, again, on the example of the Prophet, who was said to never go out to battle without leaving some people behind.[25] Likewise Qur'ān 9: 122 reads, "And the believers should not all go out to fight. Of every troop of them, a party only should go forth, that they (who are left behind) may gain sound knowledge in religion, and that they may warn their folk when they return, so that they may beware." The experience of the early Islamic community was

21 Ibn Rushd al-Ḥafīd, *Bidāyat al-Mujtahid*, I: 376.

22 Ibn Rushd al-Ḥafīd, *Bidāyat al-Mujtahid*, I: 377.

23 Ibn Rushd al-Ḥafīd, *Bidāyat al-Mujtahid*, I: 378.

24 Another point of debate was under what conditions women could perform the ḥajj. Mālik allowed for a woman to travel with her husband, a *dhū maḥram*, or a trustworthy female companion, Ibn Rushd al-Ḥafīd, *Bidāyat al-Mujtahid*, 1: 378.

25 Ibn Rushd al-Ḥafīd, *Bidāyat al-Mujtahid*, I: 455.

filled with examples of jihād and how and why it should be waged. A comprehensive theory was developed. Generally, it is understood to be incumbent on free men, who are of age (*bāligh*), have the means, and are of sound health.[26] Permission from parents is deemed appropriate, except when circumstances make the need or obligation universal, and except when the parents themselves are unbelievers. The majority of jurists also allow for a man in debt to go to war by leaving something behind as a security "for the satisfaction of his debts."

While Ibn Rushd's answer to ʿAlī b. Yūsuf's question was not original, it set an important precedent in the legal tradition of the Maghrib. "The obligation (*farḍ*) of the ḥajj," he wrote in opening his opinion, "has fallen from the people of al-Andalus in this, our time."[27] This was because, he argued, "ability" is one of the preconditions that God set for the obligation to be effective upon an individual. Ibn Rushd thought this "ability," which he defined as the capacity to arrive safe of body and possessions, was "non-existent today." The inability to fulfill this condition (which he characterized as an *ʿilla*) renders the performance of the ḥajj not only supererogatory, but reprehensible, in view of the accumulation of danger and risk involved (*li-taqaḥḥum al-gharar fīhi*). Under these circumstances, and given that the performance of jihād enjoys "countless merits according to the Qur'ān, *mutawātir* Sunna, the traditions (*āthār*)" – that is, with the backing of the most authoritative sources – waging jihād is more virtuous than performing the ḥajj. "This," Ibn Rushd wrote, "is clear beyond any need for clarification."[28]

However, the crux of the *istiftā'* according to Ibn Rushd, is the question of the individual who has already performed the pilgrimage safely. Is pilgrimage for this person more virtuous than waging jihād? He rephrased and amplified the scope of the question. Should a person who has already performed the ḥajj feel compelled to wage jihād, if only to secure more favor with God and not just out of obligation? Ibn Rushd wrote that, in his opinion, jihād is more virtuous for this person "because of the great merit mentioned in its regard."[29] Someone who has performed the ḥajj should, therefore, feel strongly encouraged to wage jihād. Ibn Rushd concluded this first opinion by taking up the problem of time and the performance of the ḥajj. When the individual has not performed the ḥajj, current circumstances precludes (*yatakharraj dhālika ʿalā*)

26 Based on Qur'ān 48:17: "There is no blame for the blind, nor is there blame for the lame, nor is there blame for the sick."

27 Ibn Rushd, *Fatāwā Ibn Rushd*, 1022.

28 Ibn Rushd, *Fatāwā Ibn Rushd*, 1023.

29 Ibn Rushd, *Fatāwā Ibn Rushd*, 1023.

disagreement over the issue of immediate performance or postponement, making it besides the point. This is the case, he said, in communities where it is felt that the obligation of jihād is being fulfilled by a sufficient number of individuals. In cases in which the obligation of jihād is deemed to fall on everyone in the community, he added, waging jihād is more virtuous than fulfilling the duty of pilgrimage. Ibn Rushd's opinion thus construes jihād as a central and foremost obligation to God, for which he felt the need to adduce little textual support.[30] This is the end of the first opinion.

The compiler now informs us that the opinion was further refined and developed in a second query from ʿAlī b.Yūsuf to Ibn Rushd. He tells us the time and place during which this exchange supposedly took place: the beginning of the year 515/1121 in Ceuta. This second *istiftāʾ* asks how the question of jihād versus ḥajj affects the people of al-ʿIdwa, i.e., whether they enjoy the same status in this regard as the people of al-Andalus. Ibn Rushd responded:

> Indeed, aside from the people of al-Andalus, there are the people of al-ʿIdwa [the Far Maghrib], whose route is the same as that of the people of al-Andalus, and they can only travel to (*lā yaṣilūn illā*) Mecca fearing for themselves and their possessions. [Even] when they don't fear for themselves and their possessions in traveling to Mecca, jihād remains for them [an obligation] more virtuous [to fulfill] than hastening the pilgrimage, since it has been said that it may be deferred (*innahu ʿalā al-tarākhī*). This is correct according to the school of Mālik – may God have mercy on him – and to which his *masāʾil* [opinions to questions of Islamic law] point. This concerns one who has been excepted (*ʿadā min*) from performing the duty of jihād. As for one who performs the duty of jihād for the protection (*min ḥimāt*) of the Muslims and their soldiers, jihād is incumbent upon him. Hastening of the pilgrimage is not specified (*lā yataʿayyanu*) as obligatory from [such a person], except for he who has already engaged in battle. This is because the obligation to defer [applies to] a specific situation, when it appears preponderantly likely to the *mukallaf* (one legally capable) that [the opportunity] will slip away by its postponement. The *ḥadd* punishment for this [according] to the words of the Messenger of God – peace and blessings upon him "For the one fighting my Umma between sixty and seventy."[31]

---

30 A point both conforming with his style and with the regional prominence of jihād in this period.

31 Ibn Rushd, *Fatāwā Ibn Rushd*, 1025–26.

Ibn Rushd concedes that *after* waging jihād an individual may be obliged to hasten the pilgrimage, that is, to perform it the first time he gets a chance, because of diminishing time and opportunity. The thrust of his opinion, however, as can be easily appreciated, is that, for Maghribīs, jihād is a religious duty of the highest virtue, the performance of which is to be prioritized. This is the case even for individuals who are technically "exempted" by the fact that others have met the minimum deemed necessary for the communal obligation to be met. For those deemed obligated to wage jihād to defend the community, Ibn Rushd re-emphasizes the opinion that this obligation trumps the obligation of performing the ḥajj. Jihād being an obligation to God, non-fulfillment involves punishment, the nature of which Ibn Rushd spelled out.[32]

•••

The Maghrib and al-Andalus were increasingly unified, not only by Almoravid policy, but also by developments in the peninsula. The centrality of jihād to the Almoravid movement and Ibn Rushd's specification of its virtue and obligation for *both* Andalusīs and Maghribīs mirrored these developments marked by the intensification of religiously defined conflict and the southward movement of the Christian-Muslim frontier.[33] The experience of the frontier profoundly affected the religio-political identity of Iberians and Maghribīs. One of the ways in which it did so was by channelling religio-political energy and symbolism in its direction, by religio-political authorities and cultural production with indelible effects for the Muslim community on both sides of the strait.[34] The Almoravids did not bring jihād to al-Andalus, as is often suggested. Rather, the economic and demographic development on both sides of the frontier, in Iberia and in the Maghrib, led to, among other things, the militarization, transformation, and movement of the frontier, which in turn galvanized religio-political identities – a process that would last into the nineteenth century and

32 This would appear to be a rather lax law of defection.

33 This movement, it must be noted, did not stop at the strait (just as al-Andalus and the Maghrib were not categorically divided by this stretch of water, arguably much easier to cross than the High Atlas mountains); it crossed and continued southward, across Ceuta, Malīla, Mogador, and Mazagan, to name but a few of what became the Luso-Hispanic strong-holds and presidios in the Far and Central Maghrib in the early modern period.

34 Likewise and in a remarkably similar fashion, as A. Bennison has persuasively argued, for the Christian community north of the frontier, Amira K. Bennison, "Liminal States: Morocco and the Iberian Frontier between the Twelfth and Nineteenth Centuries." On the development of the concept of jihād into the modern period, see Amira K Bennison, *Jihad and its Interpretations in Pre-Colonial Morocco: State-Society Relations during the French Conquest of Algeria* (London: Routledge Curzon, 2002).

persists in popular culture. The Almoravid movement, the relationship between the Andalusī religio-legal establishment and the Almoravid leadership, and the formulation and justification for a central place for jihād in the movement's identity was an important chapter and example of this regional process as it impacted the Far Maghrib.

3 Two Technical Questions from al-ʿIdwa: Ritual and Murder

The next two fatwās reinforce the notion, introduced in Chapter One, that Ibn Rushd performed the role of expert elucidator of intricate questions of law for Far Maghribī jurists. The first question deals with a symbolically significant detail in ritual law. The second concerns a case of double murder.[35]

The Man who Forgot to Wipe his Head[36]

This question – described by the compiler as coming from al-ʿIdwa – concerns the omission of an action from the sequence of ablutions for prayer and its rectification. The *mustaftī* wrote that a man reportedly performed all five prayers of the day, but that, while performing his dusk prayers, he remembered that he had forgotten to wipe his head when washing to remove an impurity incurred between the morning and noon prayers. While the omission most likely took place during the ablutions for the noon prayer, the man said he was unsure for what specific set of prayer ablutions (noon, afternoon, sunset, or dusk) he forgot to wipe his head. The man was instructed (presumably by a local imām) to wipe his head and repeat all of the prayers. This he did. However (and almost comically), he appears to have repeated his mistake, not wiping his head during ablutions. The *mustaftī*, making no explicit query, wanted to know what course of action should be followed.

Wiping the head is an integral part of the performance of ablutions. There is some disagreement within the Sunnī schools of law over how much of the head must be wiped. Mālik said it was obligatory to wipe the entire head,[37] while other Mālikī jurists said the minimum surface to be wiped is one-third of the head.[38] Historically, Muslim jurists agreed that praying without being in a state of ritual purity – whether intentionally or out of forgetfulness – invalidates a prayer and necessitates its repetition. Naturally, the repeated prayer

35 Unfortunately, generic in presentation of detail, but intriguing nevertheless.

36 Ibn Rushd, *Fatāwā Ibn Rushd*, 175–76.

37 Ibn Rushd al-Ḥafīd, *Bidāyat al-Mujtahid*, I: 7–10.

38 Ibn Rushd al-Ḥafīd, *Bidāyat al-Mujtahid*, I: 7–10.

should be performed correctly.[39] In the present case, the key issue was when in the day he had forgotten to wipe his head and, therefore, how many prayers were to be repeated.

Ibn Rushd addressed the question succinctly. He answered that if this man has performed his last prayers of the night, as he was instructed to locally (*qabla ʿan yafʿala mā uftiyā bihi*), but before wiping his head – having forgotten –, then he must repeat the ablutions correctly as well as the last set of prayers. "Prayer is only correct [when performed] in a state of purity," he wrote.[40] The man need only perform the last prayers, however, because when he performs this last set correctly, in a state of ritual purity, "all [preceding prayers] are obtained with complete purity." Ibn Rushd closes by citing precedent from the Mālikī tradition, which underscores what he considered the most relevant point of the question. This is highlighted in the case of a person who prays several sets of prayers, but then realizes that some action was performed incorrectly for one set (as in our case, unspecified because of forgetfulness). Ibn Rushd wrote,

> This is like the case of a man who performs ablutions for one of the day's prayers and prays, and then incurs an impurity and performs ablutions but forgets that he has already prayed and so he prays a second time. When he completes his prayers, however, he remembers that he had already prayed. But then he remembers that he forgot to wipe his head, for one of the two performed ablutions (which one he isn't certain). [In this case] there is no [need for] repeating the [prayer or ablutions, as has been established] by consensus, since one of the two prayers has been correct. And in God is success.[41]

The fact that the example cited by Ibn Rushd from the legal tradition is so similar to the question coming from al-ʿIdwa invites speculation into whether the *istiftāʾ* was hypothetical, in which case the exchange between the Maghribī jurist and Ibn Rushd would have been more pedagogical than practical in nature.[42] We have no direct indication here that the question was purely hypo-

39 Ibn Rushd al-Ḥafīd, *Bidāyat al-Mujtahid*, vol. 1, 201.

40 Ibn Rushd, *Fatāwā Ibn Rushd*, 176.

41 Ibn Rushd, *Fatāwā Ibn Rushd*, 176.

42 Such general questions from students of jurisprudence are attested. An example of a purely theoretical question from a group of students is Ibn Rushd, *Fatāwā Ibn Rushd*, 1494–507. This is explicitly stated, however, and the construction of the question is, unlike all of the fatwās analyzed here, not problem-based or framed as a situation eliciting a question but outright asks what, in the opinion of Ibn Rushd, are the qualities an

thetical, and thus it remains open to question. While many fatwās are clearly rooted in practical reality, appearing almost inconceivable as hypotheses, the possibility that fatwās also served pedagogical or scholastic purposes should not be discounted. The present question, along with that of the conflicting testimonies over the number of repudiations a couple has accumulated, in Chapter One, are of a scholastic nature. This character, however, does not invalidate the point made here that one of the key functions of the fatwā, and of the correspondence between jurists, was the development of Mālikism through a learning network.

A Question Concerning the Shedding of Blood in a Double Murder[43]

Another question reached Ibn Rushd – also coming from al-ʿIdwa – concerning a double murder and its aftermath. The *mustaftī* reported that a man, somewhere in the Far Maghrib, had been murdered by a group of four men (*bayn arbaʿati nafar*[in]). There was a single eye-witness – a woman – who could not identify which of the four had perpetrated the crime. Two of the four men exculpated each other and were released. The remaining two then attempted to lay the blame for the crime on each other, offering conflicting versions. The relevant local authority (*al-wālī*) detained both of them under his supervision (*bi-naẓarihi*). Meanwhile, the brother of the victim (*al-maqtūl*) came across one of the men who had been set free (after exculpating each other) and killed him in revenge. Perpetration of this last act – described literally as blood-letting or shedding (*dammā ʿalayhi*) – was confirmed by trustworthy witnesses before the judge; the father of this second murder victim then demanded "the perpetrator's blood," in retaliation. The father of the first victim, however, appealed (*qāma*) to the judge, arguing that his son's blood "was on" the second victim (i.e., had been requited by the death of the second victim). In support of his argument, the father of the first victim brought forth the woman, who was the single witness of the first murder, and swore fifty times, "as is required," in support of his claim. The *mustaftī* wrapped up his *istiftā*ʾ with the

individual who acts as muftī should possess. The fatwā's distinctly belletristic style further distinguishes it as an exercise more scholastic than the fatwās treated here. It is however an important text on an important question. Coming from Tangier, it almost falls within the scope of this book. I have chosen to omit it, however, because Tangier, as discussed in the historical background presented in Chapter Three, had close ties to Ceuta and had cultural and institutional ties to al-Andalus pre-dating our period, very much like Ceuta. For a discussion on *futyā* and the qualities and qualifications of muftīs, see N. Calder, "Al-Nawawī's Typology of Muftīs and Its Significance for a General Theory of Islamic Law," *Islamic Law and Society* 3, no. 2 (1996): 137–64.

43 Ibn Rushd, *Fatāwā Ibn Rushd*, 577–78.

basic question: "Do you consider this permissible?"[44] Foremost in his mind, it appears, was the issue of the permissibility and validity of the argument that the father of the first victim put forth and the procedure by which he established his claim.

The law of retaliation or *qiṣāṣ* grants a specific network of relatives of a victim, known as *awliyāʾ al-dam*, the right to *qiṣāṣ*, that is, the right to extract from their counterparts among the relatives of the perpetrator, a punishment equivalent to what they have suffered. The right of *qiṣāṣ* is limited to death and dismemberment. The issues concerning the application of the laws of *qiṣāṣ*, on which Muslim jurists focused, have included intentionality, the status of the victim in relation to that of the perpetrator, and the nature of rights and obligations once the right of *qiṣāṣ* has been established or granted. The perpetrator and victim must meet certain criteria in order for *qiṣāṣ* to be invoked or granted; there is general agreement among Muslim jurists that the right of *qiṣāṣ* is granted when someone has been murdered intentionally by another person of equal or lesser status. Individuals to whom the right is granted – the *awliyāʾ al-dam* – then have the option to exact punishment or pardon with compensation – blood money or *diya* – or even without compensation if so desired.[45]

As a rule, establishing with certainty that a crime was committed is paramount for the full punishment to be exacted. On this point the prophetic tradition, "Avert the *ḥudūd* in cases of doubt," was often invoked.[46] Several factors, when present, are deemed to obligate *diya* (monetary compensation) instead of *qiṣāṣ*. Issues concerning intentionality (e.g. who is liable in cases in which the perpetrator has been coerced or under orders) and status (e.g. when a Muslim kills or maims a slave, an unbeliever, or a *dhimmī*) were among the most contentious for Muslim jurists; but they played no role in the present case. It was, rather, a set of two related issues that gave the judge pause: These arise in cases in which an individual responsible for an act liable to *qiṣāṣ* commits the act in association with someone else, and cases in which a group acts against a single individual.

Several jurists, including Abū Ḥanīfa, argued that in the first scenario, both individuals must pay the *diya* but they are not liable to *qiṣāṣ* because of the doubt resulting from their co-participation (i.e., the second individual may have been the perpetrator). Others argued, in the interest of deterrence, that both are liable.[47] The second scenario caused similar disagreement, with a

44 Ibn Rushd, *Fatāwā Ibn Rushd*, 578.

45 Ibn Rushd al-Ḥafīd, *Bidāyat al-Mujtahid*, II: 479–490.

46 Ibn Rushd al-Ḥafīd, *Bidāyat al-Mujtahid*, II: 480.

47 Ibn Rushd al-Ḥafīd, *Bidāyat al-Mujtahid*, II: 480–481.

majority of jurists, including Mālik, maintaining that every member of the group should be liable, again in the public interest (*maṣlaḥa*) of deterring conspiracy and collusion. The argument against this position was based on the perceived imbalance between the crime and the retaliation (i.e., the death of several individuals for one victim), which violates the principle of retaliation, strictly defined.[48] The *mustaftī* in our case, most likely wondered whether the presence of multiple individuals at the scene of the first crime deserved consideration – and was greatly complicated by the retaliation exacted by one of the victim's *awliyā'* (his brother), before guilt had been clearly established, and the ensuing claim that the retaliation had been just.

Ibn Rushd, however, deemed the relevant factors in the case to be altogether different. In his view, the issue of multiple perpetrators and a single victim was moot as long as the testimony to the first homicide remained weak or unsubstantial. That the judge allowed the father of the first victim to swear fifty times as means to move the case forward, Ibn Rushd considered a procedural mistake (*khaṭa' min al-ḥukm*). This was on account of the doubt or uncertainty (*lawth*) introduced by the weak testimony, being based on the word of a single woman who did not identify the individual responsible for the murder.[49] Not being based on the "testimony of a trustworthy witness," therefore, the only way for the procedure to become valid, Ibn Rushd wrote, was by oath-taking of the legal guardians/relatives (*awliyā'*) of the second victim to the effect that the second victim's blood "was on" the brother, who they could then demand executed in retaliation.[50]

The correct course to follow according to the tradition of Ibn al-Qāsim, which considered the testimony of a single woman to be weak (introducing uncertainty, *lawth*), would have been for the father of the first victim to swear fifty times to the relatives of the second victim that he was responsible for the death of their relative (*walī himā*). This would entitle the relatives of the second victim to the blood of the father of the first victim, which would in turn render null the claim of his own relatives for blood or retaliation. Ibn Rushd's point being simply that the father of the first victim did not have grounds to claim the second murder as proper retaliation. What he could do was assume responsibility, but incur liability for *qiṣāṣ* himself.

• • •

48 Ibn Rushd al-Ḥafīd, *Bidāyat al-Mujtahid*, II: 484.

49 Along with the fact that the four individuals either exculpated or contradicted each other.

50 Ibn Rushd, *Fatāwā Ibn Rushd*, 578.

Intriguing on a formal level, if both questions are assumed to refer to cases that took place in the southern Far Maghrib, we may speculate that they represent transformations in customary practice, as Mālikism and its ritual practice and criminal law were being adopted; a comparison of the law of retaliation in Mālikism and Berber practice would be in order. But the generic description of the location of the cases, as simply al-ʿIdwā, precludes such speculation. These two fatwās – compounded by the possibility of the first fatwā's academic or non-practical origin – stand, chiefly, as evidence of a correspondence between al-Andalus and the Almoravid Far Maghrib, cultivating the development of Mālikī learning in the latter. This should not lead one to believe that all such correspondence was academic and hypothetical or that it bore little local relevance, as the cases in the following section attest. While also lacking geographic specificity, the detail and character convey a powerful sense of the unique nature of the Far Maghribī context and of its impact and engagement with the process of Mālikī institutional development.

4 The Islamicization of Property: Partitioning and Gifts from Plunder

The following questions arose from a concern over the status, according to the Sharīʿa, of property that has passed hands, whether through inheritance, the expansion of settlements, or usurpation. In both cases below, the moment and precise nature of the transformation of property from one status to another was of chief concern to the *mustaftī*. While the details of the cases are scant, their implications may have been far ranging, as they seem to capture social changes occurring on a broad level: These include the redistribution of land said to have characterized the Almoravid period, the increase in private landholdings and in the buying and selling of land, and the mutual transformation of two different social orders through encounter, represented here by a group of Ṣanhāja tribes (who customarily plundered or usurped cattle from each other) with the local Muslim authority, whose practice included receiving gifts.

On the Privatization of Communal Property[51]

This question – also described as having reached Ibn Rushd from al-ʿIdwa – revolves around the permissibility of partitioning communal property. The *mustaftī* wrote of a group of villages (*qurā*) that had been, over the years, "alternately, abandoned and seized [and passed on in ownership] as inheritance" by their inhabitants, from original owners to their sons "and to the sons of their

51 Ibn Rushd, *Fatāwā Ibn Rushd*, 1155–56.

sons after them."[52] The "villages" are described as having changed hands between different groups – presumably clans or tribes. In these villages there was no custom of giving precedence to certain individuals or clans (even of property owners, *arbāb*) over others in matters of grazing rights over pasture lands (*masāriḥ*) traditionally owned or associated with the villages. The question was triggered when several "property owners" in the villages agreed to partition the lands amongst themselves, decommunalizing them, as it were, on the basis of the idea that since they had inherited the use of the land collectively they likewise could dispose of it collectively. They thus partitioned the lands with the approval of all involved and "according to the calculation of their shares" (*ʿalā ḥisāb ḥiṣaṣihim*). The judge of the region (*balad*), who was present at the partitioning, made it effective, certifying this process, in which the share (*ḥaẓẓ*) of each owner became specified and public. The *mustaftī* wanted to know whether the procedure and action of partitioning was lawful,[53] and whether it was "permissible and legally effective" (*nāfidha*). Whether the action was contested, so prompting the question from the *mustaftī*, is uncertain. It appears most likely that it was the arrangement itself that elicited the question in the mind of the *mustaftī*, who may have been the judge or whomever he consulted.

The legality of the partitioning (*qisma*) of property is accepted and common practice in the Sunnī legal schools. The Qur'ānic sources typically cited in justification of this practice are: "And when kinsfolk and orphans and the needy are present at the division (of the heritage) bestow on them therefrom and speak kindly unto them," and "Whether it be little or much–a legal share."[54] It was generally considered lawful practice to partition inheritable property. The act of partitioning was treated as a sales transaction, yielding similar consequences to a sales contract.[55] While the partitioning of movable objects and benefits presents several complications – over which jurists disagreed – land is, on the whole, deemed partitionable; and most of the conditions and limitations involved were aimed at ensuring equitable results.[56]

Land may be partitioned between a group of people by drawing lots or by consent, after "valuation and equalization (of shares)." The drawing of lots was

52 Ibn Rushd, *Fatāwā Ibn Rushd*, 1155.

53 Engaged in by the inhabitants of the villages, transforming the status of communal grazing land into delimited properties owned by (presumably) specific *arbāb* of the villages – likely the clan leaders.

54 Qur'ān 4: 8 and 4: 7.

55 Not revokable, other than when cheating has occurred, a defect found, or the rights of a third party have been violated. Ibn Rushd al-Ḥafīd, *Bidāyat al-Mujtahid*, II: 323–324.

56 Ibn Rushd al-Ḥafīd, *Bidāyat al-Mujtahid*, vol. II, 323–324.

considered to aid in producing an equitable outcome. As suggested by the Qur'anic phrases, "And then [he] drew lots and was of those rejected," and, "Thou wast not present with them when they threw their pens (to know) which of them should be the guardian of Mary," cited as support.[57] A finer point of disagreement within the Mālikī school over the drawing of lots revolved around concerns about equity and avoiding public harm, e.g. how to determine equal attributes, value, and utility of the sections resulting from the partition, as well as with the sections having at least a minimum level of utility or value. The relative equality of the sections and the value derived from their use was, therefore, a key point of debate, especially when difficult to establish, as, for example, when the lands (or other immovable property such as buildings) were of different qualities (e.g., orchards, baths, fields). If the drawing of lots resulted in a partitioning that was deemed unfair by the beneficiaries, it could be repeated or adjusted.

The partitioning of land through mutual consent, on the other hand, presents far fewer problems. "Division through agreement, irrespective of whether it is after valuation and adjustment or without it, is permitted in similar and differing properties as it is a kind of sale, but whatever is prohibited in sale is prohibited here."[58] The fact that the lands in the present case were of relatively homogeneous value and utility as grazing lands, meant that the partitioning process was simple. This was how Ibn Rushd understood it to be:

> If it is the case that those pastures, which they partitioned are within their villages, and not outside of them, that they alone graze in them (*yanfaridūn bi-l-sarḥ fīhā*), and that no one but them can graze there other than by entering through their villages, then the partitioning [of these pastures] is permissible and effective, according to what they agreed upon. [This is] because [the pastures] are [the villagers'] property [and] no one of them has cause (*ḥujja*) for criticizing [the partition] since they [have all] approved of it.[59]

In Ibn Rushd's opinion the partitioning of the grazing lands was lawful. In his brief response, he shows little concern for the manner in which the property became inheritable.[60] As always, he leaves room for interpretation; implicit in the opinion is something we detect the *mustaftī* to have been concerned about:

57 Qur'ān 37:141 and 3:44.
58 Ibn Rushd al-Ḥafīd, *Bidāyat al-Mujtahid*, II: 320.
59 Ibn Rushd, *Fatāwā Ibn Rushd*, 1156.
60 That is, how these villages came to own the property.

the existence of a third party with a claim to the property – it not being fully known to the *mustaftī* how grazing rights over these lands came into the possession of the villagers in question. Nevertheless, Ibn Rushd's one criterion is simply that no one else has a claim.

On Purchasing, Giving, and Receiving Gifts Acquired through Plunder or Usurpation[61]

This question investigates the legal status of movable property originally acquired through usurpation (*ghaṣb*) and the consequences of various transactions in which it may be involved. For all practical purposes, the property in question was stolen. However, the *mustaftī* selected a different term to designate its status and contextualize the question. The term *ghaṣb* is usually associated with land and certain types of benefits. The action by which the property in question was acquired was understood here to be distinct from theft (perhaps more akin to seizing booty). Significantly, the choice of term demonstrates a kind of cultural sensitivity capable of parsing what could otherwise be an irreconcilable difference in the encounter of the social practices between the Ṣanhāja and the discursive tradition of Mālikīsm. This is not to say that the *mustaftī* was foreign to this custom (he is identified as Ṣanḥāja), but rather that, whether Berber or Arab, strategies were available for reconciling different legal and ethical values. Such strategies would have borne special import for Almoravid leaders, for whom the conflicting practices or traditions intersected in a visible or public manner.

A man identified by the compiler[62] as one of the "desert *Mulaththamūn*" (veiled or muffled ones) wrote to Ibn Rushd with this question concerning "the usurpation taking place among them" (i.e. the *Mulaththamūn*).[63] He wanted to know what should be done concerning a group of tribes who wintered in the desert and whose custom was to raid each other's cattle, a long-standing custom in the community – practiced by "fathers and grandfathers." This property "usurped from each other" had been inherited and passed on from generation to generation. The Ṣanhāja *mustaftī* posed a series of questions related to the general problem of the Muslim who trades in property the procurement or origin of which is unlawful according to the Sharīʿa. He asked whether a person who "strove for piety" and avoided "compromising" situations could purchase cattle from these tribes. He asked whether the tribes could offer their cattle to the "Amīr al-Muslimīn wa-Nāṣir al-Dīn," and whether a "pious" person, in turn,

61 Ibn Rushd, *Fatāwā Ibn Rushd*, 1017–20.

62 Ibn al-Wazzān (d. 543/1148).

63 Ibn Rushd, *Fatāwā Ibn Rushd*, 1017.

might receive the gift of this cattle from the Amīr al-Muslimīn. May the amīr of the Almoravids reward (*yuthību*) members of these tribes in reciprocation for a gift he has received from them consisting of this cattle? And may he use public money from the "treasury of the Muslims" (*bayt al-māl al-muslimīn*)? He also asked whether it is permissible for a man belonging to one of those tribes who is appointed commander (*amīr*) by the amīr of the Almoravids (and who also has participated in these raids) to receive such gifts of cattle and make or receive them from the Almoravid amīr. The unnamed *Mulaththam mustaftī* ended his *istiftā* with the question of whether the fact that the raiding activity was limited to this community of tribes had any bearing on the ruling (*ḥukm*).[64]

This case was discussed under the rubric of usurpation (*ghaṣb*) rather than theft (*sariqa*) because of the different liability attached to each offense, even when the effect of actions is identical. The terms are thus understood to refer to the liability rather than the offense. As is well known, *sariqa* is subject to the *ḥadd* liability of amputation. "Substantial doubt with respect to ownership," however, "has the effect of waiving this *ḥadd*."[65] Certain conditions must be met for something to be termed theft, among them: the testimony of two trustworthy (*ʿadl*) witnesses, a confession, and the clear identification of what was stolen and from whom. All of these are absent from the case in question.

Usurpation, defined as the act of acquiring or causing the destruction or loss of property belonging lawfully to someone else, is chiefly subject to the liability of restitution of the usurped property.[66] Generally speaking, when someone is proven to have unlawfully taken possession or caused the destruction of someone else's property, whether intentionally or by mistake, the person is liable for replacing or compensating the owner for the property. Camels and other livestock were considered, across the schools, to be usurpable, i.e., liable for restitution by the usurper. According to Mālik, this restitution should amount to the value of the animals (and nothing beyond this value) on the day of the usurpation. Mālik's source for this opinion was a tradition transmitted on the authority of Abū Hurayra, which reads: "If one sets free a slave in whom he has a share, he is obliged to pay the value of the remainder through fair

64 Ibn Rushd, *Fatāwā Ibn Rushd*, 1018. In other words, can goods which have been procured through un-Islamic practice, even through unlawful means, be "laundered" into lawful property? And can this be done repeatedly and systematically? This is an important, and presumably not unique problem, since so much property lawfully owned inside Dār al-Islam had once resided outside and had at some point been acquired in a way that did not necessarily conform to Islamic practice. It should come as no surprise that a model or concept to legalize such property existed within the Islamic legal tradition.

65 Ibn Rushd al-Ḥafīd, *Bidāyat al-Mujtahid*, II: 543.

66 Usurpation is considered a tort.

valuation." Usurpation of movable goods, such as livestock, was thus understood to necessitate the restitution of value and not necessarily of the property or its identical counterpart.[67] According to an alternate opinion, however, the restitution of the property should be made in identical kind, based on the Qur'ānic verse: "Whoso of you killeth out of set purpose he shall pay its forfeit in the equivalent (*mithl*) of that which he hath killed, of domestic animals."[68] Thus once usurpation was determined to have occurred, there was a great deal of disagreement among jurists – within Mālikism and among the other schools – over the exact nature of the liability, i.e. what was to be restituted. The principle variables around which the debates revolved included the determination of intentionality or accidentality – whether caused by man or God – the nature of the property, and its valuation, including whatever benefits the usurper may have drawn from the property since usurpation. A variety of further possible contingencies were considered and discussed in the legal literature – including what the usurper was liable for when he/she has added value or labor to the usurped property.[69]

In the present case, however, all these considerations turn out to be irrelevant, since no specific party claimed to have lost the property (the stolen camels). What concerned the *mustaftī* was not whether or how to effect restitution, but how property deemed to have been usurped could be lawfully traded or gifted. This concern is addressed in legal manuals under the topic of *hibāt* or gifts. And while the legal dimension of gift-giving revolved mostly around issues of inheritance (such as under what circumstances and with what limitations appertaining to the relevant portion of an individual's wealth could this be given away as gifts) and *ribā* restrictions,[70] proven and lawful ownership was certainly deemed an essential condition for the act to be lawful. Thus, for a gift transaction to occur, the property in question must be rightfully owned by the gift giver, a concern which Ibn Rushd addressed in his opinion.

Ibn Rushd answered this question in a fair amount of detail, acknowledging the significance of the issue and its bearing on the power and behavior of military-political leaders. The gist of his opinion was that the property need not be considered usurped, but rather "found" (*luqṭa*), meaning that the status of the property should be conceived in a wholly different manner from that posited

67 Ibn Rushd al-Ḥafīd, *Bidāyat al-Mujtahid*, II: 384.

68 Qur'ān 5: 95.

69 Ibn Rushd al-Ḥafīd, *Bidāyat al-Mujtahid*, II: 386.

70 Having the effect of a sale, certain *ribā* restrictions apply. Ibn Rushd al-Ḥafīd, *Bidāyat al-Mujtahid*, II: 401.

by the *mustaftī* in his question.[71] The camels in the possession of this group of tribes, Ibn Rushd wrote, should be considered found instead of usurped, because they were inherited ("from fathers and grandfathers") and because of the great length of time elapsed (*li-qidam al-ʿahd*) since they came into their possession. The original owners of the camels are thus not identifiable. Restitution of the property, "or of any portion of it," to a rightful owner is therefore impossible. If such is the case, Ibn Rushd continued, "let it be judged to be in the [rightful] possession of those who possess it ... by inheritance from their fathers and grandfathers" and let the property be deemed, therefore, to have been "found." In support of this opinion Ibn Rushd adduced the tradition in which the Prophet reportedly said to someone who had found something: "Do as you like with it."[72]

It is commendable, Ibn Rushd added, for a person who finds such property to donate it to charity. But this is not obligatory, especially in a case such as this, in which the current animals are the offspring of those that were usurped. He said it is permissible for anyone to purchase such livestock from the present owners and likewise permissible for the Amīr al-Muslimīn to receive and bestow such property as a gift and for the recipient to receive and own it. "He incurs no crime (*ithm*) or sin (*ḥaraj*) through this." It is also lawful for the amīr of the Almoravids to reward the person or tribe who gave him this gift from "the treasury of the Muslims," the *bayt al-māl.*

What is a more sensitive issue, however, is for the holder of an office (*wālī*) who has been appointed by the Amīr al-Muslimīn to receive such a gift.

> For him it is not permissible to accept it from them, due to what has been said [in the Prophetic ḥadīth, which is] that "the gifts of commanders are malicious (*ghalūl*)," unless he reimburses it (*yukāfiʾu ʿalayhā*). If he reimburses with a value equal to it, [by means of] a reward, and he gives some of it [as a gift] to the Amīr al-Muslimīn – may God perpetuate his success and sanction – and [the amīr in turn] gives this to someone, this giving is sound and permissible for him. [This remains so] whether the usurpers of this cattle usurped it from someone who has not usurped from them or from one who has from their fathers before them. Since the tribe has plundered the tribe, each individual does not know that he took specific property [or] to whom particular property has gone.[73]

71 Ibn Rushd al-Ḥafīd, *Bidāyat al-Mujtahid,* II: 369.

72 Ibn Rushd, *Fatāwā Ibn Rushd,* 1018–19.

73 Ibn Rushd, *Fatāwā Ibn Rushd,* 296.

Receipt by the *wālī* of such property without redistribution is thus deemed corrupting. The original source of the property – once the property itself is declared "found" with certainty (meeting certain conditions) – is not relevant. Overall, Ibn Rushd placed great emphasis on the redistributive role and protocol of political authorities with regard to receiving gifts.[74] Naturally, if the conditions above are not met, and the current owners in fact usurped the camels, or they know the owner and can return the property to a specific person or to his/her heirs, they are obliged to return the property. All other transactions excluding this – giving them as gifts, purchasing, or receiving – would be unlawful. Any person receiving usurped property knowingly will be liable for that usurpation.

•••

In the two cases above, both *mustaftī* and muftī leave many questions unanswered. We do not know how the possession of communal lands by certain villages came to be recognized or even what the result of the partitioning process was – whether they resulted in individual ownership or, more likely, family or clan ownership. Likewise, in the second fatwā, the opinion, while detailed, appears disarmingly simple (they just "found" the camels). We are left wondering how the value of the property was estimated, and more importantly, how its equivalence was estimated for the gift giving process and what role such exchange played in the fiscal economy and in local political relationships.

These texts are but windows onto a greater landscape. They intimate a set of processes of widespread significance for the period: the expansion of land settlement, use, and re-distribution attendant to Almoravid unification; the gradual entry of property into fiscal and commercial systems regulated (if only loosely) by Mālikī practices; and the gradual and adaptive encounter of Mālikī

74 The issue of usurpation and sale of usurped property was not limited to the hinterland of the Far Maghrib but was also contentious in al-Andalus where political instability and change over a century saw a great deal of property changing hands. When the issue of the legality of the sale of such property (which had been usurped or acquired and then sold by *taifa* ruling families or by Almoravid governors themselves acting on behalf of the public treasury) was brought up in Cordoba toward the end or soon after Ibn Rushd's tenure as chief judge there, he appears to have taken the very unpopular position that the legality of such properties and purchases could be questioned – an opinion his opponents believed would lead to chaos. Ibn Rushd and those who supported his opinion were forced to make a public apology. Delfina Serrano, "Ibn Rušd al-Ŷadd," 619. Aḥmad al-Wansharīsī, *al-Mi'yār al-mu'rib wa-l-jāmi' al-mughrib 'an fatāwā 'ulamā' Ifrīqiyā wa-l-Andalus wa-l-Maghrib*, 13 vols. (Rabat: Ministry of Culture and Religious Affairs, 1981), 97–102.

discursive traditions with Ṣanhāja and other Berber and Far Maghribī custom. The existence of extra-Mālikī custom is openly acknowledged and, in a very real way, sanctioned in both of these texts. This process of sanction and synthesis characterized in significant ways the development of social practice during the Almoravid period and ensuing Berber Islamic states. The legacy of this process is visible today across the Far Maghrib, from High Atlas irrigation to dowry practices. It is this process of synthesis on the popular level of daily transaction and conflict resolution that was most influential in the development of Islamic institutions in the Maghrib – more significant than the elite political history or even intellectual history of the ʿulamāʾ and their legalistic debates, upon which so much of the historiography of the last century has focused. Unfortunately it is one of the most difficult aspects to glean from the textual sources. The text analyzed in the following chapter, affords a rare glimpse into the details of a long case, giving us a bit room to imagine what such processes in daily life may have looked like.

CHAPTER 3

Fatwās to Ceuta: Water Rights, Judicial Review, and Ibn Rushd's Correspondence with al-Qāḍī ʿIyāḍ

1 Introduction

This chapter traces the development of a single case that pits a group of garden owners living in a province in the border region between al-Andalus and the Far Maghrib against a miller over the use of a stream. Its analysis serves to illustrates the process, on both micro and macro levels, whereby the institution of Mālikism – a network of jurists backed by the state and whose relative independence afforded it a high level of legitimacy among the population – began its consolidation in the countryside of the Far Maghrib. As described in the two previous chapters, much of this institution was absorbed or imported from its highly structured and established counterpart in al-Andalus, in a manner transformed to meet local needs.

2 Historical Background

Ceuta may have been on the edge of al-Andalus, but it had a claim to authority[1] of the highest kind in the peninsula. The city had played a key role as an Andalusī enclave and bridge to the Maghrib, a role which grew in importance under the Almoravids.

The capture of Ceuta, a Mediterranean port of strategic significance, was a critical step for the extension of Almoravid power to the Iberian Peninsula. The Sabtī regime of Suqūt al-Barghawāṭī and his son Yaḥyā Diyā'[2] al-Dawla (453–476/1061–1083) was the obstacle that had prevented Almoravid armies from crossing in force to Iberia, to which they had been summoned by several *taifa* leaders with increasing urgency beginning in the 460s/1070s. Barghawāṭī Ceuta was much like an Andalusī *taifa*. It attracted notable poets, and legal and religious scholars, who left an indelible mark (ʿIyāḍ's first teacher was taught by one of the most prominent legal authorities of al-Andalus who lectured in Ceuta for a spell). The city, which controlled Tangier and sometimes Algeciras,

1 And a history of claiming, representing, and holding Andalusī caliphal authority.

2 Also known as Bahā' al-Dawla.

 | DOI 10.1163/9789004279841_005

vied for power with the other *taifas*, most notably Seville, against which it contended for control of the strait.

The history of Ceuta can be broken down into three periods: 1.) the city's inclusion in the Umayyad Caliphate; 2.) its prominent position in the struggle for power in al-Andalus, during the *Taifa* Period;[3] and 3.) its incorporation into the Almoravid Empire, under which it became the state's principal North African port, experiencing great commercial and demographic growth.[4]

Ceuta developed strong ties with the peninsula after the Andalusī Umayyad Caliphs made it, in 319/931, one of two North African bases in its struggle with the Fāṭimids. Later, ʿAlī b. Ḥammūd, an Idrīsid prince appointed governor by the restored Umayyad Caliph Sulaymān al-Mustaʿīn, would himself take Cordoba and assume the caliphate (the first non-Marwānid to do so after the restoration) in the turbulent first half of the fifth/eleventh century. Ceuta became the home of the Ḥammūdid princes, successors to the caliphate and thus deeply involved in the power struggles of Cordoba and Seville. A lieutenant of the Ḥammūdids named Suqūt (originally captured as a boy in an expedition against the Barghawāṭa, and purchased and manumitted by ʿAlī b. Ḥammūd for his good services) proclaimed himself independent of the Ḥammūdids in 453/1061 and assumed the double and unusual caliphal title of al-Manṣūr and al-Muʿān.[5] Suqūt minted coins in the name of the Abbasid Caliph al-Qāʾim bi-Llāh ʿAbd Allāh (422–467/1031–1075) as well as himself and his successor.[6]

While Suqūt warred against al-Muʿtadid of Seville after 457/1065 for control of the strait, which he preserved, the Almoravids consolidated their power in the Far Maghrib, arriving at borders of the Barghawāṭi *taifa* in the 1070s. By this

---

3 This process entailed in turn the city's progressive isolation as the struggle between the *taifas* came to a standstill.

4 The resulting pressure on the city's agricultural hinterland is intimated in our case as farmers and millers contended for declining water resources to feed a population growing at a rate requiring a double extension of Ceuta's great mosque during ʿIyāḍ's lifetime.

5 J. Vallvé Bermejo, "Suqūt al-Barghawāṭī rey de Ceuta," *Al-Andalus* 28 (1963), 177.

6 J. Vallvé Bermejo, "Suqūt al-Barghawāṭī rey de Ceuta." This spirit of independence and entitlement to authority inherited by the Barghawāṭī from the Ḥammūdids may explain the behavior of Ceuta's last Almoravid judge-cum-city ruler, Qāḍī ʿIyāḍ (the presiding judge in our case), who, sixty years after Suqūt, stubbornly held out against the Almohads, minting his own coins with the Almoravid slogan, in the last city in the Far Maghrib to do so. Hanna E. Kassis, "Qadi Iyad's Rebellion against the Almohads in Sabtah (AH 542–543/AD 1147–1148) New Numismatic Evidence," *Journal of the American Oriental Society* 103, no. 3 (1983): 504–14. For a more critical reading of these coins, see Maribel Fierro, "Sobre monedas de época almohade: I. El dinar del Cadí ʿIyāḍ que nunca existió. II. Cuándo se acuñaron las primeras monedas almohades y la cuestión de la licitud de acuñar moneda," *al-Qanṭara* XXVII, no. 2 (2006): 457–76.

time the new leader of Seville, al-Muʿtamid, threatened by Alfonso VI from the north, called upon Yūsuf b. Tāshufīn for help. Yūsuf responded that he could not intervene in Iberia while Tangier and Ceuta remained unconquered. Eventually al-Muʿtamid offered Yūsuf b. Tāshufīn diplomatic, legal, and naval assistance against Ceuta. In 471/1078–1079, Yūsuf was met in battle by Suqūt, aged ninety, and his son Yaḥyā. Suqūt was slain and Tangier lost, while Yaḥyā Diyāʾ al-Dawla fled to Ceuta, where he assumed the title al-ʿIzz and held out against Yūsuf until 476/1083. In 475/1082, after an altercation with Alfonso VI, al-Muʿtamid organized a delegation that included judges from Badajoz, Granada, and Cordoba as well as his own vizier. The delegation travelled to Tangier to entreat Yūsuf to intervene against Alfonso VI. When al-ʿIzz showed himself uncooperative and unresponsive to calls from Yūsuf for permission to cross the strait, both Yūsuf and the delegation convened judges to issue fatwās against al-ʿIzz. For eleven months, in 475–476/1082–1083, Yūsuf laid siege to Ceuta. He then asked for and received naval help from al-Muʿtamid, making the siege total, and forcing al-ʿIzz into a confrontation which he lost. He was said to have been carrying the seal of Yaḥyā b. ʿAlī, one of the Ḥammūdid caliphs.[7]

Qāḍī ʿIyāḍ was born six months after the Almoravid occupation of Ceuta. As a boy he witnessed the armies of Yūsuf b. Tāshufīn crossing four times to Iberia, most determinedly in 483/1090, when he undertook the conquest and unification of all of the Islamic lands of al-Andalus. Yūsuf's son and successor, ʿAlī b. Yūsuf, was born in Ceuta in the same year as ʿIyāḍ and was brought up in the city (another sign of its newfound importance). After assuming leadership of the state in Marrakesh, ʿAlī would sponsor ʿIyāḍ's education by financing his short but productive trip to al-Andalus.

•••

Set on a peninsula which provides a natural port, Ceuta depended for much of its food on the agricultural town of Balyūnsh, nine kilometers away, richer in water and the site of the gardens to which the inhabitants of Ceuta retreated for leisure. ʿIyāḍ is said to have taught in a mosque there, and the town fell under his jurisdiction as chief judge of Ceuta. This is why a group of farmers – whose gardens were in Balyūnsh – approached ʿIyāḍ in the case below seeking redress. The Barghawāṭīs, the last rulers of the city before the Almoravid conquest, had had their summer residences in Balyūnsh. At one point in time, a large portion of land directly involved in our case appears to have been in their

7 María Jesús Viguera, *Los reinos de taifas y las invasiones magrebíes: (al-Andalus del IX al XIII)* (Madrid: Editorial MAPFRE, 1992).

possession – or that of a close relation – into the beginning of the Almoravid period.

3 The Qāḍī

At the time of our case, ʿIyāḍ had been a judge for between three and five years. He was, to some extent, still learning the ropes of his job.[8] Through his later written works of piety, poetry, and law, and, in an altogether different way, because of his obstinate resistance to the dynasty that would defeat the one to which he was inextricably bound, ʿIyāḍ would become one of the preeminent jurists of his time (as well as one of the most important Maghribī scholars of ḥadīth). The fame of his best known work spread far beyond the geographical and ideological confines of his own legal school.[9] ʿIyāḍ was born into an established family of Arab origin in Ceuta where he spent most of his life.[10] He left Ceuta only twice, to al-Andalus, for relatively brief periods of time: the first, as an advanced student to meet the scholars of the peninsula and gather transmitting licenses (*ijāzāt*); and the second, to assume the judgeship of Granada. ʿIyāḍ's career came to an end with the collapse of the Almoravid dynasty; he led the city in open rebellion against the Almohads, capitulated, and was exiled to Marrakesh where, according to several sources he appears to have met a violent death.

8 Which is perhaps why most of his extant *istiftā*'s date to this period.

9 The most popular work by ʿIyāḍ – a large number of manuscripts and commentaries from the middle and early modern period exist throughout the Islamic world – is his *al-Shifāʾ bi-taʿrīf ḥuqūq al-Muṣṭafāʾ* (The healing in knowing the truths of the Chosen One). Its success and diffusion point to the emergence from popular religion into mainstream Islamic society of the figure of the Prophet Muḥammad as a figure of veneration. See Annemarie Schimmel, *And Muhammad is His Messenger: the Veneration of the Prophet in Islamic Piety* (Chapel Hill: University of North Carolina Press, 1985), 33. This phenomenon in the Far Maghrib is manifest in the mystical or Ṣūfī tradition, as well as in the political and social institution of Sharīfism. For a reading of ʿIyāḍ's work in the context of religious and intellectual developments in the Islamic West, see Maribel Fierro, "El tratato sobre el profeta del Cadí ʿIyāḍ y el contexto almohade," in *Legendaria Medievalia: En honor de Concepción Castillo Castillo*, ed. Raif Georges Khoury, et al. (Córdoba: Ediciones el Almendro–Fundación Paradigma, 2011).

10 Some of the material in this section also appears in Camilo Gómez-Rivas, "Qāḍī ʿIyāḍ (d. 544/1149)," in *Islamic Legal Thought: A Compendium of Muslim Jurists*, ed. Oussama Arabi, et al., Studies in Islamic Law and Society, Vol. 36 (Leiden: Brill, 2013), 323–338. See also Delfina Serrano, "ʿIyāḍ b. Mūsà," in *Biblioteca de al-Andalus*, ed. Jorge Lirola Delgado (Almería: Fundación Ibn Tufayl de Estudios Árabes, 2009), 404–434.

Of particular significance are the facts that ʿIyāḍ, who was linked inextricably to the institution of Mālikism, was canonized in the very center of the Almohad state (whose early and unsuccessful radical project included the eradication of this school),[11] and that he wrote the works that would define the network of the institution itself (through a description of its principal figures, past and present).[12] Working on the edge of the two greater regions of the empire, in its major African port, Iyāḍ personally transmitted a great deal of the legal and religious knowledge that would be used in the growing south, especially by consulting jurists he had met during his *riḥlat al-ṭalab fī al-ʿilm* (journey in search of knowledge) to al-Andalus. Many of these consultations, once compiled, became references for legal practice for Far Maghribī jurists. Also of significance is that ʿIyāḍ's career was directly sponsored by the Almoravid amīrs (especially by ʿAlī b. Yūsuf), who first financed his studies in al-Andalus and appointed him judge of Ceuta, later Granada, and finally reappointed him to Ceuta in the last days of the empire.

ʿIyāḍ, whose full name was Abū al-Faḍl ʿIyāḍ b. Mūsā b. ʿIyāḍ b. ʿAmrūn b. Mūsā b. ʿIyāḍ b. Muḥammad b. ʿAbd Allāh b. Mūsā b. ʿIyāḍ al-Yaḥsubī al-Sabtī,[13]

---

11 However, Qāḍī ʿIyāḍ only came to be venerated as one of the seven saints of Marrakesh in the Marinid period. Maribel Fierro, "La Religión," 445–46.

12 The *Tartīb al-madārik wa-taqrīb al-masālik li-maʿrifat aʿlām madhhab Mālik* (Organizing the faculties and revealing the methods for discovering the signs of the school of Mālik) is the most influential of ʿIyāḍ's biographical works. It traces the history, development, and diffusion of the Mālikī legal tradition from Mecca to the different regions of the Islamic world, by identifying and describing its main proponents and practitioners, from Mālik b. Anas, through nine generations or *ṭabaqāt*. The book opens with a brief apologetic of the school's epistemological method and is followed by a detailed biography of Mālik, after which the jurists of the school are presented chronologically, through generations and regions. ʿIyāḍ's second biographical work, *al-Ghunya* (The Riches), is, in a sense, a more autobiographical work, describing ʿIyāḍ's recent contemporaries in the Mālikī school, placing special emphasis on his own teachers and on those from whom he garnered transmission licenses or *ijāzāt*.

13 See Delfina Serrano's introductory study in Muḥammad b. ʿIyāḍ, *Madhāhib al-ḥukkām fī nawāzil al-aḥkām* (*La actuación de los jueces en los procesos judiciales*), 13–141. M. Talbi, "ʿIyāḍ b. Mūsā," EI². M. José Hermosilla Llisterri, "En torno al Qāḍī ʿIyāḍ I: datos biographicos," *Miscelánea de Estudios Árabes y Hebraicos* XXVII-XXVIII (1978): 149–74; Muḥammad b. ʿIyāḍ, *al-Taʿrīf bī l-qāḍī ʿIyāḍ* (Muḥammadiya: 1982); al-Maqqarī al-Tilimsānī, *Azhār al-riyāḍ fī akhbār ʿIyāḍ* (Rabat: 1978). For a complete annotated bibliography of Arabic works on ʿIyāḍ to 1994, see Ḥasan al-Warāgilī, *Abū al-Faḍl al-Qāḍī ʿIyāḍ al-Sabtī* (Beirut: Dār al-Gharb al-Islamī, 1994). On Muḥammad b. ʿIyāḍ and the Banū ʿIyāḍ family thereafter, see Delfina Serrano, "Los Banū ʿIyāḍ: de la caída del imperio almorávid a la instauración de la dinastía nazarí," in *IX*, ed. M. Luisa Ávila, and M. Fierro, Estudios Onomástico

was born in Ceuta toward the middle of Shaʿbān 476/January 1084. Shortly thereafter, Yūsuf b. Tāshufīn made the city into the base of operations for his military excursions into Iberia. As a scion of a notable scholarly family, ʿIyāḍ was able to learn from the best teachers Ceuta had to offer. The qāḍī Abū ʿAbd Allāh Muḥammad b. ʿIsā al-Tamīmī (d. 505/1111) was ʿIyāḍ's first important teacher and is credited with his basic academic formation. Growing up, ʿIyāḍ benefited from the traffic of scholars from al-Andalus, the Maghrib, and the eastern Islamic world.

At the age of 31 and as a fairly established scholar, ʿIyāḍ made his *riḥlat al-ṭalab fī al-ʿilm*, a traditional requirement for Muslim scholars who sought employment in certain public functions, such as the judgeship. The northward direction of ʿIyāḍ's scholarly journey is novel and somewhat unique in the literature. This *riḥla* had been traditionally performed together with the pilgrimage to Mecca, and thus, from al-Andalus and the Maghrib, it was most often an eastward journey. Historically, the Islamic East had been the source of all trends, intellectual and otherwise, that swept through this part of the Islamic world. ʿIyāḍ's northward journey underscores a crucial historical development, to wit, the creation of the first large-scale bureaucratic structure in the Far Maghrib and the cultural and institutional know-how that was imported southward from al-Andalus.[14] The contacts that ʿIyāḍ made during his eight-month journey to the cities of al-Andalus, and the sustained correspondence he would carry on with these once he returned, put him at the center of this crucial flow.

ʿIyāḍ spent part of 507/1113 and 508/1114 visiting the cities of Cordoba, Murcia, Almería, and Granada. He received *ijāzāt* from the most important traditionist of his time, Abū ʿAlī al-Ṣadafī (d. 514/1120) in Murcia, and met with some of the most celebrated scholars of the moment, such as Ibn al-Ḥājj[15] (d. 529/1134), Ibn Rushd al-Jadd, and Ibn Ḥamdīn[16] (d. 508/1114). Upon returning

Biográficos de al-Andalus (Madrid-Granada: Centro Superior de Investigaciones Científicas, 1999).

14 Al-Andalus had been especially attractive to the Almoravids for the stability and legitimacy of its state institutions and their freedom from the Ismāʿīlī "heresy" of the Fāṭimids, against whom the Andalusī Umayyads had fought a proxy war through Berber client tribes in the Far and Central Maghrib in the tenth and eleventh centuries. Earlier alliances to Fāṭimids and Andalusīs and later rivalries among the three largest Berber groups in the Maghrib played a crucial role in the history of the region. These major groups are the Ṣanhāja (associated with the Almoravids), the Maṣmūda (associated with the Almohads), and the Zanāṭa (once allies of the Umayyads and later associated with the Marinids).

15 Abū ʿAbd Allāh b. al-Ḥājj, qāḍī of Cordoba.

16 Muḥammad b. Ḥamdīn, qāḍī of Cordoba.

to Ceuta, ʿIyāḍ participated in a public debate on Saḥnūn's *Mudawwana*, a kind of rite of passage that was followed by his appointment to the *shūra*.[17] He was first appointed judge of Ceuta in 515/1121 and served in the position until 531/1136.[18] It is presumably during his double tenure as judge of Ceuta (where he served again from 539–543/1145–48) that ʿIyāḍ was most prolific. Most of the consultations and cases compiled by his son are from this period, and his overall fame as a jurist and as a writer of fiqh (jurisprudence) was most probably founded on the work he did in this city.

In 515/1136 ʿIyāḍ was appointed judge of Granada, where he was initially well received but after a little more than a year fell into disfavor with the amīr of al-Andalus, Tāshufīn b. ʿAlī, who deposed him, according to one source, on account of his excessive censoriousness. After this episode, ʿIyāḍ stepped back from public life. He appears to have been active only once and briefly, acting in an official capacity in the southern Iberian town of Algeciras. Then, in 539/1144, having recovered the favor of the Almoravid administration, ʿIyāḍ was again appointed judge of Ceuta by the briefly-reigning Ibrāhīm b. Tāshufīn, second to last amīr of the Almoravids.

Two late eastern biographer's of ʿIyāḍ, Ibn al-ʿImād (d. 1089/1679) and al-Shaʿrānī (d. 973/1565), claim that ʿIyāḍ instigated the public burning of al-Ghazālī's (d. 505/1111) *Iḥyāʾ ʿulūm al-dīn*. The claim is doubtful, as it is found in no earlier western sources. It would appear, rather, as a gloss on ʿIyāḍ's perceived close ties to the pro-Mālikī Almoravid dynasty and his subsequent fate at the hands of the anti-Mālikī Almohads, a conflict that, on a symbolic and rhetorical level, involved al-Ghazālī's very famous work and the notion of the proper role of the Muslim jurist in society, pitting the members of a series of rebellious Ṣūfī movements and other discontents against the Mālikī jurists.[19]

The earliest source on ʿIyāḍ is the *al-Taʿrīf bi-l-Qāḍī ʿIyāḍ* by his son Muḥammad b. ʿIyāḍ.[20] As D. Serrano has argued, Muḥammad struggled with the problem of honoring his father in a political environment that was hostile to the dynasty to which the latter had remained steadfastly loyal. Filial piety and a desire to make his father acceptable to an antagonositic generation (and perhaps a lack of acquaintance with the actual man)[21] may account for

17 In al-Andalus and the Maghrib, a consultative body at the service of the judge and, in this period, often a preliminary position toward the judgeship.

18 ʿIyāḍ's tenure as judge was as follows: Ceuta (515/1121–531/1136), Granada (531/1136–532/1138), Ceuta (539/1144–542/1147), and possibly, whilst briefly exiled in Dāy (543/1148).

19 Maribel Fierro, "La Religión," 439.

20 Muḥammad also compiled the *Nawāzil* from which this case is taken.

21 Muḥammad b. ʿIyāḍ, *Madhāhib al-ḥukkām fī nawāzil al-aḥkām* (*La actuación de los jueces en los procesos judiciales*), 22.

Muḥammad's stock description of 'Iyāḍ as the ideal jurist: a man of pleasant appearance and smell, a smart dresser, an elegant rider, a tireless worker who was quick to chastise leaders when they departed from the truth, and a man of self-abnegating magnanimity (Muḥammad reports inheriting a debt of 500 dīnārs; money his father reportedly spent in the public interest out of his own pocket). This desire for acceptability may also account for Muḥammad's reticence about the events surrounding his father's rebellion, surrender, and subsequent exile to Marrakesh.[22]

The Almoravid government crumbled precipitously with the death of Tāshufīn b. 'Alī, the dynasty's last capable military leader. Marrakesh, the Almoravid capital, fell in Shawwāl 530/March 1147, and the dynasty's last amīr, Isḥāq b. 'Alī, was slain. By then most of the cities of the Maghrib had capitulated, including Tangier and Ceuta. But when the Almoravid governor of al-Andalus managed to retake Algeciras, an Almoravid leader on the African side of the strait, Yaḥyā b. Abī Bakr al-Ṣaḥrāwī, was stirred to launch his own, last ditch rebellion, starting from Ceuta and Tangier and eventually moving south until petering out in the deserts of Mauritania. In what had become a recurrent pattern in al-Andalus and the Far Maghrib in times of political turmoil, 'Iyāḍ, as judge of the city, assumed Ceuta's leadership, which now stood in open rebellion against the Almohads as a result of al-Ṣaḥrāwī's doomed revolt. The armies of 'Abd al-Mu'min were quick to surround the city and, defeat being imminent, 'Iyāḍ sued for peace. The Almohads then took the city without bloodshed and 'Iyāḍ was exiled to Marrakesh. Muḥammad b. 'Iyāḍ casts a positive light on these events, in which, according to his version, 'Iyāḍ submitted docilely to the Almohads and ingratiated himself with the Almohad leader when he arrived in Marrakesh. According to Muhammad's account, his father died, after falling ill, during a military campaign in which he was fighting *alongside* the Almohad amīr.

---

22 It may also be an issue of the parameters of the genre. On the construction of character in the biographical genre, see Fernando Rodriguez Mediano, "El Género Biográfico Árabe: Apuntes Teóricos;" Omayra Herrero, "Ṭariq b. Ziyād: las distintas visiones de un conquistador beréber según las fuentes medievales," in *Biografías Magrebíes. Identidades y Grupos Religioses, Sociales y Políticos en el Magreb Medieval*, ed. Mohamed Meouak, Estudios Onomástico-Biográficos de al-Andalus (Madrid: Consejo Superior de Investigaciones Científicas, 2012); C. de la Puente González, "La caracterización de Almanzor: Entre la epopeya y la historia," in *Biografías y género biográfico en el occidente islámico*, ed. María Luisa Ávila, and Manuela Marín, Estudios Onomástico-Biográficos de al-Andalus, VIII (Madrid: Consejo Superior de Investigaciones Científicas, 1997).

Other sources describe much different endings. Ibn Khaldūn (d. 808/1406) puts ʿIyāḍ at the time of his death in Dāy, a village north of Marrakesh, where he reportedly served as a rural judge in exile. Others describe ʿIyāḍ dying dejectedly, murdered by order of the Almohad amīr, either strangled (al-Bunnahī, d. after 793/1391) or poisoned by a Jew (Ibn Farḥūn, d. 799/1397).[23]

• • •

The case analyzed below comes from ʿIyāḍ's *nawāzil*, compiled and annotated by his son Muḥammad. These record the questions ʿIyāḍ directed to several muftīs concerning cases that came before his court, as well as opinions he produced as a muftī. The *Madhāhib al-ḥukkām fī nawāzil al-aḥkām* (The procedures of judges in judicial practices) provides important information on ʿIyāḍ's legal work and thought, as well as that of a few of his most distinguished contemporaries. It shows how ʿIyāḍ corresponded with jurists of al-Andalus, such as Ibn Rushd and Ibn Ḥamdīn, and acted as a link in the transmission of ideas into the Maghrib. Like Ibn Rushd's fatwās, the collection also presents a wealth of legal-historical and socio-historical information, including the practice and composition of Ceutan courts, the qualities of witnesses, the use of documents, the jurisdiction of judges, the nature of the cases tried, and the power of recourse to the law demonstrated by jurists and laymen. Several of these facets are featured below.

4 Islamic Water Law

The principles relevant to this case are those governing one of three types of water source recognized by Islamic water law (rivers and canals; wells; and springs). In principle, the water of a river is "the common property (*mubāḥ*) of all living things and cannot be owned or sold."[24] Regarding rivers there is the important qualification, however, that if the river is small enough that shortages can result from diversion, then water use is determined by taking into account the consequences of building diversions and canals. Islamic water doctrine distinguishes a further type of small river or water course that is dammed and its water allocated at fixed times in order to provide enough

23 As later legend has it, ʿIyāḍ died suddenly in the baths of Marrakesh from an overheard invocation to al-Ghazālī, or was strangled by the spiritual leader of the Almohads, the Mahdī b. Tūmart, for secretly practicing Judaism. Both accounts are chronologically unfeasible.

24 David S. Powers, *Law, Society, and Culture in the Maghrib, 1300–1500*, 104.

water for irrigation. Such a water course is generally regarded as the joint property of the cultivators who inhabit its banks. The share of water that may be taken by upstream users depends on circumstances such as season and crop.[25] The river or stream at the center of the dispute in the case below could be construed as either of these two kinds, diversions of its water causing major shortages to other users. Damming is at no point discussed in the case, from which I infer (as did the judge and muftīs) that the stream falls under the first category.[26]

In principle, the water of a stream such as the one in our case is ownerless; its use is established on a first-come, first-served basis. Since the water was insufficient to meet the needs of all of its users, usufructuary rights had to be established. These are generally granted according to specific criteria, of which priority of use and proximity to the source are two of the best recognized. On this basis, the judge and muftīs recognized and wished to preserve the rights of the users with established priority and proximity. They also took into account two further criteria of equal weight: first, that upstream water users may retain water to fulfill their needs, but must also allow the surplus to flow down to the next user. This principle of allowing surplus to flow to other users, or, put differently, of prohibiting one user from obtaining exclusive possession of the water rights, may be applied to both upstream users regarding downstream ones and vice versa. Furthermore, Islamic water doctrine distinguishes types of water users and water usage, assigning priority to some over others. Milling and other industrial use was defined as subordinate to irrigation. The precise articulation of this principle in the Far Maghrib can, to some extent, be attributed to Ibn Rushd, whose opinions concerning the case below are found in his *al-Bayān wa-l-Taḥṣīl*, as well as in later Maghribī cases.[27]

5 The First Ruling[28]

The biography of the presiding judge, al-Qāḍī ʿIyāḍ b. Mūsā, is of particular importance to the contextualization of the case within the history of this

25 David S. Powers, *Law, Society, and Culture in the Maghrib, 1300–1500*, 103–05.

26 This would not preclude the possibility of a future arrangement between the irrigators treating the stream as of the second kind.

27 Cited in a complicated water dispute between two mountain communities of the Middle Atlas mountains, adjudicated sporadically from the late thirteenth to fifteenth centuries and analyzed in David S. Powers, *Law, Society, and Culture in the Maghrib, 1300–1500*, 25–140. Especially 125 and 130.

28 Muḥammad b. ʿIyāḍ and ʿIyāḍ b. Mūsā, *Madhāhib al-ḥukkām*, 109–21. The case spans 41

institutional development. As discussed above, Qāḍī ʿIyāḍ was instrumental to the transmission of juridical knowledge from al-Andalus to the Far Maghrib and represents a key link between the regions. A native of Ceuta, educated partly in al-Andalus, posthumously venerated as a saint in Marrakesh, Qāḍī ʿIyāḍ was the most significant jurist of his generation in the Far Maghrib, where he is enshrined as a founding figure. Through his work as a jurist and in his writings on fiqh and biography, ʿIyāḍ set significant legal precedents, articulated a justification for the school's hegemony, and defined the network and genealogy of Mālikism both within the region and without. Qāḍī ʿIyāḍ was a particularly important figure as a bridge between the great Andalusī jurists of his time and those of the Far Maghrib. This is well attested in the text analyzed here, as three of the four identified muftīs were Andalusī. It is no coincidence, moreover, that the dominant muftī of the case was Ibn Rushd al-Jadd, whose highly developed responses to ʿIyāḍ's questions gained added influence through the prominence achieved by ʿIyāḍ, his best known student in the Far Maghrib. The consultation analyzed below thus illustrates the process of institutional development in which Cordoban judicial theory and practice – under the aegis of the Almoravid State – were brought to bear on the countryside of the Far Maghrib, where it was adapted to local practice and eventually transmitted into the countryside of southern Morocco by later generations of Mālikī judges.

The dilemma this case presented for ʿIyāḍ lay in the conflict he perceived between: 1.) the deference due to the standing ruling or decision (*ḥukm*) of his predecessor, and 2.) the necessity of averting harm, whether to an individual or the community, embodied here by a number of fruit-bearing trees that were endangered by a lack of water. To avert this harm, a legal deficiency was to be sought as the basis for overturning the standing decision. When this was not found, another principle was applied, which prioritizes agricultural production over industrial. In the ensuing water dispute, the principle of equitable distribution of riparian rights, irrespective of a user's location on the stream or history of use, was also invoked. Both principles were applied in contravention of the existing decision.

---

years and contains eleven sets of questions (thus possibly eleven letters sent by ʿIyāḍ) with at least one and most often two answers to each set. The case describes two judicial decisions (*ḥukm*), the first of which appears in a summarized version of the court record left by ʿIyāḍ's predecessor, and which he used to introduce the first set of questions.

The case thus began as an appeal[29] for the review of a ruling made by a Mālikī judge in the interest of saving a number of fruit-bearing trees.[30] It then turned into a process of mediation and redistribution of irrigation rights between the beneficiaries of a stream. During this second phase, one of the parties (the defendant) raised a series of demands in an effort to preserve the status quo. The most significant of these demands involved the demonstration of ownership rights and benefits (*manāfiʿ*) through proven use and documents of purchase. Finding himself in the position of mediator, Qāḍī ʿIyāḍ consulted with the muftīs of al-Andalus on procedural matters. These consultations concerned the treatment of the object in dispute, the effect of an owner's ignorance of previous litigation involving his/her property on his/her rights to that property, and the strategies and time frames allowed the disputants to come to a resolution. The muftīs remained in disagreement throughout the case.

The case, then, proceeds as follows: Within the first three years of the fall of Ceuta to the Almoravids, a *muḥtasib*[31] presented a complaint to the city's new judge, ʿAbbūd b. Saʿīd al-Tanūkhī[32] on behalf of the neighbors of a relative of the former ruling dynasty (of the Barghawāṭīs), a certain ʿAbd al-Salām. These neighbors of ʿAbd al-Salām, who lived in the village of Balyūnsh, testified to the *muḥtasib* that ʿAbd al-Salām had unlawfully diverted water from a stream

29 Not in the sense of appealing to a higher court to overturn the decision of a lower court, but rather, in the form of an appeal to a judge to overturn the decision of a predecessor, a legal practice D. Powers terms *Islamic successor review*. As described by Ibn Qudama, a successor judge has the discretionary right to investigate his predecessor's rulings "either in response to a request by a defeated litigant or on his own initiative." David S. Powers, *Law, Society, and Culture in the Maghrib, 1300–1500*, 323.

30 It is likely, although by no means certain, that many of these were olive trees.

31 A municipal inspector with enforcement powers. On the office of the *ḥisba* in al-Andalus, see Pedro Chalmeta Gendrón, *El "señor del zoco" en España: edades media y moderna: contribución al estudio de la historia del mercado* (Madrid: Instituto Hispano-Arabe de Cultura, 1973).

32 Bencherifa identifies him as "the judge ʿAbbūd b. Saʿīd al-Tanūkhī, known as Ibn al-ʿAṭṭār al-Sabtī, whom Yūsuf b. Tāshufīn appointed. He gained predominance in the judgeship. He ascended through righteousness and was not diffident with princes. He stayed in the judgeship until his death in 480/1086–1087." ʿIyāḍ b. Mūsā, *Tartīb al-madārik wa-taqrīb al-masālik li-maʿrifat aʿlām madhhab Mālik*, 8:197–198. His son Abū ʿAbd Allāh Muḥammad b. ʿAbbūd was also judge of Ceuta, see ʿIyāḍ b. Mūsā, *Tartīb al-madārik wa-taqrīb al-masālik li-maʿrifat aʿlām madhhab Mālik*, 8: 203.

known as al-Sayyāj[33] across a path (*maḥajja*)[34] in order to irrigate his own gardens. ʿAbd al-Salām's action, the witnesses said, digging across the path and diverting water across it, had made the path impassable, to the detriment of those who used it. Furthermore, they testified that ʿAbd al-Salām had no established rights to this water. They expressed this in an ambiguous way, however, at least as it was preserved in Judge ʿAbbūd's court record: The stream of al-Sayyāj, they said, does not pass through the gardens of Ibn Hudhayl, nor does it flow through the road that goes to the mill.[35]

Presented with the evidence furnished by the *muḥtasib* and unintimidated by ʿAbd al-Salām's connections, Judge ʿAbbūd took immediate action – perhaps precisely because he was the representative of the new government and saw himself as a righter of wrongs. Satisfied with the probity of the *muḥtasib*'s witnesses, he summoned ʿAbd al-Salām, informed him of the claim and set a deadline for ʿAbd al-Salām to counter the claim with credible evidence. ʿAbd al-Salām's first response to the accusation was to admit that he had diverted the water but that he had done so with the sanction of a local authority (*bi-ḥukm ḥākim*),[36] and that he had possessed the right and use of this water for a

33 Bencherifa writes that al-Sayyāj is mentioned in the "*Ikhtiṣār al-akhbār* in the context of a list of irrigation ditches (*ḥafāʾir*, s. *ḥafīr*): *ʿal-ḥafīr al-hāʾil al-maʿrūf bi-l-sayyāj*ʾ, according to al-Bakrī, which separated the outskirts from the town, and there were two bridges crossing it: the bridge of the gate of al-Mashāṭīn and the gate of al-Faraj. The word appears as al-Sayyāḥ, and in the *Ikhtiṣār* as al-Sahāj. Al-Sayyāj seems to be the most correct." Muḥammad b. ʿIyāḍ and ʿIyāḍ b. Mūsā, *Madhāhib al-ḥukkām*, 109.

34 *Maḥajja* means road or way. It is important to note, however, that this landscape was one of intensely irrigated gardens, with irrigation ditches, the shapes and courses of which where liable to change. A ditch could double as a path, and a path may simply be conceived of, as the Arabic word used suggests, as a place passed through or to. Therefore the "path" originally may have been quite rudimentary.

35 Muḥammad b. ʿIyāḍ and ʿIyāḍ b. Mūsā, *Madhāhib al-ḥukkām*, 109. This ambiguity would prove problematic when the record was consulted forty years later, since the boundaries of the gardens of Ibn Hudhayl had been left undefined. This particular mill, as well, would never be mentioned again. Presumably, the gardens of Ibn Hudhayl were somewhere in between ʿAbd al-Salām's orchard and the path (or they may have been one and the same). Being a man of wealth and power (Judge ʿAbbūd stated that no action had been brought against ʿAbd al-Salām out of fear of his links to the ruling family), the mill may well have been his as well. Thus when the record was consulted after so many years, and probably due to political change within Ceuta as a result of the Almoravid conquest, ʿAbd al-Salām's gardens had passed to multiple, unrelated owners, and no one knew precisely what "the orchards of Ibn Hudhayl" meant.

36 The nature of this authority, *ḥākim*, is uncertain. The first authority in irrigation matters tended not to be the municipal qāḍī, but another local authority.

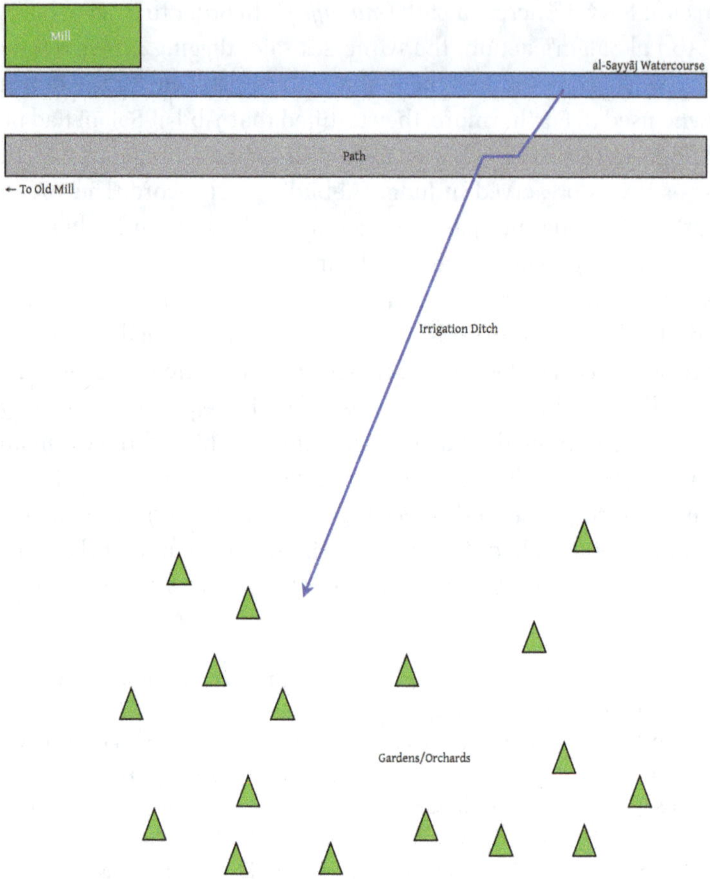

FIGURE 1 *Schematic map of Gardeners vs. Miller*

long time: twenty years. In all these twenty years, ʿAbd al-Salām claimed, the witnesses adduced by the *muḥtasib* had not raised any sort of claim against him. He said the witnesses were now testifying tendentiously, in order to secure the water for their own use.

ʿAbd al-Salām then produced his own document in which witnesses testifed to the water's flow through the path and into his gardens. Judge ʿAbbūd did not accept the document as valid evidence, because, in his opinion the witnesses were ignorant of the circumstances of the lands and water in question. Drawing on his own knowledge of the community of Balyūnsh, Judge ʿAbbūd determined that only because of ʿAbd al-Salām's relationship to the former regime had he not been challenged for unlawfully diverting the water. ʿAbbūd deferred the deadline for ʿAbd al-Salām more than once before he ruled against ʿAbd al-Salām and ordered that he immediately interrupt the flow of water across the path to his gardens. As a final plea, ʿAbd al-Salām proposed burying the water under the path, building a tunnel to channel it to his gardens. ʿAbbūd summoned locals who were knowledgeable of the conditions on the ground, and, based on their testimony, ruled that such a canal was liable to break and cause damage, possibly leading to the collapse of the walls of the neighboring gardens.[37]

ʿAbbūd thus set the stage for the case that ʿIyāḍ would try. He had ruled decisively in favor of the plaintiff (here the *muḥtasib*), based most apparently on the principle of preventing damage to the public interest, here represented by the *maḥajjat al-muslimīn* or path of the Muslims. The determination of ʿAbd al-Salām's historic water rights also played a role in the decision. The relative importance of each of these rights, as well as the validity of a new set of claims questioning the integrity of the original processes, was left for ʿIyāḍ to determine.

6 The Case Re-opened: Judicial Review and Avoiding Harm

Sometime between 517/1123 and 520/1126, during his first five years as the judge of Ceuta, Qāḍī ʿIyāḍ was approached by a group of farmers with an urgent plea. It was watering season, and the water sources used by these farmers in the past to irrigate their gardens had run dry. Their trees were in danger of dying unless another source could be tapped. Such a source did exist: the stream known as al-Sayyāj. But they could draw from it only by diverting its water across a country road, in the direction of their gardens. In fact, in recent years, they had occasionally resorted to this method to alleviate water shortages (perhaps made more acute by an increase in population and food production). This year drought had exacerbated the situation.

The garden owners of Balyūnsh asked for the revision of a forty-year-old judicial order by ʿIyāḍ's predecessor (Judge ʿAbbūd). This decision or *ḥukm* had effectively barred the diversion of water from al-Sayyāj to their gardens because of the damage it was liable to inflict on the country road and because of the resulting inconvenience for those who used the road. The garden owners now wanted legitimate and habitual use of water from al-Sayyāj to irrigate their gardens.[38]

37 Muḥammad b. ʿIyāḍ and ʿIyāḍ b. Mūsā, *Madhāhib al-ḥukkām*, 110.

38 Muḥammad b. ʿIyāḍ and ʿIyāḍ b. Mūsā, *Madhāhib al-ḥukkām*, 110.

Their strategy to convince the judge that review was appropriate rested on producing testimony demonstrating that they had long-standing and uninterrupted use of water from al-Sayyāj, dating to a time before the decision against diversion. They questioned the validity of the testimony upon which 'Iyāḍ's predecessor had based his ruling. They hoped to strengthen this argument by pointing out that they had continued using water from al-Sayyāj *after* the ruling, thereby establishing continuous possession or productive use (*ḥiyāza*).[39] They argued that they were in dire need of this water and that there was only one path of access to their gardens (i.e., the road). Finally, they argued that the physical conditions of the road itself had changed in the forty years since the decision, lessening the possibility of damage, and therefore invalidating the original grounds for prohibition. The road had been paved with stone, they said. Diverting water over it would mean that passersby would get their shoes wet, while their trees would survive. The garden owners asked for judicial review, or the overturning of the previous judge's ruling, based on the faulty evidence on which the ruling had been based (new witnesses disproved old ones) and on a change of the physical circumstances governing the premises of the original case.

'Iyāḍ heard them out and considered their evidence and arguments. He may have had cursory knowledge of this area of Balyūnsh and its community, but later developments show that such knowledge was indeed limited. From the beginning, it seems clear that 'Iyāḍ was favorably disposed toward the plight of the garden owners and sought the means to grant them access to the water of al-Sayyāj. This is especially clear from the questions he posed after his first deliberations. After studying the court record closely and formulating what he believed were the key questions, 'Iyād wrote a concise summary of the record followed by a series of questions. He sent this to the muftīs Ibn Rushd al-Jadd, Muḥammad b. Aḥmad b. al-Ḥājj, Muḥamad b. Ismā'īl, as well as to Mūsā b. Ḥammād. The first three occupied prominent judgeships in Seville and Cordoba. The last was the chief judge of Marrakesh.[40]

It is likely that before sending the formal consultation, 'Iyāḍ deliberated with local jurisconsults, two of whom would have been employed in the office of the chief judge of a city of the size of Ceuta. However, such routine consultations – unfortunately for the historian – would not have been recorded in writing. What has been preserved is 'Iyāḍ's correspondence with the jurisconsults

---

39 *Ḥiyāza:* usucaption, or possession by long use or occupation.

40 See the Introduction and Chapter One. There is an anonymous answer in this case as well. Presumably the name of the jurist was lost, dropped from the letter or in the process of compilation or transcription.

further afield. These succinctly describe the case and pose a set of questions, a process which, due to the ongoing nature of the case, would be repeated eleven times.

The group of gardeners who lived on what had been ʿAbd al-Salām's property (across the path from the stream of al-Sayyāj), pressed by their need for water, considered the course taken previously by ʿAbd al-Salām to be the best solution to their problem: channeling the water from al-Sayyāj over the path to their gardens. Judge ʿAbbūd's decision barred them from doing so. Acting collectively, they formulated a strategy to procure this water for their gardens, the record of which we have in the *nāzila*.

Later developments in the case point to another possible, unspoken calculation on the part of the garden owners. (This calculation would prove to be powerful, in spite of its formal weakness). The garden keepers had one principal riparian competitor who they failed to mention in their complaint: a miller who had established himself on al-Sayyāj, downstream of the gardeners, some two years prior to presenting the claim to ʿIyāḍ. Although this information is omitted from the first stage of the case, it is relevant because it played an important role on two levels. Firstly, the miller's increased water use may have exacerbated the water shortage and the pressure on the available water resources in the area. Secondly, the garden owners may have considered themselves to be more entitled to the water than the miller on the basis of their activity and social function. Even though the garden owners were trying to gain access to al-Sayyāj against an existing legal decision, it is likely they believed they could elicit sympathy as irrigators, more entitled than a miller, whose use of water (as a manufacturer) was traditionally given a position secondary to irrigation.[41] The existence of such sympathy is impossible for us to determine, but is good to keep in mind.

The case can be divided into three clear stages, dealing principally with the following legal problems: 1.) the conditions for judicial review, 2.) the obligation to avoid harm (*nafy al-ḍarar*), and 3.) the adjudication of water rights in the light of a former judgment, the different functions of riparian users, and the possible injury resulting from this distribution. As can be seen in the qualification of this last problem, the key difficulty facing ʿIyāḍ and his muftīs (hence the need to write many sets of questions) is how these three concerns overlapped. The later stages of the case, dealing with the formal problems of distributing the water rights and setting the limits to legal recourse available to the different parties, point to a second possible reason for the case's length: The judge's reticence to pronounce a final judgment in the face of a riparian

41 David S. Powers, *Law, Society, and Culture in the Maghrib, 1300–1500*, 119.

dispute (a sensitive issue) meant he preferred for the parties to reach a settlement (*ṣulḥ*) while limiting himself to procuring authoritative consultations from highly regarded muftīs.[42]

ʿIyāḍ's First Set of Questions: Judicial Review and Avoiding Harm[43]

ʿIyāḍ's first set of questions illustrate how he understood the case, and what options were available to the gardeners, whose situation he regarded as a kind of harm to be avoided. ʿIyāḍ first conceived of the case as one in which this harm to the public interest should be avoided, although this would mean overturning a decision made by his predecessor, grounds for which were generally limited. His first concern was the problem presented by contradictory evidence. Addressing Ibn Rushd, Muḥammad b. Ismāʿīl, and Muḥammad b. Aḥmad b. al-Ḥājj, ʿIyāḍ asked what should be done with the gardeners' claim that the decision's application was limited to the individual named in the document (ʿAbd al-Salām) when the record also clearly stated that ʿAbd al-Salām diverted the water across the path over which "it had never flowed." This statement contradicted the gardeners' assertion of long-standing use before the judgment. ʿIyāḍ asked which evidence was valid and how it would effect the status of ʿAbbūd's judgement.

In a series of associated questions, ʿIyāḍ inquired into the points on which the decision could be overturned. Does the decision, which singled out ʿAbd al-Salām, apply to the entire area of the gardens of Ibn Hudhayl, the precise boundaries of which were uncertain in ʿIyāḍ's time? What was the effect of this uncertainty on the decision? Did the ambiguity concerning the location affect the implementation of the decision today?

ʿIyāḍ then raised a more serious suspicion. Judge ʿAbbūd, it seems, had owned property in the area. A wall of his appears to have been directly affected by ʿAbd al-Salām's proposal to bury the water, and, although he did not elaborate on this, ʿIyāḍ asked whether this fact could invalidate the judge's decision. ʿIyāḍ also asked whether new evidence, relating to the state of the road and the quality of the walls (unlikely to collapse), should be considered. He asked how other changes in physical conditions affected and were affected by the decision. What was to be done with the appearance of a new water source that may also potentially cross the path. What if another canal was proposed when the judge only prohibited ʿAbd al-Salām from such an endeavor. Lastly, how did the garden owners' knowledge (or lack thereof) of the forty-year-old decision affect their rights to the water, especially when they had not been given the

42 David S. Powers, *Law, Society, and Culture in the Maghrib, 1300–1500*, 137.

43 Muḥammad b. ʿIyāḍ and ʿIyāḍ b. Mūsā, *Madhāhib al-ḥukkām*, 110–11.

chance to defend their water rights? They were thus affected by a decision without having had the right to state their own claim. Did they buy the land with its rights and benefits (*bi-ḥuqūqihā wa-manāfiʿihā*)? Perhaps most importantly, did their need for irrigation give them legitimate claim to the water, regardless of the previous decision?[44]

The muftīs consulted by ʿIyāḍ disagreed over how to approach the case. For some, the case presented no grounds for revision of the standing decision, while, for the key muftī (Ibn Rushd), the necessity of providing water for irrigation overrode other considerations. His opinion proved the most influential, as we shall see, but remained controversial.

On Judicial Review and Contradictory Evidence

A tradition of judicial review has existed in Islamic law from its earliest stages of development, in a shape different from the processes of appeal in Western legal systems. This difference may account for its having been largely unknown to Western scholarship (for a half century),[45] as well as for the difficulty of mapping its structure and development. Islamic judicial review is not based on a hierarchical structure, in which appeals progress from lower to higher courts, but rather, through a more informal process.

By the sixteenth century, the process of review in Andalusī and Maghribī judicial practice had assumed a few clearly defined forms. A judgment could be reversed by the issuing judge or by a contemporary "under limited and precisely defined circumstances,"[46] namely, that the issuing judge had lacked "jurisdictional authority" (viz. he was "unjust") or had engaged "in the improper use of independent reasoning by issuing a judgment that is in conflict with the Quran, Sunna, or consensus."[47] Then there is *successor review*, which occurs when a judge reverses the decision of a predecessor. To do this he must have been acting within his jurisdiction, and be of equal or higher rank than his predecessor. As in the first type, successor review proceeds on grounds of law, not of fact. A rudimentary hierarchical structure of appeal also seems to have existed, in which provincial judges were subordinated to chief judges of capital cities, whose decisions, in turn, were reversible by *maẓālim* courts. The structure and process, as stated above, were marked by relative informality.[48]

---

44 Muḥammad b. ʿIyāḍ and ʿIyāḍ b. Mūsā, *Madhāhib al-ḥukkām*, 111.

45 David S. Powers, "On Judicial Review in Islamic Law," *Law and Society Review* 26:2 (1992), 316–17.

46 David S. Powers, "On Judicial Review in Islamic Law," 324.

47 David S. Powers, "On Judicial Review in Islamic Law," 324.

48 David S. Powers, "On Judicial Review in Islamic Law," 324.

ʿIyāḍ complicates our understanding of the practice of judicial review in the Far Maghrib, since a number of his documented cases admit considerations of fact, not only law (or technical procedure) as grounds for review.[49] ʿIyāḍ's *nawāzil* contain several examples of judicial review which admit factual and evidentiary errors. Our case is one such example. Judge ʿAbbūd did not commit, nor was he accused of, committing a formal error in delivering his judgment. Rather, the gardeners based their appeal on the introduction of new evidence that contradicted that upon which ʿAbbūd made his judgment. Ibn Rushd, who provided the "winning" opinion in the case, from the outset stated that contradictory evidence provides legitimate grounds for appeal. He wrote that the gardeners had irrigation even if their testimony over possibility of damage was found inadmissible. The other muftīs were very hesitant in the matter of reviewing, changing, or modifying ʿAbbūd's judgment. Ibn al-Ḥājj and Muḥammad b. Ismāʿīl, held steadfast to their opinions against review and, to some extent, were proven correct (formally), when the garden owners' evidence was later almost entirely disqualified. "If the matter is as you have described it, the judge's decision remains effective and nothing else is to be considered. In God is success. Said Muḥammad b. Aḥmad b. al-Ḥājj."[50]

Ibn Rushd and ʿIyāḍ considered revision to be legitimate. The reasons for accepting the appeal appear to have been multiple, with one key consideration: Drought presents special dispensation for riparian users, especially when these are irrigators. Ibn Rushd would need to write more than one opinion to untangle the different factors of the case, but from the beginning, the irrigators' special entitlement is prominent in his deliberations, as is clear when he states that if testimony of the first judgment can be recused then "the garden owners are the party that is more entitled to the water to irrigate their gardens in times of need."[51]

The centrality of the shortage of water notwithstanding, other grounds for appeal were presented and discussed. The ones ʿIyāḍ considered important were the following: 1.) New evidence disproved the evidence upon which the first judgment was based; 2.) There was a need to prevent harm greater than

49 On this point, as illustrated by ʿIyāḍ's *Nawāzil*, see Delfina Serrano, "Legal Practice in an Andalusī-Maghribī Source from the Twelfth Century CE: The Madhāhib al-ḥukkām fī nawāzil al-aḥkām," 214–20. While, in general principle, decisions may be reversed only on grounds of an error of procedure or law, in certain cases, fact may be admitted. Drought, specifically, "may also force the modification of an agreement reached by judicial order, by virtue of necessity (*ḍarūra*)." Delfina Serrano, "Legal Practice in an Andalusī-Maghribī Source from the Twelfth Century CE: The Madhāhib al-ḥukkām fī nawāzil al-aḥkām," 218.

50 Muḥammad b. ʿIyāḍ and ʿIyāḍ b. Mūsā, *Madhāhib al-ḥukkām*, 112.

51 Muḥammad b. ʿIyāḍ and ʿIyāḍ b. Mūsā, *Madhāhib al-ḥukkām*, 112.

that averted by the first judgment; 3.) Changing physical conditions and the passage of time made the previous judgment impractical; and 4.) The self-interest of the judge may have impaired his opinion regarding a part of the judgment. Ibn Rushd limited the grounds for appeal to one of two possibilities: 1.) The new evidence displaces the old (especially given that the irrigators are prioritized over other users); and 2.) If evidence can be provided that the harm prevented by the first judgment no longer exists, then, the gardeners are entitled to the water (i.e., a change of physical conditions allows for review). This last opinion, however, was not formulated until later in the case. ʿIyāḍ moved to modify his predecessor's judgment based on Ibn Rushd's opinion, which allowed for new evidence to supersede the evidence that informed ʿAbbūd's judgment: a clear case of judicial review based on an error of fact (an exception to a general rule, in which water scarcity, most probably, played the determining factor.)

On Nafy al-Ḍarar

Iyāḍ's preoccupation with *nafy al-ḍarar*, or the avoidance of harm, reflects the growing prominence of the judge's function as the protector of private property. Developing this function involved a more elaborate understanding of the harm individuals cause to the public interest and to each other.[52] Originating from ḥadīth and opinions scattered across different chapters in early works, the concept of *nafy al-ḍarar* was gradually separated and discussed independently.[53] The late fifth/eleventh century jurist al-Bājī wrote a treatise on the damage neighbors caused to each other. And an early fifth/eleventh century *nawāzil* collection is the first to group together cases dealing with damage to buildings and watercourses.[54] This new grouping facilitated reference to a concept gaining legal-conceptual foothold in the Almoravid period.[55] ʿIyāḍ's

52 Delfina Serrano, "Las demandas particulares como limitación de las construcciones privadas en el Occidente islámico medieval," in *L'Urbanisme dans l'Occident musulman au Moyen Âge: Aspects juridiques*, ed. P. Cressier, et al. (Madrid: Casa Velázquez-CSIC, 2000), 24. On the development of the concept of avoiding damage, urban environments, and jurisconsultative texts in al-Andalus and the Maghrib, see A. I. Kahera, and O. Benmira, "Damages in Islamic Law: Maghribī Muftīs and the Built Environment (9th-15th Centuries CE)," *Islamic Law and Society* 5, no. 2 (1998): 131–64. Also R. Brunschvig, "Urbanisme medieval et droit musulman," *Études d'Islamologie* 2 (1976): 7–35.

53 Delfina Serrano, "Las demandas particulares como limitación de las construcciones privadas en el Occidente islámico medieval," 18.

54 *Nawāzil* al-Shaʿbānī. Delfina Serrano, "Las demandas particulares como limitación de las construcciones privadas en el Occidente islámico medieval," 20.

55 Delfina Serrano, "Las demandas particulares como limitación de las construcciones privadas en el Occidente islámico medieval," 20.

concern with *nafy al-ḍarar* in this case reflects his interpretation of his predecessor's judgment, which ʿIyāḍ understood to be aimed precisely at avoiding harm inflicted by one individual on the public interest (the public path). ʿIyāḍ wondered whether the case before him presented a situation in which a harm greater than that avoided by ʿAbbūd's judgment had appeared, and thus required (as well as permitted) the reversal of the original judgment, in order to avoid the greater of the two harms.[56]

The Muftīs' Responses[57]

Ibn Rushd, on the other hand, did not conceive of this case as one involving two harms, but rather, as two separate cases, or legal situations: one involving riparian users where one user was more entitled than the other, and a second involving the possibility of harm, which could be prevented in more ways than one. The muftīs' answers to Iyāḍ's first set of question were in disagreement. Ibn Rushd's opinion would sway ʿIyāḍ and dominate the remainder of the case. By convincing ʿIyāḍ, Ibn Rushd also influenced Maghribī judicial practice in later centuries, as evinced by the presence of this case in the reference literature and its citation, in another case 300 years later.[58] Later influence notwithstanding, Ibn Rushd was here in the minority.

Ibn Ismāʾīl and Ibn al-Ḥājj were united in their oppposition to revision. "The judge's (*al-ḥākim*) decision," Ibn Ismāʿīl wrote, "in this matter remains effective and is to be caried out to completion" (*maḥmūl ʿalā al-kamāl*). Ibn al-Ḥājj, after cordially greeting ʿIyāḍ, stated that what the qāḍī ʿAbbūd b. Saʿīd – God have mercy on him – recorded [in the court register] is efffective, in force, and contains nothing objectionable."[59] They would (with one possible exception) stick to their positions.

Ibn Rushd al-Jadd conceded that the irrigation rights of the garden owners would be invalidated were it to be established that judge ʿAbbūd, supported by unimpeachable evidence, had ordered the cessation of the water's flow across the path, and that there was no testimony in support of the garden owners and no other road through which people may pass. But this formulation opened possibilites for the garden owners to make their case: They can disqualify the evidenced used by ʿAbbūd, present counter-evidence, or provide an alternate route for people to walk on. Ibn Rushd then stated explicitly: "If the document's witnesses [provided by the *muḥtasib* to ʿAbbūd], who established the

56 Muḥammad b. ʿIyāḍ and ʿIyāḍ b. Mūsā, *Madhāhib al-ḥukkām*, 112.

57 Muḥammad b. ʿIyāḍ and ʿIyāḍ b. Mūsā, *Madhāhib al-ḥukkām*, 112.

58 David S. Powers, *Law, Society, and Culture in the Maghrib, 1300–1500*, 130.

59 Muḥammad b. ʿIyāḍ and ʿIyāḍ b. Mūsā, *Madhāhib al-ḥukkām*, 112.

possibility of damage before the judge (*al-ḥākim*), were recusable... [then] the garden owners are the party more entitled to the water to irrigate their gardens in times of need." Ibn Rushd added that the record's effectiveness was uncertain, there being such ambiguity regarding the precise definition of the area in question, and he urged ʿIyāḍ to drop the record from his consideration. "The case (*al-amr*)," he wrote, "is to be reopened, and the garden owners are not to be prevented from chanelling water through the road to irrigate their gardens, upon which they are dependent for farming."[60] He added, somewhat confusingly, "This is unless the damage to passersby is [too] great." Lastly, addressing the question of burying the canal, he argued that "it is impossible to bury the water or reinforce its course, because, as you mentioned, the path has been paved in stone. In God is success." Ibn Rushd's opinion opened up for ʿIyāḍ the possibility of review, with a concession to ʿAbbūd's intention of keeping the path passable. The harm must not be great. But the gardeners are entitled to the water.[61]

60 Muḥammad b. ʿIyāḍ and ʿIyāḍ b. Mūsā, *Madhāhib al-ḥukkām*, 112.

61 There is a fourth, anonymous, response to ʿIyāḍ's first set of questions. The name of the muftī must have been dropped at some point. The answer appears anonymously in al-Wansharīsī's collection as well. This anonymous opinion is followed by a curious note by the work's first editor, ʿIyāḍ's son Muḥammad, stating that this respondent was the only one who had addressed the judge's interest in the case, by owning property on the path in question, because the respondent had not received the remainder of ʿIyāḍ's question. "This answer," he wrote, "was the only one to comment on the suspicion cast upon the judge, because the section asking him what would happen were the testimony to the deep foundation of the wall so that in the most part it would be unharmed, was dropped from the copy of the question." It is difficult to know what Muḥammad meant by this terse note. Was a page dropped? Had a copyist (perhaps ʿIyāḍ sent out more than one copy of his questions) suppressed the rest of the question from one copy? Or did the accusation, without the shift of focus away from ʿAbbūd's possible corruption to the physical characteristics of the wall, prompt Muḥammad to explain away the comment? There are two more anonymous opinions in the case, and there is no reason to believe they have the same author, other than a certain similarity in content and style; these are the least careful opinions in the case. They agree with Ibn Rushd regarding the general direction ʿIyāḍ should take, but along different, more rushed lines of reasoning. To ʿIyāḍ's first question, the anonymous muftī said he found the testimony contradictory and containing elements added to the original, facts which, taken together, justify reopening and independently rethinking (*iʿmāl al-ijtihād*) the case. "And with what you said regarding the suspicion cast on the judge because one of the walls of his orchard [was involved], the slightest suspicion involving the witnesses invalidates both testimony and decision." The anonymous muftī provided two legal principles to justify review. The first was the principle that a decision affecting one individual should not be transmitted to others, and the second was the principle that if two injuries should occur, neither having the prerogative

7 ʿIyāḍ's Case Part II: Riparian Dispute, Avoiding Harm, and Water Rights Adjudication

After hearing the garden owners' evidence and arguments and weighing the opinions of the (mostly) Andalusī muftīs, ʿIyāḍ proceeded to grant irrigation rights to the garden owners.[62] The arrangement resulting from ʿIyāḍ's reversal was put immediately into question, however, when the opposing party, so conspicuously absent from the first deliberations, stepped forward and vigorously demanded the preservation of the status quo ante.[63] This party's efforts to prevent the reversal of ʿAbbūd's judgement and against ʿIyāḍ's decision to aid the gardeners propelled the remainder of the case. The ensuing litigation can be characterized as an effort to define the rights of both parties, based on their function, water usage history, and the existence of a judgment that had precluded water use by one side for forty years. Considerations were further complicated by the fact that the judgment had prevented harm to the public interest, protection ʿIyāḍ wished to maintain. The ensuing sets of questions and answers unfolded in two stages: 1.) questions produced by the appearance of a second party required a redefinition of the terms of the case (Ibn Rushd, in his role as muftī, was moved to redefine his opinion); 2.) questions concerning the procedure ʿIyāḍ should follow in his role as water rights adjudicator and the extent of the limitations that may be set on the second party's vigorous and resourceful use of the law against his riparian contenders.

The final three responses, especially those given to questions six and eight, written by Ibn Rushd, put the case to rest by articulating the principle upon which the irrigators' right was based, and then, by restating how meeting their needs along with avoiding the harm to the path could be dealt with as separate issues with separate solutions. The case thus moved away from the revision of an existing judgment to the mediation of water rights, to which end the judge took decisive action and set a series of deadlines to be met by the litigating parties. While Ibn Rushd's opinions untangled the separate legal issues (the *ʿilal*) behind each judgment (ʿAbbūd's and ʿIyāḍ's), ʿIyāḍ asked how exactly he

---

(*al-maziya*), "the lighter of the two prevails." It is difficult to know what effect this anonymous opinion had on ʿIyād, besides the fact that he provided only two or three opinions, whereas Ibn Rushd, whose opinions I believe steered the course of the case, provided ten. Muḥammad b. ʿIyāḍ and ʿIyāḍ b. Mūsā, *Madhāhib al-ḥukkām*, 109–21.

62 The case thus offers a clear example (and conclusive evidence) of judicial review based on the availability of new evidence and changed physical conditions, where the operative factor behind this exceptional kind of successor review was the exacerbation presented by drought and the entitlement of irrigators in such conditions.

63 Muḥammad b. ʿIyāḍ and ʿIyāḍ b. Mūsā, *Madhāhib al-ḥukkām*, 113.

was to implement this mediation procedure, especially in response to the miller's attempt to defend the status quo ante (questions six through eleven).

ʿIyāḍ's Second Set of Questions[64]

After ʿIyāḍ heard and moved to concede water use of al-Sayyāj to the garden owners, an unnamed man who had built a mill on the water course downstream from the gardeners stepped forward and challenged the gardeners' rights to irrigation, stating that he had gained legitimate possession (*ḥuztu*) of the water in question, especially the water resulting from ʿAbbūd's decision. This miller said he had built his mill and incurred expenses, counting on this water, the use of which had been explicitly denied to the garden owners. As ʿIyāḍ understood the situation, the water channeled away from the road fed the mill during the "days of winter," but in those of summer, the garden owners had decided to challenge his use of it, as described above. The development prompted ʿIyāḍ to ask the muftīs what was to be done with the miller's evidence, testimony gathered from witnesses who had likely lived and worked on the river for a long time. He asked what to do if the miller's evidence proved stronger than that presented by the garden owners, who, it now appeared, may have testified in self-interest, urged by the immediate necessity of procuring water. ʿIyāḍ then asked explicitly what had more weight in this situation, the irrigator's need or the miller's use (*manfaʿa*). He also wanted to know what was the exact effect of ʿAbbūd's judgment on the miller's claim (i.e., should he be able to claim more than he would have without it?).

Muftīs' Answer

All three named muftīs reiterated their positions: Ibn Ismāʿīl[65] and Ibn al-Ḥājj maintained that the record prevented the gardeners from using the water, while Ibn Rushd simply stated that the garden owners were more entitled, because of their need to irrigate.[66]

64 Muḥammad b. ʿIyāḍ and ʿIyāḍ b. Mūsā, *Madhāhib al-ḥukkām*, 113.

65 This is Ibn Ismāʿīl's last response in the case.

66 The second anonymous answer is given to this question. The anonymous muftī had a position similar to Ibn Rushd's, if a bit more facile. His emphasis on time lapse as a determinant for establishing rights is interesting, however. These rights, he wrote, should be given to the garden owners if the evidence were established to be in their favor, for "they are the party more entitled," as long as the miller was not in possession of the water for a "long-enough period of time, during which he would have been able to deny [the garden owners] use and they had kept silent." They could not justify this silence with the passing of any judgments if the time lapse was long enough. If this was the case, the anonymous

ʿIyāḍ's Third Question[67]

Having conceded something to the gardeners, and facing the miller's defense, ʿIyāḍ chose to act cautiously, suspending the case while he studied the facts and set deadlines for all parties to present further arguments and evidence. Approaching the case as a dispute over an object, ʿIyāḍ was faced with the obligation of confiscating the disputed object, which, not surprisingly, made him uncertain of the procedure to follow. ʿIyāḍ asked whether and how to confiscate the object in question, "since the purpose of confiscation is having the challenger withdraw the disputed object from the defendant (*min yad maṭlūbihi*) while the latter's right to the object is at issue (*tawajjaha ḥaqq al-maṭlūb ʿalā al-ikhtilāf*)." This question has only one anonymous answer (the third of its kind) recorded. The anonymous muftī held that the testimony presented in the case thus far required the wholesale confiscation of the water, meaning its diversion away from both the gardeners and the miller. This could be done physically or financially, by charging the party most likely to win its use (which can be seen again, as a concession to the gardeners who were in desperate need), or otherwise.[68]

Response of Mūsā b. Ḥammād[69]

At this point in the litigation, ʿIyāḍ directed a question to Mūsā b. Ḥammād, who answered according to what I believe was the majority or more common opinion, conservative and cautious when confronted with the option of review. For Judge Mūsa, as far as he could tell, the existing judgment fulfilled the duty of removing or avoiding harm to the community of Muslims. "The damage inflicted upon the road of the Muslims must be removed," he said, and he did not see how ʿAbbūd's decision had failed to do so. Mūsā does, however, offer an interesting and telling caveat, especially for a Far Maghribī jurist of our time period, sensitive to the diversity of legal practice and knowledge in the region, where arbitration in this sort of dispute was most often effected by tribal authorities and other community figures who were not Mālikī qāḍīs. Referring to ʿAbbūd, Mūsā said that if he, as judge (here using the term *ḥākim*) had been properly qualified or, literally, "belonged to the people of knowledge

---

judge wrote, then both parties had equal rights to the water (a rather generous concession to the garden owners). Muḥammad b. ʿIyāḍ and ʿIyāḍ b. Mūsā, *Madhāhib al-ḥukkām*, 113.

67 Muḥammad b. ʿIyāḍ and ʿIyāḍ b. Mūsā, *Madhāhib al-ḥukkām*, 113–14.

68 The editor, ʿIyāḍ's son, added that Ibn Rushd was against confiscation, a position made clear in the following opinion. Interestingly and perhaps uniquely in the case, ʿIyāḍ followed the course provided by the anonymous muftī and not that provided by Ibn Rushd. Muḥammad b. ʿIyāḍ and ʿIyāḍ b. Mūsā, *Madhāhib al-ḥukkām*, 114.

69 Muḥammad b. ʿIyāḍ and ʿIyāḍ b. Mūsā, *Madhāhib al-ḥukkām*, 114.

(*min ahl al-ʿilm*)" then his judgment still stood. It was "effective and decisive confronted with the disagreement and hazard to which you point in your questions concerning the case over which you are presiding." This qualification referred to the judge's having received training from a qualified figure in the recognized network of scholars, such as those ʿIyāḍ describes in his historical and contemporary biographical dictionaries, *Tartīb al-Madārik* and *al-Ghunya*.[70] Belonging to this network provided a judge and his decisions with a kind of legal authority that was new to the Far Maghrib, backed, as it was, by the region's largest heretofore known indigenous Islamic state.

ʿIyāḍ's Fourth Question[71]

The developments of the case up to this point drove ʿIyāḍ to rethink and restate it as a whole, as well as to restate the question of confiscation. The order of events, of cause and effect, had become clearer in ʿIyāḍ's mind.

> Please answer – may God grant you success – [this question] concerning a judge's decision to cut water flowing through a road of the Muslims that lies between gardens after it was established that this caused damage to passersby, that a particular person (*fulān*) diverted it through that road, and that it had never flowed through the road before. The resulting enforceable decision was passed on this one person (*ʿalā fulān waḥdihi*), preventing the water from flowing through the road in his direction.
>
> Forty years after this decision, a group of people sued to irrigate their gardens with this water, claiming they had a right to it, that the decision was passed on one particular person, that the only way for said water to benefit them was through the aforementioned road (through which the judge ordered the water cut), and that that particular person had made the water run through it. They testified (*athbatū*) that they continued to irrigate their gardens with this water for a period of time that was long enough to suggest that they irrigated with the water before the judgment, and after it up to this day. They claimed that the witnesses who had testified in the document to the damage and cause (upon which the judge based his decision) acted out of self-interest (*al-madāfiʿa*).[72] The more so

70 ʿIyāḍ b. Mūsā, *al-Ghunya* (Beirut: Dār al-Gharb al-Islamī, 1982).

71 Muḥammad b. ʿIyāḍ and ʿIyāḍ b. Mūsā, *Madhāhib al-ḥukkām*, 114.

72 Bencherifa has *manāfiʿa*. Muḥammad b. ʿIyāḍ and ʿIyāḍ b. Mūsā, *Madhāhib al-ḥukkām*, 114. Serrano bases her reading on Ibn Rushd, *Fatāwā Ibn Rushd*. I follow her here. Muḥammad b. ʿIyāḍ, *Madhāhib al-ḥukkām fī nawāzil al-aḥkām* (*La actuación de los jueces en los procesos judiciales*), 253.

> as no statement (*iʿdhār*) is recorded for any of them excepting the individual upon whom judgement was passed.
>
> Two years ago, a mill was built on the water, [flowing] through a different way. The owner of this mill challenged the evidence furnished by the garden owners. He used the water for his mill after the decision, to which there is testimony. He claimed that those who testified in favor of the garden owners' right to use this water in irrigation did so out of self-interest (*ṭalaba al-madāfiʿa fī-man shahida lahum*).
>
> Should the water to the mill and to the gardens be cut until judgment is passed (*yufṣalu fī-hi*), the deadlines have passed, and its course altered? Or does [the fact that] the judge passed judgement on some [of the parties involved] prevent this (unless they present evidence of something in which there is no self-interest involved, God willing)?[73]

The case is restated succinctly, with well-defined points, and a question regarding the qāḍī's role as mediator now moved to the fore. How does ʿAbbūd's judgment, now in the process of being revised or reversed in its entirety, affect the process of confiscation during the process of review, which here involved setting deadlines for the parties to furnish evidence. Should the water be cut from both the garden owners and the miller, in spite of the fact that ʿAbbūd's decision, which would still be effective, benefited the miller?

Muftīs' Answer[74]

ʿIyāḍ's restatement of the case provided Ibn Rushd with the occasion to produce his own clearer opinion of the procedure ʿIyāḍ should follow. In this, together with his response to ʿIyāḍ's eighth question, Ibn Rushd provided the two most forceful opinions of the case. Taken together, they appear to have settled it, allowing him to simply repeat his answer in subsequent questions. As mentioned above, Ibn Rushd, separated the entangled problems of avoiding harm and meeting the irrigation needs of the farmers, by identifying two *ʿilal* (sing. *ʿilla*: *ratio juris*) of entangled problems. Once the *ʿilla* which occasioned the first judgment was satisfied, the necessity of irrigation could be fulfilled without invalidating the beneficial object of the first judgment. In other words, although spatially, so to speak, the principle of avoiding damage to public property conflicted with providing water to the irrigators, conceptually they do not have to conflict. Therefore, the new evidence provided by the garden owners, stating their continued use of the water before and after ʿAbbūd's judg-

73 Muḥammad b. ʿIyāḍ and ʿIyāḍ b. Mūsā, *Madhāhib al-ḥukkām*, 114.

74 Muḥammad b. ʿIyāḍ and ʿIyāḍ b. Mūsā, *Madhāhib al-ḥukkām*, 115.

ment, did not present grounds for reversing judgment. All the gardeners had to do was present evidence satisfying the object of ʿAbbūd's judgment, viz., that the damage to the road had been removed. Ibn Rushd thus left the miller without a defense.

> I have studied and thought about the question. The judge's decision is not to be rejected because the orchard owners testified to their continued irrigation with the water, before and after the decision up to this day. There is no way for them to irrigate with it, unless they provide proof that there will be no damage in that inflicted on the road with evidence that has greater probity than that upon which the judge based his decision, or the witnesses who established before the judge the possibility of damage are recusable, or they are able to prevent such damage by reinforcing the water's course, in such a way that it can be known that the damage has been suppressed. In this case, they will be the party more entitled to the water to irrigate their gardens in time of need, even if the gardens appeared after the mill was built. It is also unnecessary to hold the water during the litigation, until the deadlines expire, in the way that disputed objects are (*al-shayʾ al-muddaʿ fī-hi*), since it is not something that is owned. It is rain that only God gives people to drink and that only He distributes among them. The approach to the decision then is to give each individual owner of mills and gardens right to the water while the others are summoned to present their plea (*fī muddat al-iʿdhār ilā aṣḥābihim*), instead of cutting it off from all of them at once. [Right to irrigate] should move from person to person as the summons to plea moves from person to person, and as they furnish evidence against each other. In God is success. Said Muḥammad b. Rushd.[75]

ʿIyāḍ's Fifth Question[76]

Ibn Rushd's solution, in which the evidence provided by the garden owners doesn't constitute the grounds for the reversal of ʿAbbūd's judgment, presented the problem for ʿIyāḍ of what then to base himself on, as he proceeded in attempting to establish the parties' water rights. He thought, again, that the prin-

75 Muḥammad b. ʿIyāḍ and ʿIyāḍ b. Mūsā, *Madhāhib al-ḥukkām*, 115. Ibn al-Ḥājj responded to this question as well, reiterating his position that ʿAbbūd's decision stands, a position which the emerging evidence seems to support. The case, however, has turned to what Ibn Rushd had envisioned.

76 Muḥammad b. ʿIyāḍ and ʿIyāḍ b. Mūsā, *Madhāhib al-ḥukkām*, 115.

ciple of avoiding the greater injury could provide a guideline for settling the dispute, and asked whether he could apply this.

Muftīs' Answer[77]

Ibn Rushd kept to the logic of his last opinion, albeit providing no simple solution for 'Iyāḍ to follow. The testimony presented in 'Abbūd's case, he says, remains effective (as does the judgment). The testimony presented by the gardeners regarding "their irrigating with the water before and after the judgment should be disregarded, since their use of it before the judgment is made void by the judgment, but not their use of it after." Again, in Ibn Rushd's opinion, the case did not present an instance of the lesser of two harms prevailing, because of the, presumably deleterious, effect of this reasoning on the miller's rights.[78]

'Iyāḍ's Sixth Question[79]

After some time had elapsed, 'Iyāḍ restated the case to the muftīs, bringing them up to date with recent developments. One interesting detail was a change in wording. 'Iyāḍ now explained that the miller cut the water off from the gardens, which impelled the gardeners to appeal to the qāḍī. As understood above, the garden owners produced testimony, which the miller disputed with counter testimony, and afterwards, demanded an investigation into the testimony produced by the garden owners, claiming it was fallacious, influenced by the self-interest of the witnesses (who, presumably, would benefit from gaining access to the water of al-Sayyāj).

In response to this demand 'Iyāḍ made the bold decision to confiscate the disputed object: "I therefore cut off the water to the mill and the gardens, [diverting] it in another direction, and set a deadline for the mill owner to present witness testmony (*al-bayyināt*)."[80] This witness testimony would, again presumably, establish the miller's claim over the garden owners' testimony, upon which suspicion had been cast by the miller's argument.

'Iyāḍ's confiscation produced a series of problems for him. When the period of irrigation and pressing ended before the miller's deadline for producing evidence to prove self-interest in the garden owners' testimony, the miller asked

---

77 Muḥammad b. 'Iyāḍ and 'Iyāḍ b. Mūsā, *Madhāhib al-ḥukkām*, 116.

78 Ibn al-Ḥājj restated his position that 'Abbūd's decision remained in force and was effective in removing the damage. Ibn Rushd's opinion now concured with the opinion of the two muftīs he disagreed with in the beginning, but to a different effect.

79 Muḥammad b. 'Iyāḍ and 'Iyāḍ b. Mūsā, *Madhāhib al-ḥukkām*, 116.

80 Muḥammad b. 'Iyāḍ and 'Iyāḍ b. Mūsā, *Madhāhib al-ḥukkām*, 116.

that the confiscation be terminated, since, he said, the garden owners' claim to the water applied only to this period and not to the rest of the year.[81] 'Iyāḍ asked the muftīs whether the miller's claim was valid. Should the confiscation of the litigated object be lifted, as the claim of one of the parties of the object was seasonal, or should the object remain confiscated so long as the litigation lasted?

Muftīs' Answer[82]

Ibn Rushd did not quite adress 'Iyāḍ's immediate concern. But the restatement and time elapsed had allowed him to clarify his position. Concerning the issue of water rights at hand, he responded forcefully:

> The orchard owners are more entitled to irrigate their gardens than the owner of the mill is, even if they planted (*ansha'ū*) their gardens after the miller built his mill. When they are no longer in need of irrigating, the miller can channel the water to his mill. This is what I think and say concerning this question, based on its sense as it appears in the ḥadīth of the Prophet (the peace and blessings of God be upon him) concerning the flow of Mahzūr and Mudhaynab, because he judged (*qaḍiya*) that upstream users take water up to the ankles and then send it downstream. Therefore since [the Prophet] (the peace and blessing of God be upon him) did not, on any account, allot the entirety of the water to upstream users excluding downstream users, so the mill owners should on no account take exclusive possession of the water for their mills, excluding the garden owners, even if the latter were upstream and even if the [millers] built before the [garden owners]. What is left to be resolved, then, concerns your question about confiscation and summoning [the parties to present their pleas] (*al-tawqīf wa-l-i'dhār*).[83]

For Ibn Rushd, the miller's water rights are to be respected or preserved, but they are not such that they can deprive the gardeners of their claim, their position on the river and history notwithstanding.[84] This opinion would remain the most important in the case, even when it transpired that the garden own-

81 This is the first time we, and quite possibly 'Iyāḍ, learn of the time specificity of the garden owners''claim, presumably one of the many strategies employed by the miller.

82 Muḥammad b. 'Iyāḍ and 'Iyāḍ b. Mūsā, *Madhāhib al-ḥukkām*, 117.

83 Muḥammad b. 'Iyāḍ and 'Iyāḍ b. Mūsā, *Madhāhib al-ḥukkām*, 117.

84 He does not, it should be noted, explicitly mention the miller's industrial use as less entitled.

ers had no real historical claim to irrigation rights in al-Sayyāj. Ibn Rushd gave the garden owners this right because of the priority afforded to agriculture over manufacturing: "They are more entitled to irrigate." He would restate this in an even clearer form in response to question eight.

Ibn al-Ḥājj responded to the new circumstances of the case succinctly: the miller should retain his rights to use (*al-infāʿ*) the water during the season in which the garden owners have also claimed need, and unless he is able to show the garden owner's testimony to have been self-interestedly tendentious, the gardeners should be given what they claim.

ʿIyāḍ's Seventh Question[85]

The miller produced the witness testimony to support his claim that the testimony produced for each of the witnesses supporting the garden owners' claim had been self interested except for one. At this point the miller demanded once again that the confiscation be lifted, based on the Mālikī doctrine that stipulates that such a confiscation of disputed property requires more than one witness to be implemented. When the garden owners offered to produce more witnesses, the miller claimed that these should also be inadmissible. ʿIyāḍ was uncertain whether the confiscation should be lifted, as demanded by the miller, since the decision about confiscation had already been taken and implemented. Should not, he asked, all of the witnesses be recused before the confiscation is rescinded?

Muftīs' Answer[86]

Ibn Rushd answered simply that his previous opinion sufficed and remained applicable to this question, since he had already argued that the gardeners have legitimate irrigation rights regardless of the evidence they produced. The muftī Ibn al-Ḥājj stood once again with the miller: if all but one of the witnesses has been recused, he wrote, then the confiscation must be lifted according to the Mālikī doctrine that stipulates that two witnesses are required to confiscate a disputed object. This doctrine, he continued, follows current legal practice. He added provocatively: "This is, of course, in so far as confiscation is the correct approach," thus reminding ʿIyāḍ that he was against revisising ʿAbbūd's decision to begin with.[87]

---

85 Muḥammad b. ʿIyāḍ and ʿIyāḍ b. Mūsā, *Madhāhib al-ḥukkām*, 117.

86 Muḥammad b. ʿIyāḍ and ʿIyāḍ b. Mūsā, *Madhāhib al-ḥukkām*, 118.

87 Muḥammad b. ʿIyāḍ and ʿIyāḍ b. Mūsā, *Madhāhib al-ḥukkām*, 118.

ʿIyāḍ's Eighth Question[88]

After a short restatement of the case focusing once again on the fact that a former judge, ʿAbbūd, had issued a judgment against a certain ʿAbd al-Salām, and that forty years later, none of the property owners who currently wanted access to the water were mentioned or connected to the documents pertaining to the first case, ʿIyāḍ wrote that some of the garden owners argued once again that the first decision was not binding on them since they were ignorant of the decision at the time of purchase. The miller argued that none of them in fact had such rights, that only ʿAbd al-Salām had had any claim to the water in the area where the new garden owners had their property, and that this is precisely why ʿAbd al-Salām is mentioned in the decision denying him these rights. On the heels of this argument, principally concerning the gardeners' knowledge of their water rights at the time of purchase, they asked again whether the improvement of the road changed anything. A new source, or water channeled through a slightly different source, also appeared, prompting ʿIyāḍ to ask again whether the first judgment remained in effect. Ibn Rushd was more than certain now of how to distinguish the problem of respecting the first judgment from the problem of procuring water for irrigation.

Muftīs' Answer[89]

Ibn Rushd began by restating the conditions for the first decision to remain effective, thereby opening a series of ways to revise it completely. If, he wrote, ʿAbbūd judged to cut the flow of water through the road because of the damage inflicted on this one and only road, based on trustworthy evidence that was not skewed in favor of those testifying, then the garden owners have no right to the water. However, this is not the case if,

> in their plea they offer to suppress the damage to the road by reinforcing the water's course in such a way that it is [clearly] known that the damage has been eliminated, or they furnish testimony of greater probity than that upon which the decision was based, that no such damage to the road exists. Or, they recuse the witnesses of the document upon which the judge personally established the [existence of] the damage. In [any of] these cases, they are more entitled to irrrigate their gardens because of their need. If a water source appeared in the road after the decision, then [the case should be] reopened for reconsideration, God willing.[90]

88 Muḥammad b. ʿIyāḍ and ʿIyāḍ b. Mūsā, *Madhāhib al-ḥukkām*, 118.

89 Muḥammad b. ʿIyāḍ and ʿIyāḍ b. Mūsā, *Madhāhib al-ḥukkām*, 118–19.

90 Muḥammad b. ʿIyāḍ and ʿIyāḍ b. Mūsā, *Madhāhib al-ḥukkām*, 119.

Once the damage is removed and evidence to that effect is produced, then the gardeners are entitled to use the water owing to the priority of irrigators over industrial users. Having solved the basic legal problem of the case, Ibn Rushd, in the ensuing questions, saw it necessary merely to restate his opinion.

ʿIyāḍ's Ninth, Tenth, and Eleventh Questions[91]

In the last remaining questions, the role of written documents, primarily documents of sale, but also the court register, came to the fore as the miller stepped up his defense, or, put differently, availed himself of the available strategies to keep water distribution as favorable as possible for his industry. The questions sent by ʿIyāḍ to the muftīs reflect not only the remarkable resourcefulness of the miller, in contrast to the lack of sophistication of the garden owners (the latter always seemed to be proven wrong, while, astonishingly, gaining some of their objectives). The questions also provide an excellent example of the relative force of such documents in resolving disputes, and illustrates questions associated with their use in court. From the ensuing questions it is clear that the documents played an important part in resolving the dispute and were of paramount importance in establishing claims. The fact that the miller seemed[92] to be unable to defend his position rests less on the fact that the documents do not support the gardeners' claims, than on the fact that his use of the water (milling) was not prioritized as highly as the irrigation of the gardens, as Ibn Rushd made clear (had it been up to Ibn al-Ḥājj and Ibn Ismāʿīl, on the other hand, the miller would have kept his rights intact). The discussion betweeen the judge and the muftīs revolved around how these documents would influence the water rights adjudication and what scope the litigants would be allowed in using (or concealing) these.

The miller's first demand was to ask to see the documents relating to ownership of the gardens in order to determine the existing water rights. This became especially complicated for ʿIyāḍ when, after an initial perusal (we are unsure by whom) it became clear that some of the garden owners' documents of purchase did indeed include mention of water rights, but not to al-Sayyāj. Should the miller be allowed to demand that these documents be produced, ʿIyāḍ asked, and should each individual gardener be allowed to claim rights without producing such documents? The miller followed this demand with another, more exacting one: the gardeners should provide copies of all documents of purchase to him. The garden owners refused to produce the documents stating that the relevant material already had been produced in the

91 Muḥammad b. ʿIyāḍ and ʿIyāḍ b. Mūsā, *Madhāhib al-ḥukkām*, 119–21.

92 I say "seems" because, as in most such records, the final deision went unrecorded.

evidence (the testimony) which established their claim. ʿIyāḍ asked the muftīs whether the miller should be accorded this right, and, what, he asked, should be done if either one of the parties demanded to see the court register (containing ʿAbbūd's decision), especially when, as ʿIyāḍ put it, none of them were mentioned?

The final question reveals that much documentation was produced, at least for the qāḍī's eyes, and that little of it substantiated the garden owners' claims. What, ʿIyāḍ asked, should be done if "no irrigation rights are established for the litigating [garden owners], other than that they occasionally diverted water to their gardens more or less since the time the mill was built?"[93] The evidence they provided established that their former source had run dry. Meanwhile, the miller had fallen back on his argument that he had established full possession of the water through use (*aḥajj bi-ḥiyāzatihi*), expending a great deal of financial resources. If the garden owners could establish possession of al-Sayyāj through occasional use, "it would be unlawful possession (*ḥawz bi-ghayr ḥaqq*)," he argued, since judge ʿAbbbūd's decision remained in force when they began to do so.

Ibn al-Ḥājj remained opposed to revision, arguing to the last that, since the gardeners were unable to substantiate their claims, ʿAbbūd's decision should remain efffective and nothing else should be considered. He also supported the miller's motion to demand the garden owners' document of purchase, the result of which made him revert to his long-held position against revision of any sort.

Ibn Rushd adhered to the reasoning of his previous opinions. The gardeners, he said, are not obliged to produce the documents of purchase since it had already been established that they had rights on the grounds of their need to irrigate, and that such documents that might be produced, including the court register, would be useful only at a later date, when the irrigators needed to work out irrigation rights amongst each other. Copies of the documents of purchase, likewise, were "irrelevant to any argument against them." Even when it had been fairly well established that the garden owners had no historic rights to al-Sayyāj, Ibn Rushd persisted:

> The garden owners have greater rights to irrigate their gardens than the owner of the mill, even if the mill were older than the gardens, because of what we said above concerning the first question, and because the fruit trees, if not watered at the right time, will perish, while the mill does not

93 Muḥammad b. ʿIyāḍ and ʿIyāḍ b. Mūsā, *Madhāhib al-ḥukkām*, 120.

perish when water is cut from it. Only its profit (*al-manfaʿa*) is cut during this time. In God is success. Said Muḥammad b. Rushd.[94]

Conclusion

This last opinion of Ibn Rushd became an important part of Mālikī practice in the Far Maghrib, as can be appreciated by the fact that this opinion, along with a similarly formulated principle in his commentary of the *ʿUtbiyya*, were cited more than three centuries later, in a water dispute in a community deep in the Middle Atlas mountains. In the beginning of the sixteenth century, it was also simplified (or stripped of it's particulars) and introduced by al-Wansharīsī into the *Miʿyār*.[95] In the long run, therefore, we can appreciate the effect of ʿIyāḍ's questions, the muftīs' consultations, and the Almoravids' financial and logistical support, on the history of the penetration of Mālikī law, its practices and network of practitioners, into the Far Maghrib and eventually its countryside, where it would increasingly work alongside existing authorities and practices.

As in most such texts, we are left ignorant of the final resolution of the dispute, if there ever was one. This extraordinarily rich, and long, case reveals a great deal of significant information about its time and place, as well as about the institutional change ushered in by the Almoravid unification of the Far Maghrib. It has featured the Mālikī judge of the nearest city acting as a careful mediator in a riparian dispute, attempting to balance local practice and needs with Islamic legal principles. The case also features actors and physical changes introduced as a direct result of the Almoravid conquest: the judges, the jurisconsults in Cordoba and Seville, the displaced landowner (connected with the former regime), the redistributed land, and the demographic pressure resulting from a growing population and increased economic activity, evident in the increased food production and diminishing resources over which producers increasingly came into conflict. Presiding over this growth – in a sense, concomitant with it – was the developing institution of Mālikism, whose members we see discussing so articulately, if not always harmoniously, here.

94 Muḥammad b. ʿIyāḍ and ʿIyāḍ b. Mūsā, *Madhāhib al-ḥukkām*, 121.

95 Aḥmad al-Wansharīsī, *al-Miʿyār al-muʿrib*, VIII: 385–394.

Epilogue

The collapse of the Almoravid state and its replacement by the Almohad state presented a profound disruption to the development of the institution explored in this book: Maghribī Mālikism. During the reign of its first three dynastic rulers (ʿAbd al-Muʾmin, Yūsuf I, and al-Manṣūr), Mālikism as a network of learning, corpus of texts, and perhaps primarily, as a vehicle for state legitimation, came under sustained attack by an Almohad ideology that championed radical religio-political change. On the whole, the kind of consultative correspondence between Andalusī and Maghribī jurists that produced the texts analyzed above was greatly diminished as the Almohads instituted a new administrative structure, which favored installing its own members in key positions across its territories. Mālikī texts were ordered burned and Almohad caliphs attempted to remake not only the judicial system but its culture and hermeneutics. Almohadism, therefore, understood as a coherent and unified ideology, coupled with the aims and effects of this anti-Mālikī agenda, may be construed as having resulted in a complete rupture in Maghribī history. And some of the discontinuities implied by these developments should definitely not be discounted. The success of the Almohad movement constitutes a major chapter in Maghribī history, a significant period of change.[1]

This change, however, was an evolution of trends existing in the Far Maghrib and not, I would argue, a sudden break. Too often in the modern historiography of the Islamic Maghrib ideology and dynastic change are construed as the sole, or at least most significant, agents of change. Many of the significant social historical trends described above, however, continued into the Almohad period, in which the Far Maghrib became even more engaged with the wider Mediterranean as a major political-economic entity. The confluence of what

1 The classic study of the Almohad period is Miranda Huici, Ambrosio., *Historia política del Imperio Almohade* (Tetuán: Editora Marroqu, 1956). For an excellent collection of relatively recent work on the period, see Patrice Cressier, et al., *Los almohades: problemas y perspectivas* (Madrid: Consejo Superior de Investigaciones Científicas, 2005). Two volumes of the series Estudios Onomástico-Biográficos de al-Andalus are also particulary noteworthy: Maribel Fierro, and María Luisa Ávila, eds. *Biografías Almohades I*, vol. IX, Estudios Onomástico Biográficos de al-Andalus (Madrid-Granada: Consejo Superior de Investigaciones Científicas, 1999); Marīa Luisa Ávila, and Maribel Fierro, eds. *Biografías Almohades II*, vol. X, Estudios Onomástico Biográficos de al-Andalus (Madrid-Granada: Consejo Superior de Investigaciones Científicas, 2000). Together, these last three titles point to important dimensions of continuity across the dynastic and ideological change from Almoravids to Almohads.

 | DOI 10.1163/9789004279841_006

one might term "international" or pan-Islamic intellectual and religio-political currents with local, Far Maghribī social movements were likewise at play in the rise of the Almohads. This confluence, in important ways, accounts for the dynamic of ideological confrontation that was so important in the period. While it is true that without Ibn Tūmart's pronouncing himself Mahdī and rallying the Maṣmūda tribes of the High Atlas to his cause, there would have been no Almohad movement, it is equally true that there would have been no Almohad movement without the emergence of Marrakesh, and the economic production and intellectual flow and ferment it entailed. It was in the direct vicinity of Marrakesh that Ibn Tūmart organized his movement, which was rooted in the local population (for whom the Lamtūna were also foreigners, in a way perhaps not as pronounced as they were for the Andalusīs, but nevertheless, distinctly so). The urban transformation of the sixth/twelfth-century Far Maghrib, that is, is largely responsible for the rise of the Almohads, to which it made an important contribution.

This book has argued that the rise of the Almoravid state coincided with an urban transformation of the Far Maghrib, that Andalusī-influenced Mālikī legal institutions developed in these new urban spaces both responding to the administrative needs of the state (the first large-scale indigenous state in the region) as well as, crucially, to the social needs of these urban societies. There is no more eloquent evidence for the success of this social institution than the attack by the Almohad leadership on Mālikism and the ultimate failure of this attack. By the time of the fourth Almohad caliph, al-Ma'mūn (624–629/1227–1232), it became clear that the institution was deep-rooted and that the Almohads' intitial agenda was pointless. It would not be the first time in the Maghrib that this legal tradition (through "conservative" popular resistance) survived the attempt of a regime to replace it. It was precisely in surviving such attempts that the tradition had gained social force and cohesion in Ifrīqiya, from where it was first transmitted to the Almoravid south. The Mālikī *madhhab* was to develop into the dominant legal tradition of the Maghrib, from where it spread to West Africa. And in a variety of ways it informs the modern legal systems of the region's contemporary nation states.

All of the above, of course, is not meant as a simple paean to Mālikism, to imply that it was "tolerant," or even that it was a particularly enlightened tradition. It is to show, rather, how this Islamic legal tradition and institution of learning, developed and adapted to real social needs beyond those of supplying political legitimation or identity construction and group cohesion. In its North African historical development, Mālikism was a flexible institution that developed and responded to a variety of social needs, and was transformed in the process. It is through its fusing, perhaps, of essential Islamic concepts of justice and morality with a set of adaptive practices with social management and self-regulatory functions, that this institution contributed to, and, in significant ways, encoded, the constitutional stability of the Islamic pre-modern Maghrib.

Appendix A: Breakdown of the Fatwās in al-Wansharīsī's *Miʿyār* by Subject and Region

	IX-XIth c.	Almoravid Era	XII-XVth c.	Non-identified
I. Religious Life (Ritual, Heresy, Inter-Religious Relations, Apostasy, Jihād)				
Ifrīqiya	69	6	47	12
C. Maghrib	0	0	22	6
F. Maghrib	1	1	24	0
al-Andalus	43	30	23	12
Non-Identified				6
II. Family (Marriage, Divorce, Guardianship, Inheritance, Dowry)				
Ifrīqiya	39	33	15	0
C. Maghrib	2	0	4	0
F. Maghrib	0	4	26	0
al-Andalus	47	24	4	0
III. Economic I (Sales, Exchange, Transactions)				
Ifriqīyā	58	15	37	5
C. Maghrib	5	0	40	8
F. Maghrib	1	1	71	2
al-Andalus	43	38	77	5
Non-Identified				30
IV. Endowments and Properties (Cemeteries, Forts, Mosques, Funduqs, Administration)				
Ifrīqiya	28	2	22	0
C. Maghrib	0	0	15	0
F. Maghrib	0	3	79	1
al-Andalus	56	18	50	3
Non-Identified				11

	IX-XIth c.	Almoravid Era	XII-XVth c.	Non-identified
V. Economic II (Water, Joint Ownership, Partitioning, Agricultural Contracts, Rents)				
Ifrīqiya	92	14	46	3
C. Maghrib	7	0	13	1
F. Maghrib	2	4	22	1
al-Andalus	83	52	25	0
Non-Identified				12
VI. Judicial (Qāḍī's Jurisdiction, Deposits and Loans, Donations, Alms, Wills, Students)				
Ifrīqiya	88	11	15	0
C. Maghrib	2	0	3	2
F. Maghrib	0	2	12	0
al-Andalus	43	26	21	2
Non-Identified				6
VII. Procedure (Litigation, Testimony, Pleas, Oaths, Confessions, Debts)				
Ifrīqiya	47	17	24	1
C. Maghrib	5	1	4	1
F. Maghrib	0	7	11	0
al-Andaus	18	20	8	5
Non-Identified				5

	IX-XIth c.	Almoravid Era	XII-XVth c.	Non-identified
VII. Procedure (Litigation, Testimony, Pleas, Oaths, Confessions, Debts)				
Ifrīqiya	47	17	24	1
C. Maghrib	5	1	4	1
F. Maghrib	0	7	11	0
al-Andaus	18	20	8	5
Non-Identified				5

	IX-XIth c.	Almoravid Era	XII-XVth c.	Non-identified
VIII. Miscellaneous				
Ifrīqiya	13	3	9	1
C. Maghrib	0	0	9	0
F. Maghrib	0	0	19	0
al-Andalus	9	1	22	1
Non-Identified				1

Appendix B: Fatwās Chapter One

Translation of *Fatāwā Ibn Rushd* # 299, p. 1030

Question 299. Concerning someone who owed a man some dīnārs, payed him the weight of the dīnārs in pieces of gold jewelry of the same or of lesser gold quality.

And as to the second question, it concerns a man who owed another man some dīnārs. He paid the man the weight of the dīnārs in pieces of gold jewelry of the same, or of lesser weight/quality than the dīnārs, without charge (*ʿāda*), condition, or specified number (*ʿidda*). When the weight of each dīnār was examined separately, however, some were found to be more complete than others (*awfā min baʿḍ*). If one hundred of them were gathered on a balance with the stone weight, the weight may prove correct or may come short. Furthermore, what is to be done if the man settled the debt using Murābiṭī dīnārs instead of ʿAbbādī ones?

The answer: I have examined this, your question, and have considered it carefully. As to being paid in pieces of gold jewelry that quantitatively exceed or fall short of the weight of the corresponding dīnārs (*tajūzu ʿadad*[an] *ḥulīy dhahab bi-wazn danānīrihi mithl ʿaynihi*), this is not permissible because of the absence of an equivalence (*mumāthala*) with the original object of the pledge (*maʿ al-qaṣad ilā al-mubāyaʿa*), and the resulting discrepancy between [the original] intentions [of the parties].

As to the settlement of a debt with Almoravid gold in substitution of ʿAbbādī gold, on the other hand, this is permissible, because the surplus (*faḍl*) in this exchange is one sided, when the ʿAbbādī gold falls short in quality or weight. In God – may He be exalted – is success. He has no equal.

Translation of *Fatāwā Ibn Rushd* #333, p. 1095–1097

Question 333. Concerning pieces of jewelry (*ḥulīy*) cast in pure, impure, and counterfeit gold (*al-khāliṣa wa-ghayr al-khāliṣa wa-l-maghshūsha*).

And [Ibn Rushd] – may God be contented with him – was asked a question concerning jewelry and this is the text: Give us your answer – may God be contented with you – concerning gold cast for jewelry for the adornment of women, according to the different standards of gold (*ʿalā ikhtilāf ʿiyyārāt al-dhahab*): the pure, noble metal (*ṭīb khāliṣ*) with no impurities, the kind that is partial or half gold, and that which is of an eighth, two-thirds, three-fourth, seven-eighths gold and the like. These standards are known to experts and merchants of gold, from whom a little added or subtracted cannot be concealed.

Also, people's objectives in acquiring gold are various. There is he who wants the noble kind as treasure for savings (*li-zamānihi*) and as ornament for his women. Others desire the kind widely available, which is bought and sold according to people's wealth or lack of means. Then there is he who goes for the lowest standard. His objective is slightness of weight at maximum size and insignificant price.

Noble gold is heavy in weight, contemptible (*ḥaqīr*) to the eye, and great in price.

So – may God grant you success – is the sale of gold for dirhams, across this range of standards, permissible or not? And is it permissible to weigh these different qualities of gold by the pound (*al-murāṭala*), against non-minted gold (*al-ghayr al-maskūk*), weight for weight, one amount for another (*yad bi-yad*) or not? Is it permissible to weigh the noble kind by the pound excluding the lesser kind? Or the lesser excluding the noble? Or is it permissible across the range of standards? And is a judge entitled to prevent people from acquiring jewelry of a quality lesser than the noble kind? Does he have the right to keep goldsmiths (*ṣāgha*) from their smithing, for others or for themselves? And does this apply equally for he who smiths his gold for his own use as it does for he who does so to sell? May a judge destroy the non-noble jewelry that is in people's possession, to devalue it and compel people to acquire exclusively gold of the noble kind? Clarify for us what is the obligatory course to be taken in this matter – may you be rewarded and thanked, if God so wills. May He be exalted.

The answer: So [Ibn Rushd] – may God grant him success – answered this question with this text: I have studied – God have mercy upon us – your question and I have informed myself regarding it. The smithing of jewelry from pure and impure gold, alloyed with (*mashbūh bi*) silver, brass, and copper is permissible (*jā'iz*) and its use is allowed if it is characterized as you have described. For God, glorified and exalted, said: "Would they attribute to God females who adorn themselves with trinkets and are powerless in disputation?"[1] Likewise, a person is allowed to procure it in quantities as treasure for his time when *zakāt* has been paid on it (if it has reached the minimum amount on which the *zakāt* must be paid) or when that person has other wealth added to it and he incurs the obligation of *zakāt* on it. Furthermore, its sale as merchandise (*bi-l-ʿurūḍ*) is permissible, for specie and on credit (*ilā ajal*), as it is permissible to sell it for silver and dirhams, one amount for another (*yad bi-yad*).

As to weighing some of it against other gold by the pound (*al-murāṭala fī baʿḍihi bi-baʿḍ*) or just against pure, minted gold, this is only permissible for the pure kind, excluding the lesser. It is also not proper (*lā yanbaghī*) to prohibit goldsmiths from working their trade for people, for pay, or for themselves, to sell or use, because all of this activity is lawful and permissible. As it is also not permissible to destroy what is in

1 Qur'ān 43:18.

people's possession, because it is their property, and because smithed jewelry is a kind of merchandise (*ʿarḍ*) that those who circulate it for commerce provide in payment of the *zakāt*. Indeed, the only gold that must be destroyed and prohibited from being wrought is that which is counterfeit, with an outer layer of gold but an interior of brass or copper. In God is success. He has no equal.

Translation of *Fatāwā Ibn Rushd* #320, p. 160–170

Question 320. From among the questions concerning exchange (*ṣarf*) and where oath-taking is obligatory upon a shortcoming of dirhams in an exchange (*ʿalā naqṣ dirham*[in] *fī-hi*)?

And [Ibn Rushd] – God be contented with him – was also written to from the capital city of Marrakesh with a question concerning exchange and the text of the question is as follows: Your answer – may God be contented with you – concerning a man who exchanged dīnārs for dirhams from another man. Having taken the dirhams, the exchanger of the aforesaid dīnārs for dirhams rose and left with them but then claimed that the dirhams were short of the number for which he had exchanged the dīnārs. "So I returned the dirhams and there was a dirham missing." The individual who bought the dīnārs from him then said: "On the contrary, I paid you the full amount." The individual who took the dirhams then said: "The dirhams did not leave my hands. You have paid me a lesser amount." Where should the oath-taking take place in this situation? Should it take place at the congregational mosque or not? Clarify this for us, may you be rewarded and thanked.

The answer: So Ibn Rushd – God grant him success – answered this by saying: I have studied – God have mercy on us – this, your question, and have informed myself on it. And oath-taking in this case is specifically required at the congregational mosque (*tataʿayyanu fī al-masjid al-jāmiʿ*) because the matter, based on what the receiver of the dirhams has claimed (*yaʾūlu bi-mā adʿāhu qābiḍ al-darāhim*) concerning the shortcoming of their amount, may result in the eventual invalidation of the exchange of the full amount of dīnārs. In God is success.

Translation of *Fatāwā Ibn Rushd* # 300, p. 1031–1032

Question 300. Concerning someone who disagrees with his companion regarding a payment over an amount of a value of less than a quarter dīnār; also concerning someone of whom an oath is required regarding the value of a defect of less than a half-dīnār: Is the oath obligatory? And is the ruling affected by the expiration of the item?

And as to the third question, it concerns two men who rescinded a sale (*taqāyalā*) in the order of a quarter dīnār and upwards. They then disagreed, however, over the settlement of the payment (*fī al-taqāḍī*). The seller said: "You still owe me (*baqiya liyy ʿalayk*) an eighth of a dīnār." The buyer said: "I already paid it to you. It was included with the total price of the merchandise." Is oath taking at the congregational mosque obligatory in this case or not? What, on the other hand, should be done if one of the men bought merchandise from the other, and the buyer proceeded to sue the seller for a defect in the merchandise (*qāma ʿalayhi bi-ʿayb*), and the seller, in response, claimed he had disclosed the existence of the defect to the buyer, which the latter denied. The value of the defect being less than a quarter dīnār, where is oath taking obligatory? And is the ruling affected by the expiration of the merchandise?

The answer: I have examined this, your question, and have informed myself about it. As to the person who is owed less than a quarter dīnār and to whom it was claimed he had already been paid, this does not necessitate oath-taking in the congregational mosque. As to the person who sued over the defect – of which the seller claimed innocence – of a value of less than a quarter dīnār for merchandise bought for a value of more than a quarter dīnār, if the merchandise is extant it is obligatory that it be returned with the defect. This action requires an oath in the congregational mosque.

This is as when two parties to a contract of sale (*mutabāyiʿān*) disagree over the price of the merchandise by a margin of less than a quarter dīnār and the merchandise is extant. They are mutually bound to take oaths at the congregational mosque, as opposed to when the merchandise has expired. This and none other is what is correct.

And it appears in the book of Ibn al-Mawwāz, in the version (*fī samāʿ*) of Ibn al-Qāsim, in the chapter on defects (*Kitāb al-ʿuyūb*) of the *ʿUtbiyya*, concerning the summoning of buyer and seller when there is a defect of outer appearance in merchandise, in a manner contrary to what we have stated above. The only correct stance is that which I have explained above. In God is success.

Translation of *Fatāwā Ibn Rushd* #298, p. 1027–1029

There is an introductory paragraph for a series of three questions (298–300), embedded in the text of question 297. It reads: A group of jurists from the capital city of Marrakesh – may God protect it – wrote to Ibn Rushd in the final months of 515, asking questions regarding three problems. Below is the text of these questions in its entirety. The response to each is appended.

Question 298. Concerning a disagreement between texts regarding testimony in cases of divorce.

The first question concerns a ḥadīth in the chapter of belief in divorce in the *Mudawwana*, on the authority of Abū al-Zināḍ and Ibn Shihāb, concerning the testimony of three men regarding another man's divorce pronouncement. One testifies to the fact that the man has pronounced the repudiation three times, another twice, and yet another once, the last thereby omitting two previous divorce pronouncements (*taṭlīqatayn*). In another copy (*nuskha*) of the *Mudawwana*, however, the men testify to the man's divorcing separately: one testifies that he has repudiated his wife once, another says he has done so twice, and another three times. As a result, it is accepted that he has accumulated only two pronouncements of divorce.

The answer: I have examined this, your question. And what you mention regarding the disagreement occurring in different copies of the *Mudawwana*, concerning the *ḥadīth* of Ibn Shihāb, has no effect on the ruling required in cases in which one individual alleges that the testimony of another is false. The requirement for an allegation of fabrication of testimony is that two pronouncements of divorce be enjoined, just as it appears in the *ḥadīth* of Ibn Shihāb in the *Mudawwana*, in accordance with the school (*madhhab*) of Ibn al- Qāsim in his transmission from Mālik, in which a different position not found in other transmissions [is embraced, and which] disregards the dating of each witness's testimony.

This position maintains that the witnesses' disagreement or agreement upon the date is to be disregarded, since dating has no bearing upon one who gives false testimony. This is because were it obligatory to accept the testimony of the one single witness concerning the specification of the day in which he witnessed the divorce, then it would be necessary to accept his testimony, by itself. When the testimony of the divorce's date by the single witness is not accepted, it follows that no single testimony should be permitted to stand alone in the assignment of a date (*fī-mā infarada bihi min al-taʾrīkh*), and that the date should not be considered, having no effect, and not being an established requirement for divorce.

Do you not consider that the *ʿidda* only begins from the day that the divorce ruling is passed, irrespective of whether the witnesses dated their testimony? Were two witnesses to concur on a date, that would require that the *ʿidda* begin from that date. Therefore the distinction al-Lakhmī makes in his *Tabṣira*, regarding the differentiation between whether the dating of the witness testifying to three repudiations occurs after the date given in the testimony of the two concurring witnesses, or before both, or one of the two, is not sound. Likewise, his stating that there is a difference when dates are absent, and his asking whether this enjoins two or three repudiations, is also not sound. This is because it is wrong to exceed a determination of two repudiations on doubtful grounds. This is furthermore unsound because there is no disagreement in the school over a judge (*ḥākim*) not deciding against one who disclaims an accusation when there is doubt (*bi-shakk*). Indeed, disagreement exists only over whether a judge shall decide against an individual, when there is doubt, when this individual corroborates this doubt upon himself. In God is success.

Translation of *Fatāwā Ibn Rushd* #541, p. 1475–1479

Question 541. Concerning one whose goodness, piety, fairness, and trustworthiness have been attested, but about whom a contract was then made public, implying that he said he had married someone who was three-times divorced from him, but whom he nevertheless remarried. What if the contract were in his handwriting? And what ruling should ensue in this matter? Would this amount to the invalidation of his testimony?

The judge of the capital city of Marrakesh, Mūsā b. Ḥammād – may God grant him prosperity –, wrote to [Ibn Rushd] – may God be pleased with him – asking about a man about whom it was testified that he had married a certain woman (*fulāna*) from whom he was three-times divorced, but married anyway. She remained married to him close to fourteen years. The text of the question is as follows:

Please give us your answer – may God be pleased with you – to a question concerning a man who married a woman in a town (*balda*), consummated the marriage with her, and remained with her for a period of three years, or thereabouts, in that town.

He then moved away from the town with the aforesaid wife to another town and established residence there for a period of ten years. A group of witnesses from this town testified that they had not seen from this man, from the time he settled in the town, anything but goodness, amiability (*al-ʿāfiya*), trustworthiness, good faith (*amāna*), virtue (*faḍl*), and piety (*al-diyāna*). This became confirmed by the judge of that town, leading to the acceptance of his testimony. The judge would deliver rulings based on his testimony, concerning all manner of legal claims (*ḥuqūq*), and regularly employed him as a witness in passing judgments. The situation of the aforesaid man continued, as has been established, and as stated above, for five years or thereabout, during which time there arose no conflict concerning what had been established about the man in the first instance. The aforementioned judge still kept up with the affairs of this individual and sought to remain knowledgeable about his situation during the aforementioned period of years, during which no lack of piety was seen from him nor lapse found.

Concerning this man, however, the aforementioned judge was then presented with a legal deed (*ʿaqd*), containing testimony about himself, which stated that when he married a certain daughter of so-and-so (*fulāna bint fulān*) she was three-times divorced from him, and in no way not lawful for him to marry, since he had thereby forbidden her to himself. This woman was the one he was still married to, and had remained so close to fourteen years. The judge queried the man about the testimony in the aforementioned contract and the latter disavowed it. The judge then established the veracity of this disavowal. But several witnesses then testified that the script of the aforesaid contract was that of the man's own hand. So the judge summoned him again to respond to what had been testified against him (*aʿdhara ilayhi al-qāḍī fī-man shahida ʿalayhi bi-dhālika*). The man maintained that he had vindicating defense (*al-madāfiʿ*) by which their testimony against him would be dropped. The judge (*al-ḥākim*) thus, based on the man's claim, granted him a deferral [to substantiate his claim].

What – may God grant you prosperity – should the judgment concerning the testimony of this man be, if he is unable to substantiate the plea he claims to have, and it is ruled against him that the aforementioned divorce be implemented? Is he thereby recused (*yujraḥu*), his testimony rejected, and the marriages contracted in which he served as one of two witnesses invalidated? Or is he not recused as a witness on account of the existing jurisprudential disagreement concerning this question? Also, what should the ruling regarding his testimony be, if this man testifies during the period of deferral that was set for him, and he requests that a judgment be passed based on his testimony, and that it be implemented with its confirmation (*wa-l-mukhāṭaba bi-thubūtihā*). Does he have the right to this or not? Clarify this for us – may you be rewarded and granted success, if God so wills.

The answer: And [Ibn Rushd] – may God be pleased with him – answered to this question in this his text: I examined your question and informed myself about it. And if the veracity of what is in the deed that was presented to the judge concerning the aforesaid man is established by the testimony of the witnesses he employed, and the man is unable to present a defense to that, then, my opinion is that what is stated in the deed should be implemented, separating the couple.

This is what I consider the correct interpretation of the known doctrines of the school: That this does not constitute an invalidation (*jurḥa*) that nullifies his testimony, unless he corroborates the fact that he married her after he swore, under oath of irrevocable divorce (*al-ṭalāq al-batta*), that he would not remarry her, and that he did so believing this unlawful, as an insolence against God – may He be glorified and exalted. This is the case since, were he to corroborate the contract in the first place, saying that he married her, after irrevocable divorce under oath, only because he believed this to be permissible on account of the disagreement among scholars concerning this matter, he should then be forgiven for what he did. It thus does not constitute an invalidation that nullifies his testimony. This is especially the case if he has studied Islamic science (*naẓara fī al-ʿilm*) or heard ḥadith.

If it is possible (*iḥtumila*) that he married her after swearing by irrevocable divorce that he would not remarry her in this manner, and that he denied it under oath, only for fear of what would be determined against him by it, leading to the couple's separation, according to the prevalent doctrine of the school, then it is not acceptable that he be recused, based [merely] on a possibility (*bi-amr muḥtamal*). This is especially the case if his situation is as you described, and he is known for righteousness and prominence of integrity. And if the validity of the deed brought against him is established only by the testimony that is in his handwriting, then he is not to be judged by it if he disavows it, and the couple is not to be separated.

This is the case even if he is unable to provide an [exculpatory] plea against the testimony of those who testified that the contract was in his handwriting, because testimony of handwriting is not admissible in cases of divorce, manumission, marriage, or in any *ḥadd* case, according to what is stated by Ibn Ḥabīb in the *Wāḍiḥa*, among others. And were he to corroborate that he wrote it in his handwriting but claimed that he did not write it with the intention of implementing it on himself but that he wrote it only as consultation and study (for had he wanted to implement it on himself he would have done so), and that he never implemented the deed and brought no witnesses to testify to it, then he should be believed in this, according to what is stated in the *Mudawwana*, among others. And in God – may He be exalted – is success. He is peerless.

Translation of *Fatāwā Ibn Rushd* # 319, p. 1065–1068

Question 319. Concerning the weak and very ill (*kathīr al-amrāḍ*) man who wishes to remove a major ritual impurity with sand (*al-tayammum min al-janāba*) and to wipe (*masḥ*) over the turban. Should this be permitted of him? And does it matter whether the major ritual impurity (*janāba*) is lawful or unlawful?

And Ibn Rushd – May God be pleased with him – was written to (*khūṭiba*) from the capital city of Marrakesh, with a lengthy question in which he was asked about a weak and very ill man who, in performing his ablutions, wanted to transfer the obligation of wiping (*masḥ*) the head to wiping his turban, as well as, in his ritual cleansing (*al-ṭuhūr*), from performing the major ablution with water (*al-ghusl*) to cleansing with sand (*al-tayammum*). The text of the question from beginning to end is as follows:

In the name of God, the Compassionate, the Merciful, please give us your answer – may God be pleased with you – to a question concerning a man, weak of body and brain, who, when he wished to wipe his head to perform ablutions, found that this augmented his illness, catching the worst cold he'd ever caught. Given his situation, is it his obligation then to wipe over the turban without removing it or not?

Because of the aforementioned condition, he is afflicted by attacks of illness, exacerbating the weakness that bedevils him. When these crises afflict him, he is unable to perform ablutions with water, even if hot, and fears catching cold from the wind. Should he then cleanse himself with sand, being in the described condition, and is his obligation in it to cleanse with sand (*al-tayammum*) or not? Otherwise what should he do? Also, were he to have relations with his wife (*law aṣāba ahlahu*) while in this condition, should he cleanse his major ritual impurity with sand, so long as the condition persists? Does this suffice?

If the major ritual impurity has been incurred by touching his wife, then, as in the aforementioned case, and the individual has been unable to wash his head with water for three to four months, more or less, due to his weakness and fear of becoming ill by pouring water on his head, whether hot or cold, is it, then, his obligation, in this situation, to wash with water (*ghusl*) or, rather, to wipe (*masḥ*) his head without water and wash his body with water? Otherwise what should he do? Go over this for us, step by step – may you be rewarded, if God so wills.

We came across this problem – may God prolong your success –, and the jurists discussed it until it was complicated by the question of the effect of the man, in the condition described above, incurring the major ritual impurity through sin (*aṣabathu janābat*[un] *min maʿṣiyya*) – may God forgive us in His grace and compassion. The question became: what should be done then? Some of the jurists said: "He will have no dispensation (*rukhṣa*) in that." And they compared it analogically (*qāsuhā*) to the problem of the traveler who has traveled with unlawful design (*al-musāfir safara al-maʿṣiyya*), who may not shorten his prayers, nor break the fast, nor eat carrion (*lā yaqṣuru wa-lā yafṭuru wa-lā yaʾkulu al-mayta*) if obliged to.

Others said: "It is not like the question of the traveler traveling with unlawful design, and there is dispensation for him concerning the wiping of his head on the basis of the aforesaid weakness, regardless of whether the major ritual impurity was incurred lawfully or unlawfully." They continued: "This is because, concerning travel with unlawful design, shortening the prayer, breaking the fast, and eating carrion is prohibited in one of two accounts (*qawlayn*), only because thereby he may be heartened in pursuing the unlawful design upon which he is intent. The question of washing (*ghusl*), on the other hand, is not like this, since the unlawful behavior has concluded, and the wiping (*masḥ*) therefore becomes allowed (*murakhkhaṣ*), while he is not persisting in the unlawful behavior or has taken it up again. God is most knowing.

Clarify for us, by your favor, this last question as well – may you be rewarded – what is correct regarding it and explain that to us clearly – May God reward and bring you success, by His omnipotence and compassion. There is no lord but Him.

The answer: Ibn Rushd – God grant him success – answered to this, all of it, by this, his text: I have studied – God have mercy on us – this, your question, and have informed myself on it. There is no dispensation for this man, concerning what he described of weakness of body and brain, to wipe over his turban to perform ablutions (*wuḍūʾ*). This is the case almost under any circumstance, unless there is a wound on his head that prevents him from wiping in any way whatsoever, because the fears you described of what will afflict him are farfetched. For it is a temptation from Satan who should not be heeded.

When he has acted in this manner, it is obligatory that he perform ablutions and resume (*iʿāda*) prayer, always. Likewise, what you said of him being afflicted by crises, which exacerbate his weakness, making him unable to perform ablutions with water, whether hot or cold, fearing the wind, well, these are fears instilled by Satan and woe to him whose faith is corrupted by him! There is no dispensation whatsoever for him to commute his ablution to cleansing with sand in this situation. For this is not one of the difficulties from which God has chosen to unburden his servants in faith, when He said: "And laid on you no burdens of the faith."

As to he who has had relations with his wife (*aṣāba ahlahu*), in the first situation, and has the ability (*sāʿ*) to commute to cleansing with sand, fearing for himself when pouring water over his head, it is not permissible for him to wipe his head while washing the rest of his body. His ability to have relations with his wife, while in this condition, provides proof that the weakness of his body and brain have not brought him to the point in which he can't wipe his head with water in performing ablution.

In that manner, for one who has had relations with his wife, as in the second situation, and is afflicted by crises, exacerbating an existing weakness, cleansing with sand, fearing for himself when washing, is more excusable than is the case in the first situation.[2] And there is no difference concerning the requirement to wash (*ḥukm al-ghusl*) between whether this obligation was incurred through lawful or unlawful action. In God is success.

Translation of *Fatāwā Ibn Rushd* # 535, p. 1462–1464

Question 535. Concerning a Christian who converts and publicly professes Islam, about whom it is then learned that he remains Christian.

Mūsā b. Ḥammād, qāḍī of the capital city (*ḥaḍra*) of Marrakesh wrote to him – may God be pleased with him – from Marrakesh asking about a Muslim man about whom rumors were circulating that he professed the religion of the Christians, which lead to an investigation into the matter.

The text of the question is as follows: Please give us your answer – May God be pleased with you – to a question concerning a man who was a Christian, who then converted to and publicly professed Islam, and after which it was reported that he remained of the Christian religion, in spite of his public profession. This was much talked about, so it was taken to the ruler (*sulṭān*), which required an investigation of his actual circumstance. His house was inspected, and in it was found a room (*bayt*)

2 Ibn Rushd understands there being two medical conditions or individual situations implicit in the question. I am not sure I see that in the text, but the operative issue appears to be the time sequence between sexual relations and the crises or attacks (or just the head injury).

[decorated] like a church, in which there was a chamber (*ḥaniya*) facing east, more narrow than the rest of the room. There was no base for a bed in the chamber, and in it there was a hanging lamp and numerous relics (*āthār*) to which candles were attached. In his residence, books written in the Christian script and many candles were found, along with a board on four legs shaped like a stretcher (*maḥmil*), a staff with a crossing piece of wood at the top of a span of the hand or more in length, and small, flat, round pieces of bread which have dried, and each of which bore an impression.

Two witnesses who have knowledge of the conditions of the Christians and the matters of their law (*umūr sharaʿihim*) testified that the aforementioned candles were of the kind that Christians favor (*yataqarrabūna bihā*) and which they bring to their priest in order to light them in their services of worship (*mutaʿabbidihm*). They also testified that the board which is on four legs was of the kind upon which a priest of the Christians places the Gospel (*al-injīl*) when he reads it, that the staff at the top of which is a crossing piece of wood was of the kind upon which a priest leans for support when he stands to read the Gospel, and that the aforementioned flat and round pieces of bread were the oblations which the Christians favor (*tataqarrabūna bihi*) when they complete their fast and which are to be found only in the possession of one of their religious leaders (*ʿinda aʾimatihim*).

Do you think – may God perpetuate your good fortune – that the aforementioned things, which were found in the residence of this man in spite of what had been heard of his public profession of Islam and suppression of his Christian religion, are evidence (*dalāʾil*) by which judgment can be passed (*yuqḍā bihā*) regarding his apostasy, since he publicly professed Islam until what was stated above was discovered of him? Should he be tried for apostasy or not? Clarify this for us, may you be rewarded, if God so wills.

The answer: [Ibn Rushd] – May God grant him prosperity – answered regarding this saying: I have studied and considered your question. If it is not proven (*idhā lam yuthbatu ʿalā*) that this Christian, who converted to Islam and publicly and willingly (*ṭāʾiʿan*) professed Islam, conceals (*yusirru*) his Christianity and practices it, by means of just and incontestable proof (*bi-bayyina ʿādila lā madfaʿ lahu fīhā*), then judgment of execution should not be passed on him on account of the objects found in his house, which Christians use to practice (*yashraʿu bihi*) their religion, without calling on him to repent (*istitāba*) for being an apostate.

This is the case even if it is most likely (*ghalaba ʿalāʾ l-ẓann*) that these belongings (*asbāb*) were present in his house, that he practiced with them (*yatasharraʿu bihā*) according the religion of the Christians, and that they do not belong to other Christians sharing quarters with him, or to those who frequent him (*aw yantābihu minhum*), particularly because of what you said concerning the rumor that this man persisted in his Christianity, in spite of his public profession of Islam, and that this was much talked about. And this is because *ḥudūd* punishments of execution and others are not applied (*lā tuqām*) on the basis of hearsay (*bi-l-sammāʿ*) or preponderant likelihood (*bi-ghala-*

bat al-ẓunūn). They are only applied on the basis of just proof witnessed by Muslims (*bayyina ʿādila min al-muslimīn*).

Do you not think that if an account about a Muslim man spread that he has drunk wine (*shārib al-khamr*), that it was found in his house, in his possession, and on his table time and again, that the *ḥadd* punishment for the drinking of wine should not be applied, even if (*wa-la'inna*) there is preponderant likelihood of his having drunk it? Or do you not think that if accounts of a man spread that he committed adultery with a woman who is a known adulteress (*fājira maʿlūma bi-l-fujūr*), and that she was found with him in his house where his door was closed with her in it for a period of time, that the *ḥadd* punishment must not be applied to him, even if (*wa-in*) there is preponderant likelihood regarding his seclusion with her for a period of time in which he may have committed adultery with her?

[For this reason] only painful punishment (*al-ʿuqūba al-mūjiʿa*) must be applied to one accused in such a case. Likewise, punishment must be applied to the one about whom you asked, due to the suspicion cast upon him stemming from the finding of those belongings which you described in his house. And only in God exalted is good fortune, He is peerless.

Appendix C: Fatwās Chapter Two

Translation of *Fatāwā Ibn Rushd* # 189, pp. 802–805

Question 189. Concerning the question of the Amīr al-Muslimīn about the imāms Abū al-Ḥasan al-Ash'arī, Abū Isḥāq al-Isfarāynī, Abū Bakr al-Bāqilānī, Abū al-Walīd al-Bājī, and their colleagues, and the answer to this.

The question of the Amīr al-Muslimīn – God be pleased with him – to the judge Abū al-Walīd b. Rushd – God be pleased with him. What does the jurist and judge, the greatest and most unique (*al-ajall al-awḥad*), Abū al-Walīd – God bless him with His success and reward and may he pursue every good deed of His way – say concerning the shaykh Abū al-Ḥasan al-Ash'arī, Abū Isḥāq al-Isfaraynī, Abū Bakr al-Bāqilānī, Abū Bakr b. Fawrak, Abū al-Ma'ālī, Abū al-Walīd al-Bājī, and the likes of those who practice the science of *kalām*, speak of the origins of the religions/sects (*uṣūl al-diyānāt*), and write in answer to the people of whim (*ahl al-hawā'*). Are these [theologians] leaders of good sense and divine guidance (*a'immat rashād wa-hidāya*) or are they caids (*qāda*) of confusion and blindness (*ḥīra wa-'amāya*)? What is your opinion of the people who disparage (*yatanaqqasū*) and revile anyone associated with knowledge of Ash'arism, accuse them of unbelief, disclaim any association from them, and turn away from them in [holy] righteousness (*bi-l-walāya*)? Those who believe [the Ash'arite thinkers above] to be in error, rushing headlong into arrogance?

What should be said to, done to, and believed about [the above said Ash'arite thinkers]? Are they to be left to their own convenience? Or shall they forbear their excesses (*ghulwā'ihim*)? Does this [excess constitute] an invalidation of and a defect in their faith? Is prayer behind them permissible)? Or not? Clarify for us in comprehensive detail the value (*miqdār*) of the aforesaid leaders (*a'imma*), their place in the faith, and inform us about the position of those who disparage and turn away from them, as well as the position of those who entrust (*al-mutawwalī lahum*) and befriend them. May you be rewarded, if God exalted so wills.

The answer: Ibn Rushd – God have mercy on him – answered: I have examined – may God protect us – this your question and informed myself about it. And these 'ulamā' are leaders of good and right guidance (*khayr wa-hudan*), and are among those who must be emulated (*mi-man yajib bihim al-iqtidā'*), because they advocate the supremacy of the *sharī'a* (*qāmū bi-naṣr al-sharī'a*) and thwarted the likes of those who sow distortion and error. They clarified ambiguities and made clear to us what beliefs (*mu'taqidāt*) must be professed. For they, with their knowledge of the origins of faiths (*dīyānāt*) are learned in the Truth, by virtue of their knowledge in God (*li-'ilmihim bi-'Llāhi*) – lofty and sublime – what is owed Him, what is permissible to Him, and what concerning Him is [to be] refuted (*wa-mā yantafī 'anhu*). This is because the branches of knowledge become known with knowledge of the origins. It is incumbent, then, that their virtues be acknowledged and their eminence recognized (*sawābiq yuqarru lahum*). For they are those whom the Prophet – peace be upon him and God is most knowing – intended with his words: "This knowledge will be carried by the trustworthy ones in every generation. They will remove from it the distortions of the excessive ones, the false claims of the liars, and the false interpretations of the ignorant." For only an ignorant dolt (*ghabī jāhil*) or a heretic deviating from the truth would believe them to be in error and ignorance. And only the wicked (*fāsiq*) reviles and ascribes controversy to what they believe.

God – lofty and sublime – said: "Those who traduce believing men and believing women undeservedly shall bear the guilt of slander and grievous sin."[1] For the ignorant must be enlightened by them, the unrighteous disciplined, and the heretic, deviating from the truth –lead by his heresy– called to repent. If he does not repent, he should be beaten relentlessly until he repents, as ʿUmar b. al-Khattāb – God be pleased with him – did with Ṣabīgh, whose belief was under suspicion. ʿUmar beat him until Ṣabīgh said to him: "Oh Amīr al-Mu'minīn, if you intend to cure me, you have brought me to illness, and if you intend to kill me, finish me off." Then ʿUmar released him. I ask God for protection and success through His mercy. Said, Muḥammad b. Rushd.

Translation of *Fatāwā Ibn Rushd* # 265, pp. 943–945

Question 265. Concerning the question put forth in this collection of questions on the imāms (*a'imma*) Abī al-Ḥasan al-Ashʿarī and those like him – may God be contented with them.

And he was written to from the city of Fās, concerning Ashʿarism and those who have adopted their path, and after which a group (or movement) has been called (*wa-sammā lahu fīhi jamāʿa minhum*). The text of the question [reads as follows]: What does the *faqīh*, great judge, and one and only imām, Abū al-Walīd – may God bestow upon him His providing and success, and bring him into the full righteousness of His path – concerning the Shaykh Abī al-Ḥasan al-Ashʿarī, and Abū Isḥāq al-Isfarayni, and Abī Bakr al-Bāqilānī, and Abī Bakr b. Fawrak, and Abī al-Maʿālī, and Abī al-Walīd al-Bājī, and the likes of those who adopt dialectical theology (*ʿIlm al-Kalām*), and speak of the origins of religions/sects (*uṣūl al-diyānāt*), and write in answer to the people of whim (*ahl al-hawā'*). Are they leaders of good sense and divine guidance, or are they caids (*qāda*) of confusion and blindness? What is your opinion of those who insult and disparage them, and revile anyone assiciated with the school of Ashʿarism, accuse

1 Qur'ān 33: 58.

them of unbelief, disclaim any association with them, turn away from them in [holy] righteousness, and believe them to be in error and rushing into ignorance?

What should be said, done, and believed about them? Are they to be left to their own convenience or shall they forbear their excesses? Does this constitute an invalidation in their religion and defect in their faith? And is prayer behind them permissible or not? Clarify for us the value of the aforementioned leaders/imāms, their place in the faith, and inform us about the position of those who disparage and turn away from them, as well as the position of those who entrust and befriend them, generally.

The answer: So he – God have mercy – answered to that with this answer, and its text from beginning to its last letter: I have examined the question and informed myself about it. And these ʿulamāʾ are leaders of goodness and right guidance (*khayr wa-hudan*), and are among those who must be emulated (*mi-man yajibu bihim al-iqtidāʾ*), because they advocate the supremacy of the sharīʿa (*qāmū bi-naṣr al-sharīʿa*) and thwarted the likes of those who sow distortion and error. They clarified ambiguities and made clear to us what beliefs (*muʿtaqadāt*) must be professed. For they, with their knowledge of the origins of faiths (*dīyānāt*) are learned in the Truth, by virtue of their knowledge in God (*li-ʿilmihim bi-Llāhi*) – lofty and sublime – what is owed Him, what is permissible to Him, and what about Him is [to be] refuted (*wa-mā yantafī ʿanhu*). This is because the branches [of knowledge] become known with knowledge of the origins. It is incumbent, then, that their virtues be acknowledged and their eminence recognized (*sawābiq yuqarru lahum*). For they are those whom the Messenger of God – peace and blessings be upon him – intended with his words: "This knowledge will be carried by the trustworthy ones in every generation. They will remove from it the distortions of the excessive ones, the false claims of the liars, and the false interpretations of the ignorant." For only an ignorant dolt (*ghabī jāhil*) or a heretic deviating from the truth would believe them to be in error and ignorance. And only the wicked (*fāsiq*) reviles and ascribes controversy to what they believe.

God – lofty and sublime – said: "Those who traduce believing men and believing women undeservedly shall bear the guilt of slander and grievous sin."[2] For the ignorant must be enlightened by them, the unrighteous disciplined, and the heretic, deviating from the truth –lead by his heresy– called to repent. If he does not repent, he should be beaten relentlessly until he repents, as ʿUmar b. al-Khattāb – God be pleased with him – did with Ṣabīgh whose belief was under suspicion. ʿUmar beat him until Ṣabīgh said: "Oh Amīr al-Muʾminīn, if you intend to cure me, you have brought me to illness, and if you intend to kill me, finish me off." So ʿUmar released him. I ask God for protection and success through His mercy.

2 Qurʾān 33: 58.

Translation of *Fatāwā Ibn Rushd* # 297, pp. 1021–1027

Question 297. Concerning which of the two actions is more virtuous today? Is it the ḥajj (pilgrimage) or jihād for the people of al-Andalus and the ʿIdwa?

And the Amīr al-Muslmīn, Nāṣir al-Dīn ʿAlī b. Yūsuf b. Tāshufīn – may God perpetuate his rule and raise his victory – wrote to him – may God be pleased with him – asking: Is the ḥājj more virtuous for the people of al-Andalus or jihād? and the text of the question [reads as follows]: In the name of God, the Compassionate, the Merciful, God's blessings and peace upon our Sayyid Muḥammad and his family – your answer – may God be pleased with you – concerning those of the people of al-Andalus who have not performed the pilgrimage in this, our time: Is the ḥajj or jihād more virtuous? And how [does it affect your opinion if the individual] has already performed the obligatory pilgrimage (*qad ḥajja ḥajjat al-farīḍ*)? Go over what you think about this for us – may you be rewarded and granted success, if God so wills.

The answer: So he – may God perpetuate his success – answered to that through this text: I have studied – may God have mercy on us – this your question, and have informed myself on it. And the duty (*farḍ*) of the ḥajj has fallen/been removed from the people of al-Andalus in this, our time, because the ability [to perform it] is non-existent today, in the absence of the precondition (*sharṭ fī al-wujūb*) laid down by God that safe arrival in person and possessions must be assured. When the obligation of the pilgrimage has fallen because of this *ʿilla* (cause; ratio juris), it has become supererogatory [and] reprehensible (*makrūh*) because of the accumulation of dangers involved (*li-taqaḥḥum al-gharar fīhi*). It is therefore clear, from what we have said, that jihād, the merits of which are countless according to the Qurʾān, the Sunna (*mutawātir*), and the traditions (*āthār*), is more virtuous than [the ḥajj]. This is clear beyond any need for clarification.

The crux (*mawḍūʿ*) of the question, in fact, concerns [the issue of] one who has performed the duty of the pilgrimage and the path (*sabīl*) safely (*maʾmūnat^{an}*): Is pilgrimage for him more virtous than jihād? What I think (*aqūlu bihi*) is that jihād is more virtuous for him because of the great merit mentioned in its regard. And as to one who hasn't performed the duty of the pilgrimage and the path safely, this precludes (*yatakharraju dhālika ʿalā*) disagreement over the point of whether the pilgrimage should be performed immediately or postponed. And this [is so] when the obligation of jihād on individuals (*aʿyān*) has been removed by virtue of its performance by others. In places where it is specifically imposed upon individuals, on the other hand, it is more virtuous [a performance] than [fulfilling] the duty of pilgrimage, there being [only] one doctrine in disagreement (*qawl wāḥid li-l-ikhtilāf fī-hi*) concerning the issue of whether it [is an obligation that should be met] immediately or [at a] postponed [date]. And in God is success.

[Addendum] And from what he – may God be pleased with him – added/corrected in his answer when the Amīr al-Muslimīn asked him in Ceuta in the beginning of the year 515 [1121] about the people of the ʿIdwa, whether their status was like that of the people of al-Andalus concerning this [question]? So he said: Indeed, along with the people of al-Andalus, there are people of the ʿIdwa, whose route is the same as that of the people of al-Andalus, and they can only travel to (*lā yaṣilūna illā*) Mecca fearing for themselves and their possessions. [Even] when they don't fear for themselves and their possessions in traveling to Mecca, jihād remains for them, in my opinion, [an obligation] more virtuous [to fulfill] than hastening the pilgrimage, since it has been said that it may be deferred (*innahu ʿalā al-tarākhī*). And this is correct according to the school of Mālik – may God have mercy on him – and to which his *masāʾil* [opinions to questions of Islamic law] point. This concerns one who has been excepted (*ʿadā min*) from performing the duty of jihād. As to one who performs the duty of jihād for the protection (*min ḥimāt*) of the Muslims and their soldiers, jihād is incumbent upon him. Hastening of the pilgrimage is not specified as obligatory (*lā yataʿayyanu*) for [such a person], except when he has already engaged in battle. This is because the obligation to defer applies to a specific situation, which is when it appears preponderantly likely to the *mukallaf* (one legally capable) that [the opportunity] will slip away by its postponement. And the [age] limit for this is [according] to the words of the Messenger of God – peace and blessings upon him: "For the one fighting for my Umma between sixty and seventy [years of age]." And in God, may He be exalted, is success, He has no equal.

Translation of *Fatāwā Ibn Rushd* # 12, p. 175–176

Question 12. Concerning an individual who performs ablutions for each of his daily prayers, for a ritual impurity (*ʿan ḥadath*), but then remembers that he forgot to wipe his head and also doesn't know for which [set of] ablutions (*al-awḍiʾa*)?

And he – May God be contented with him – was asked a question, which came from al-ʿIdwa, concerning prayer, and it [reads as follows]: [Please give us] the answer – may God be pleased with you – [to a question] concerning a man who performed ablutions for morning prayer and prayed. Then he performed ablutions for an impurity (*ʿan ḥadath*) for noon prayers and prayed. Then he performed ablutions for an impurity for afternoon prayers and prayed. Then he performed ablutions for an impurity for sunset prayers and prayed, and then he performed ablutions for an impurity for dusk prayers (*li-l-ʿatama*) and prayed. While praying at dusk he remembered that he forgot to wipe his head. He's also not sure for which of the ablutions he left this out? He was told (*fa-umira*) to wipe his head and repeat the prayer, but he forgot to wipe his head and repeated all of the prayers without wiping. Give us you opinion in answer to this.

The answer: So he – may God assist him – answered: I have studied this, your question and considered it. If the man has already repeated all of the prayers after the ablutions he performed for the last prayers of the night (*li-ṣalāt al-ʿashāʾ al-ākhira*), summarily forgetting to do so before wiping his head as he was told to (by a local muftī: *qabla an yafʿala mā aftā bihi*), then he must perform his ablutions if these have been undermined (*intaqaḍa*), or [if the opportunity] to rectify his [ablutions] has escaped him. He must also repeat the last prayers of the night. This is because he prayed them twice, having performed one set of ablutions, [the completeness of which] he is doubted, [unsure of whether he] wiped his head. Prayer is only correct [when performed] in a state of certain purity. There is no [need to] repeat the other prayers, [however], because when he repeated the night's final prayers with [correctly performed] ablutions, all [other prayers] were obtained with complete purity, without doubt in them, since he either prayed each prayer with his second set of ablutions or with the [third set] he performed for the night's last prayers, he being certain that [at least] one of the two sets performed was complete. One of the two prayers performed is, therefore, correct. This is as the case of a man who performs ablutions for one of the day's prayers and prays, and then incurs an impurity and performs ablutions, but forgets that he has already prayed and so he prays a second time. When he completes his prayers, however, he remembers that he had already prayed. But then he remembers that he forgot to wipe his head, for one of the two performed ablutions (which one he isn't certain). [In this case] there is no [need for] repeating the [prayer or ablution] [as been established] by consensus, since one of the two prayers has been correct. And in God is success.

Translation of *Fatāwā Ibn Rushd* #122, p. 577–578

Question 122. Question concerning the shedding of blood (*tadmīya*).

And he – may God increase his esteem and elevate his memory – was written to from the ʿIdwa with this question, concerning bloodletting. Its text, from beginning to end, [is as follows]: In the name of God the Compassionate and the Merciful, your answer – may God be pleased with you – concerning a man who was killed by a group of four (*bayn arbaʿat*[i] *nafar*). It is unknown which of them killed him, and no one witnessed his killing except for one woman. Two of the four individuals exculpated the other two. And these two contested each other over who perpetrated the killing. Each said to his companion: "You killed him." The respective authority (*al-wālī*) incarcerated both of them under his jurisdiction/supervision (*bi-naẓarihi*). The remaining individuals were set free. Then the brother of the victim (*al-maqtūl*) came across (*raṣada*) one of the two individuals who were exculpated by his companions and killed him and spilt his blood (incriminated himself: *dammā ʿalayhi*). The blood-letting was confirmed by two trustworthy witnesses before the judge. And the victim's father began calling for the perpetrator's blood for killing his son. But the father of the first victim (*al-maqtūl al-awwal*) sued (*qāma*), claiming that the blood of his son, the first murder victim, was on this last murder victim, to which he brought forth the testimony of the aforementioned woman concerning his death at the hands of the aforementioned group of four. He swore fifty times as is required. Do you consider this permissible or not? Clarify this for us – may you be assisted and rewarded, if God so wills.

The answer: So he – may God grant him success – answered to this with the following response. Its text [reads as follows]: I have studied the question and considered it, and the judge's ruling (*mā ḥakama bihi*) that the father of the first victim swear fifty times by the right hand, based upon (*maʿa*) the testimony of the woman, is a mistaken one (*khaṭa' min al-ḥukm*). The only way such a ruling may take place, removing the stain (or discrediting doubt: *fī anna al-lawth lā yakūn*), other than basing it upon the testimony of a trustworthy witness, according to the *madhhab* of Ibn al-Qāsim and his transmission from Mālik, is by the swearing (*an yuqsima*) of the legal guardians/relatives (*awliyā'*) of the second murder victim to what has been established concerning the blood guilt of his killer (*min tadmīyatihi ʿalā qātilihi*), and that as a result they might kill him (*wa-yaqtulūhu*). Whereas according to the *madhhab* of those who consider the testimony of the woman to be a stain/discrediting doubt (*lawth*), the father of the first murder victim [must] swear before the relatives [of the second victim] (*maʿa wulātihi*) fifty times with the right hand that he killed their relative (*walīhimā*), by which they would become entitled to his blood, rendering null the suit of his own relatives who sued demanding blood for blood. And in God is success, He has no equal.

Translation of *Fatāwā Ibn Rushd* # 363, pp. 1155–1156

Question 363. A question on partition/division (*qisma*).

And he – may God be pleased with him – was written to from the ʿIdwa with a question on partition asking for an answer to it, and its text, from beginning to final letter, [reads as follows]: The answer – may God be pleased with you – concerning the people of some villages which were alternately abandoned and seized as inheritance (*aslamū ʿalayhā wa-taʿāwarathā wirāthat[an]*) among their sons and the sons of their sons after them, with the passing years. The people of the villages owned pastures (*masāriḥ*), but no one had precedence over other owners (*arbāb*) of the villages with regard to [their use]. Then, the descendants who inherited these lands agreed as a group, coming together in their opinion (*ittafaqa mala'uhum wa-ijtamaʿa ra'iyuhum*), to partition the pastures between them. They thus partitioned them, with the approval of all [involved], according to the calculation of their shares (*ʿalā ḥisāb ḥiṣaṣihim*). The judge of their region (*balad*) was present at the partitioning and put it into effect. The share (*ḥaẓẓ*) of each owner in the villages became specified and [publicly] known. Clarify – may God have mercy on you – for us whether or not this [act] of partitioning was permissible and effective (*nāfidha*)? Explain this to us – may God make your reward great, and make abundant your compensation through His mercy.

The answer: And he – God grant him success – answered to this with the following text: I – God have mercy on us – have studied this, your question, and have informed myself about it. If it is the case that those pastures which they partitioned are within their villages, and not outside of them, that they alone graze in them (*yanfaridūna bi-l-sarḥ fī-hā*), and that no one but them can graze there other than by entering through their villages, then the partitioning [of these pastures] is permissible and effective, according to what they agreed upon. [This is] because [the pastures] are [the villagers'] property no one of them has proof (or cause: *ḥujja*) for criticizing [the partition] since they approve of it. And in God, may He be exalted, is success, He has no equal.

Translation of *Fatāwā Ibn Rush* # 296, pp. 1017–1020

Question 296. Concerning a question from among the questions concerning illegal possession arising from plunder (*al-ghaṣb*).

An Almoravid man of the Desert Mulaththāmūn (veiled ones) asked him – may God be contented with him – a question concerning the plunder taking place among them, and the text of the question [reads as follows]: The answer of the great jurist (*faqīh*) – may God prolong your success – concerning a group of tribes who winter in the desert [and] who plunder each other's possessions, which consist only of cattle. The aforesaid practice of plundering property has been a long-standing one with their fathers and grandfathers. And they have passed on these possessions, plundered from each other and not [rightfully] theirs.

Is it permissible (*hal yasūghu*) for someone owning lawful property – one who is untainted by anything unlawful, has avoided [compromising] legal consequences (*rāgha ʿan al-tibāʿāt*), and has strived for piety (*arāda al-tawarruʿ*) –, is it permissible (*yajūzu*) or not for him to purchase some of this plundered property (*min dhālika al-māl al-maghṣūb*)? And [is it permissible] for the aforementioned group (*qawm*) to offer [as a gift] the Amīr al-Muslimīn and Nāṣir al-Dīn – may God assist him – some of those camels (*ibil*), plundered from each other? Is it permissible or not, for one striving for piety, to receive some of those camels when the Amīr al-Muslimīn bestows them upon him? And is it permissible or not for [the Amīr al-Muslimīn] – may God assist him – to reward (*yuthību*) them for their gift from the treasury of the Muslims (*bayt al-māl al-muslimīn*)? And [what when] they offer to the commander (*amīr*) who was appointed to rule over them (*amarahu ʿalayhim*) by the Amīr al-Muslimīn – may God assist him – and who thus like them is in illegal possession of such plunder, and then that commander offers to the Amīr al-Muslimīn – may God assist him – [a gift] of those plundered camels, is it permissible or not for any one to accept it when given to him by the Amīr al-Muslimīn – may God assist him? And what would [the fact] that the aforementioned group only plunders from those who plunder from them or their fathers [entail for the ruling]? Clarify this question and explain it to us – may you be rewarded and thanked, if God, glorified and exalted, so wills.

The answer: So he – may God be pleased with him – answered [this question] stating: I have studied – God protect us – this, your question, and have informed myself about it. If the cattle in the possession of this group of tribes was inherited by them from their fathers and grandfathers, as you mentioned, and it is in origin [the product] of plunder, and today, because of the great length of time (*li-qidam al-ʿahd*), the owners from whom the cattle was usurped – and in consequence did not inherit it – are unknown, and [if] it is impossible to return [these cattle] to their specific owners, or any portion thereof to its specific owner out of ignorance of who that person is, then let it be judged to be in the [rightful] possession of those who possess it, as you mentioned, by inheritance from their fathers and grandfathers. [This property will thus be] deemed as "found" (*ḥukm al-luqṭa*), once specified (*baʿd al-tarīf bihā*) and once hopes for finding its [original] owner have been despaired of.

About this the Messenger of God – peace and blessings of God upon him – said to the one who found it: "Do as you like with it." It is thus preferable for them to donate it as alms. This is not incumbent upon them, however, as a legal obligation (*farḍ wājib*), especially since [the cattle] itself was not plundered, but is, rather, the offspring [of the plundered cattle]. It is thus permissible for whomever wishes to do so, to buy some of it.

And [as to] that which was given [as a gift] to the Amīr al-Muslimīn – may God perpetuate his days – [and which] he has then bestowed upon someone [else,] it is permissible for whom it was bestowed to receive it. And it is lawful for him to own it. He incurs no sin (*ithm*) or interdiction (*ḥaraj*) through this – if God so wills, may He be glorified and exalted. The Amīr al-Muslimīn – may God perpetuate his days – has the right to reward, from the treasury of the Muslims, one who has presented him with some of this [cattle as a gift], since he only receives this [gift] in order to spend it for the benefit of the Muslims.

And as to what is given [as a gift] from this [cattle] to the holder of an office (*li-wālī*) appointed by the Amīr al-Muslimīn, for him it is not permissible to accept it from them, due to what has been said about "the gifts of commanders are malicious (*ghalūl*)," unless he reimburses it (*yukāfiʾu ʿalayhā*). If he reimburses with a value equal to it, [by means of] a reward, and he gives some of it [as a gift] to the Amīr al-Muslimīn – may God perpetuate his success and sanction – and gives it [the rest] to someone, this giving is sound and permissible for him. [This remains so] whether the usurpers of this cattle usurped it from someone who has not usurped from them or for one who has or from their fathers before them. Since the tribe has plundered the tribe, each individual does not know that he took specific property [or] to whom particular property has gone.

And as to the question of [what] if this group with the cattle in its possession has plundered it themselves or have inherited it from their fathers and grandfathers before them, who may or may have not plundered it, [and] they know its owner, from whom it was plundered, and they can return [the property] to them specifically (*bi-aʿyānihim*), or to their inheritors, then it is absolutely and specifically incumbent upon them to return [the property] to its owners, since it is unlawful for them to keep any of it. If they do not do [this] and they keep [the property], then it is unlawful for anyone to buy from them any of [this cattle]. Gifts from [this group] or from whomever it winds up with, are not to be accepted, whatever the circumstances of how [this particular person] ends up with the [property]. For if [he, the person accepting the stolen property] does the like of this, knowing the [circumstances], he shall be judged in this the judgment of plunder. And in God is success, He has no equal.

Appendix D: Fatwā Chapter Three, The Case of the Gardeners vs. the Miller

Madhāhib al-ḥukkām fī nawāzil al-aḥkām
Kitāb al-miyāh, p. 109–121

1 Introduction

Question concerning irrigation with water through a path (*maḥajja*) and who is more entitled to it, mill or orchards (*wa-man aḥaqq bihi al-arḥā aw al-jannāt*). Should the water be held/sequestered/damed or not? Where should it be diverted if it must be held/sequestered? Is its sequestration lawful when one of the litigants forgoes/relinquishes it? Is it allowed to flow (*inbaʿatha*) after [revising] the decision, [since] it prescribes something different [from the original]?

[Alternative translation: Question concerning irrigation with water in the commons, and who is more entitled to it, mill or orchards. Should it be rationed or not? Where should it be diverted if it must? Is its rationing lawful when one of the litigants forgoes it? Is a decision contrary to customary use to be put into effect (*inbaʿatha*)?]

The judge of Ceuta and its districts, ʿAbbūd b. Saʿīd, declared (*ashhada an*) that a *muḥtasib* came before him and told him that ʿAbd al-Salām b. Fulān channeled the water know as the water of al-Sayyāj to such and such (*kadhā*) a place across a road of the Muslims and that he had dug across it to the detriment of passersby. The *muḥtasib* showed him a document (*ʿaqd*) he transcribed/wrote (*nasakhathu* [*yaduhu*]), in which the witness cited at the bottom of the document declare to know that the water known as the water of al-Sayyāj of the village (*qarya*) of Balyūnsh does not pass through the orchards (*janān*) of Ibn Hudhayl, that it never ran across the road that goes to the mill, that ʿAbd al-Salām caused this [diversion], and that the water had wrecked the way (*al-ṭarīq*) to the detriment of passersby. It was thus declared at the end of the document. The judge verified in the record (*al-sijill*) the probity (*al-ʿadāla*) of the mentioned witnesses and stated that he summoned and informed the defendant of the claim. The defendant admitted to diverting the water and claimed entitlement to it by judicial decision (*bi-ḥukm ḥākim*), to have possessed it for a long time. He claimed that the witnesses who testified against him, did so tendentiously, in order to benefit themselves from this water for their own use in irrigation, since, he claimed, they had now seen the water flowing [to ʿAbd al-Salām's property] for over twenty years without challenging him. The defendant (*al-marfūʿ*) presented evidence in response. The judge says in the record that the defendant presented a document containing [mention of] the water's flow across the lane (*al-zuqāq al-madhkūr*) and its entering ʿAbd al-Salām's orchard. The judge states that he did not admit the testimony of this document's witnesses because some of them, in his opinion, were ignorant of the circumstances, others were disqualified (*jurḥat ākharīn*). Because of a defect, the judge found the document invalid. He also stated that he personally knew for a fact that ʿAbd al-Salām was related to al-Barghawāṭī, whence no one had dared contest him. The judged stated that he repeatedly deferred the deadline for ʿAbd al-Salām who produced nothing worthy of consideration. So the judge withdrew ʿAbd al-Salām's ability to present evidence (*ʿajazahu*) and judged that he cut the flow of the water, prohibiting its flow across the way/road (*al-ṭarīq*) at any time. The judge also also stated in the record that the defendant had wanted to build an underground canal for the water in question, covered so that it harm no one. The judge stated that he knew with certainty through testimony [of witnesses] he summoned that such a canal was liable to break and the water spread, harming the walls of the country's neighboring orchards, and with the rise/spread of the water, it was feared the walls would collapse.

2 Questions Concerning these Sections/Points (*Fuṣūl*)

Note – may God bestow honor upon you (*aʿazzaka Allāh*) – the sections of this record. Forty years later, a party unrelated to the party found guilty (*al-maḥkūm ʿalayh*) demanded that the water be allowed to flow to irrigate their orchards. They were obliged to do this because the water with which they had been irrigating had run dry. They claimed to have irrigation rights to this water. They supported this claim with the testimony of trustworthy witnesses (*shahādat ʿudūl*) according to whom they had used the water for many years prior to – and even after – the aforementioned judge's decision to cut its flow through the road. They claimed to have farmed with it. And they claimed that, for the most part, only through the road where the water's flow was condemned could make water reach [their orchards].

The record refers only to the decision regarding ʿAbd al-Salām's orchard and no one else is mentioned. At the beginning of the witnesses' testimony, however, you can see that ʿAbd al-Salām was said to be responsible for diverting the water down a path through which it had never run. Note the testimony and words of the witnesses [who testified against Abd al-Salām] that "it never ran through it." Is their testimony therefore inadmissible, according to what you know, or is the judge (*al-ḥākim*) to uphold its validity (*yaḥkumu bi-maḍiyhi*)? And if true [and therefroe upheld], does it replace the testimony of those who testified to the irrigation [rights] of the second group [who made their claim forty years later]? Or, [would the latter group's] adding that ʿAbd al-Salām was the causer apply to them and invalidate their evidence (*qāṭiʿat^{un} bi-ḥujajihim*)? Do you think – may God bestow honor upon you – that the [prior] decision and record apply to the entire area of [the orchards of] Hudhayl (*ḥattā yajʾara mawqiʿ al-ḥukum bi-taḥdīd hudhayl*), whose present delimitation and usucaption (possession by long use or occupation) has not been established?

The witnesses also said that [the water] had never run through the road leading to the disputed land and orchards. There is only one path leading from the orchards of Ibn Hudhayl to the orchards of the aforementioned [ʿAbd al-Salām]. Does their saying "it never ran," along with the judge's decision against its diversion through the said road, prevail, when [the latter] doesn't mention the orchards of Ibn Hudhayl [explicitly]? For, as you can see, the testimony implies [that the lands in question are located] beyond the orchards of Ibn Hudhayl. The testimony implies thus that the land in question falls outside of that belonging to Ibn Hudhayl; and they testified precisely to this effect.

Or is there, rather, a contradiction, or an imprecision regarding location in the testimony? Think all of this over – may God bestow honor upon you – and give your opinion of what should be done and how – may God honor you.

[What's more], a wall belonging to the aforementioned judge lay on this path about which he heard testimony regarding the damage the water would inflict on the walls of its orchards. What would be the case if [new] testimony established that this wall had deep foundations and would, in the most part, be unlikely to suffer damage?

And what – God honor you – if the record and the delimitation of the orchards of Ibn Hudhayl are upheld against the interest of [the current claimants], thereby inflicting damage on their orchards and irrigation needs, there being no other water source around them? Is the damage to [the orchards] to have prevalence over the damage to the road in consideration of the [principle of] lesser of two damages? Especially if it is established that the road is now paved in stone, and that the only damage resulting from the water's flow would be that pedestrians would get their feet wet and the like.

What if a water source, feeding into the aforementioned water, appeared in the orchard after [Abd al-Salām's] decision, and they said this source was not included in the decision? Is the decision to be applied to it, as it was to the other, that its flow through the road be cut? Or does this require the reopening of the case?

What if they proposed to dig and reinforce a canal for the water? Should this be allowed, when the witnesses in the record testified as you can see and the judge (*al-ḥākim*) prohibited people other than themselves [from diverting the water through the road]?

Answer us in all of this, point by point.

And what – God bestow honor upon you – if the claimants bought recently? Did those who sold them the land do so ignorant of the litigation, as their plea (*iʿdhār*) does not appear in the record? Do they therefore lose their claim to the water? Or do they not, on account of the testimony to the continued use of this water to irrigate these orchards, and to their having bought the orchards with rights and yields (*bi-ḥuqūqihā wa-manāfiʿihā*)? Or do they not lose the claim to the water on account of their need to irrigate? Explain this to us. May you be rewarded, God willing, may He be exalted.

3 The Answer

I have – may God bestow honor upon you with His pity and take you into His magnanimity – studied your question and considered it carefully. I have already answered to some extent one of your questions in a previous consultation: If you establish that the judge ordered that the flow of the water, through the road to the orchard, be cut, that this was verified by the presiding judge with unimpeachable evidence, that there was no counter evidence favoring the orchard owners, and that there is no other road, then their irrigation rights are invalidated. This is not the case, however, if the document's witnesses, who established the possibility of damage before the judge (*al-ḥākim*), were recusable. In which case the orchard owners are the party that is more entitled to the water to irrigate their orchards in times of need.

If a thorough verification of the ruling (*al-ḥukm*) – without which usucaption of the place to which the water was cut cannot be properly established – is impossible, since, as you mentioned, the document states that the water doesn't reach the orchards of Ibn Hudhayl, and because of the uncertainty of the land's precise delimitation, and because no one has had usucaption of it, and [lastly] because of the [overall] ambiguity of the issue (given that the document states that the water never ran through the path to the mill), then the record must no longer be taken under consideration. It is to present no evidence in favor of the owners of the mill. The case (*al-amr*) is to be reopened, and the owners of the orchards are not to be prevented from channelling water through the road to irrigate their orchards, upon which they depended for their farming [to begin with]. This is unless the damage to the passersby is [too] great.

It is also not possible to bury the water or reinforce its course because, as you mentioned, the path has been paved in stone. In God is success. Said Muḥammad b. Rushd.

4 Second Answer to this Question

I have thought – may God give us health and inspire us with what is right – of and have informed myself on all the points of [your question]. I found the testimony patently contradictory and to contain elements that were added to the original, all of which demands that the case be reopened and independently rethought (*iʿmāl al-ijtihād*), may it be favored by God most high. And with what you said regarding the suspicion cast on the judge because one of the walls of his orchard [was involved], the slightest suspicion involving or witnesses invalidates both testimony and decision.

Another aspect to be considered is that a decision affecting a particular individual does not transfer to another. Also, in the event that two damages occur, and neither [party] has the prerogative (*al-maziya*), then the lighter of the two prevails.

In the question there are [several] points that call for reopening the case. This is what is evident to me, but God is most knowing and He grants success through His compassion. May the peace and compassion of God most high be with you.

Muḥammad [b. ʿIyāḍ] adds:

This answerer was the only one to comment on the suspicion cast upon the judge, because the section asking him what would be the case were there testimony to the deep foundation of the wall so that in the most part it would be unharmed, was dropped from his copy of the question.

5 Third Answer to this Question

The judge's (*al-ḥākim*) decision in this matter remains effective and to be carried out to its completion (*maḥmūl ʿalā al-kamāl*). Said Muḥammad b. Ismāʾīl.

6 Fourth Answer to This Question (as well as an answer to the second question which follows)

I have informed myself, dear sir – may God help you with what He has entrusted you and give us the happiness of salvation through His compassion – of this question and of the following one and have thought about it at length. What Judge ʿAbbūd b. Saʿīd – God have mercy on him – recorded is effective, in force, and contains nothing objectionable. In God is success. Said Muḥammad b. Aḥmad b. al-Ḥājj.

7 Second Question on a Point of this Case

And answer us also – may God bestow honor upon you – on the following point of the case: for a man here built a mill on the waters, gathered and channeled (*al-mujtamaʿa al-maṣrūfa*) away from the road, with which he milled on the days of winter. When it was summer, however, the owners of the orchards challenged (*nāzaʿūhu*) [his use of the water]. He in turn challenged them, after testimony had been presented in their favor in what preceded. While the record prevented [the orchard keepers from diverting the water], and while the damage or benefit they incurred through their testimony didn't concern him, he remained silent. When something was conceded to [the orchard owners] regarding this [case], however, the mill owner challenged them stating: "I gained possession (*ḥuztu*) of this water to your disadvantage, especially that produced after the decision. I have built and incurred expenses on this water. Your challenging me, and your use of it in irrigation, is in violation [of the ruling], as it was prohibited that you use it."

What if those who built on, and were in possession of, the water before the miller testify in his favor? And what if he corroborates their testimony (*shahida lahum huwa bi-sabaqihim minhu qabl bināʾihi*)?

What if whoever testified in favor of the orchard owners did so out of self-interest (*in dafaʿa fī-man shahida lahum*), just because of the damage to their orchards and their need for irrigation? Does their need of water prevail over his use (*manfaʿa*) for milling? Or is he more entitled? Is his claim to the water before the decision equal to that after it, or is it different? Answer us what you think, with success, God willing.

8 Answer to the Second Question

If it is established that [the owners of the orchards have indeed possessed] what you have mentioned, or that it was thus judged (*quḍiya*) in their favor, then they are the party that is more entitled. The water is theirs use as long as they do so, and as long as the miller was not in possession of it for a long-enough period of time, during which he would have been able to deny them use of it, and they kept silent, and thus can't justify their silence with the aforementioned decision or other. In such a case they would have equal rights [to the water]. God grants success with whaat is right, in His compassion.

9 Second Answer to this Question

I have studied and informed myself on the question posed above. The owners of the orchards are more entitled to the water to irrigate their orchards than the millers, in any case, because of their need to irrigate. In God is success. Said Muḥammad b. Rushd.

10 Third Answer to this Second Question

The record prevents them [from using the water]. I ask God for success through His compassion. Said Muḥammad b. Ismāʿīl.

Muḥammad [b. ʿIyāḍ] adds:

Judge Abū ʿAbd Allāh b. al-Ḥājj answered this question above, in his answer to the first question.

11 Third Question Concerning a Point of this Case

And what do you think – may God bestow honor upon you – of the judge's decision to confiscate the water (*ḥakama bi-ʿaqlihi*) while he studies the case and sets deadlines (*muddat al-naẓar wa-ḍarb al-ājāl*)? Is this necessary because of the judge's decision to cut the water's flow through the road, or is it not? Does this confiscation, if necessary, mean changing the water's course away from the owner of the mill and the orchards, since the purpose of confiscation is having the challenger withdraw the disputed object from the defendant (*min yad al-maṭlūb*) while the latter's right to the object is at issue (*tawajjaha ḥaqq al-maṭlūb ʿalā al-ikhtilāf*)? Or does confiscation in this matter have a different approach (*wajh ākhar*), since the dispute [here] is not over the mill itself, which would entail confiscating the profit (*fa-tuʿqalu al-ghalla*)? Here on the other hand, they are just disputing the use of the water, so this is what must be taken from the hands of the defendant, who will then be unable to claim it until the case is closed, if God, the most high, wills it.

12 Answer to this Third Question

Contradiction in the preceding testimony requires wholesale confiscation and diversion to where the judge (*al-ḥākim*) sees fit, either by renting it at cost agreed upon with whomever is most likely to receive it in judgment, or however is seen fit. In God is success.

Muḥammad [b. ʿIyāḍ] adds:

Judge Abū al-Walīd b. Rushd says that the water should not be confiscated, as he mentions below in his answer to the following question. He describes the resulting decision, God willing.

13 Another Answer on All Previous Points of this Case

If the judge (*al-ḥākim*) is properly qualified (*min ahl al-ʿilm*) then his decision is effective and decisive confronted with the disagreement and hazard to which you point. The damage inflicted upon the road of the Muslims must be removed. In God is success. Said Mūsā b. Ḥammād.

14 Fourth Question Concerning this Case

Please answer – may God grant you success – [this question] concerning a judge's decision to cut water flowing through a road of the Muslims that lies between orchards after it was established that this caused damage to passersby, that a particular person (*fulān*) diverted it through that road, and that it had never flowed through the road before. The resulting enforceable decision was passed on this one person (*ʿalā fulān waḥdihi*), preventing the water from flowing through the road in his direction.

Forty years after this decision, a group of people sued to irrigate their orchards with this water, claiming they had a right to it, that the decision was passed on one particular person, that the only way for said water to benefit them was through the aforementioned road (through which the judge ordered the water cut), and that that particular person had made the water run through it. They testified (*athbatū*) that they continued to irrigate their orchards with this water for a period of time that was long enough to suggest that they irrigated with the water before the judgement, and after it up to this day. They claimed that the witnesses who had testified in the document to the damage and cause (upon which the judge based his decision) acted out of self-interest (*al-madāfiʿa*). The more so as no plea (*iʿdhār*) is recorded for any of them excepting the individual upon whom judgement was passed.

Two years ago, a mill was built on the water, [flowing] through a different way. The owner of this mill challenged the evidence furnished by the orchard owners. He used the water for his mill after the decision, which was testified to. And he claimed that those who testified in favor of the orchard owners' right to use this water in irrigation did so in self-interest (*ṭalaba al-madāfiʿa fī-man shahida lahum*).

Should the water to the mill and to the orchards be cut until judgment is passed (*yufṣalu fīhi*), the deadlines have passed, and its course altered? Or does [the fact that] the judge passed judgement on some [of the parties involved] prevent this (unless they present evidence of something in which there is no self-interest involved, God willing)?

15 The Answer to this Fourth Question

I have studied and thought about the question. The judge's decision is not to be rejected because the orchard owners testified to their continued irrigation with the water, before and after the decision up to this day. There is no way for them to irrigate with it, unless they substantiate that there will be no damage inflicted by that on the road with evidence that has greater probity than that upon which the judge based his decision, or the witnesses who established before the judge the possibility of damage are recusable, or they are able to prevent such damage by reinforcing the water's course, in such a way that it can be known that the damage has been suppressed. In this case, they will be the party more entitled to the water to irrigate their orchards in time of need, even if the orchards appeared after the mill was built. It is also unnecessary to hold the water during the litigation, until the deadlines expire, in the way that disputed objects are (*al-shay' al-mudda' fīhi*), since it is not something that is owned. It is rain that only God gives people to drink and that only He distributes among them. The approach to the decision then is to give each individual owner of mills and orchards right to the water while the others are summoned to present their plea (*fī mudda al-i'dhār ilā aṣḥābihim*), instead of cutting it off from all of them at once. [Right to irrigate] should move from person to person as the summons to plea moves from person to person, and as they furnish evidence against each other. In God is success. Said Muḥammad b. Rushd.

Muḥammad [b. 'Iyāḍ] adds:

An opinion before this called for cutting off the water completely, stating that was the correct approach to the judgement.

16 Second Answer to this Question

If what you said concerning the judge's decision to cut the water's flow through the road on account of the damage inflicted on the passersby is thoroughly established – without there being self-interest in the witnesses statement to the judge (*a'dhara ilayhi*) [to bar the water from the road] – then the water must be held, eliminating any objections. In God is success. Said Muḥammad b. Aḥmad al-Ḥājj.

17 Fifth Question Concerning a Point in this Matter

And what – may God bestow honor upon you – if the testimony of the witnesses produced by the orchard owners contradicts the testimony of those who testified in the judgment's record, which stated that [the water's] diversion was caused [by someone] as stated above. Which [testimony] prevails? Do you think that [the principle] of the lesser of two damages applies here, since the damage inflicted on the orchards through the withering of its fruits, especially when the other water they used to irrigate has run dry during this period, is harsher and greater than the damage inflicted on the road's passersby by wetting their feet and sandals and dirtying their clothes with the splashing water. Should this be taken into consideration, even if they don't prove their right to the disputed water, when they have, however, proven their need and the other water they used to irrigate has run dry? Answer us concerning this, may you be rewarded.

18 The Answer to this Fifth Question

I have studied and thought about the question, and think that the testimony of the witnesses of the judgment's record remains effective. The testimony of the orchard owners to their irrigating with the water before and after the judgment should be disregarded, since their use of it before the judgment is made void by the judgment, but not their use of it after. And, in my opinion, this is not a matter of the greater of two damages prevailing, because of how it would affect the rights of the mill owners. In God is success. Said Muḥammad b. Rushd.

19 Second Answer to this Fifth Question

What was established by the judge's decision (*ḥukm al-qāḍī*) remains effective in removing the damage, God willing. Said Muḥammad b. Aḥmad b. al-Ḥājj.

20 Sixth Question on a Point of this Case (*Nāzila*)

May God give lasting success to the most illustrious jurist (*faqīh*), give him long life, impress in him His beauty, and give him the good things of this life and the next. My letter contains these questions which I would like answered, [may you] be rewarded and thanked, God willing. And – God bestow honor upon him – it is that a group of orchard owners sued a miller (*rajul min ahl al-arḥā'*) for cutting water off from their orchards when they were in need of irrigating with it and using it. So the mill owner claimed they had no right to it, and that his mill had made previous usucaption of the water, and that he built and milled on it for many years. Prior to this, the group produced testimony that they used to irrigate their orchards with the water before and after the mill was built. The mill owner asked for an investigation into the testimonies and the self-interest involved. So I cut off the water to the mill and the orchards, [diverting] it in another direction, and set a deadline for the mill owner to present documentary evidence (*al-bayyināt*).

What do you think should be done if the period for which the owners of the orchards demanded irrigation and water use expires before the deadline [set for the miller to produce evidence of] self-interest. And the owner of the mill asked for the confiscation to be dissolved, arguing that those suing him only did so for the period of irrigation and pressing, that outside of that time the water should flow to his mills, that they had no claim or need in the new period, and that their challenge to him was limited to that other time.

Should he be heard and must the confiscation be dissolved, while they remain claiming what they argued for? For whether or not their lawsuit expires after another year, should the water be held again when it is irrigation time again next year? Or do you think the confiscation remains effective until their lawsuit is complete, since they argued that the water was something to which rights were disputed, and therefore, which should not remain in the possession of our adversary until the lawsuit is concluded. Explain this and be rewarded, God willing.

21 The Answer to this Sixth Question

I have studied and considered you question. The orchard owners are more entitled to irrigate their orchards than the owner of the mill, even if they planted (*ansha'ū*) their gardens after the miller built his mill. When they are no longer in need to irrigate, the miller can channel the water to his mill. This is what I think and say concerning this question, based on its sense as it appears in the ḥadīth of the Prophet (the peace and blessings of God be upon him) concerning the flow of Mahzūr and Mudhaynab, because he judged (*qaḍiya*) that upstream users take water up to the ankles and then send it downstream. Therefore since [the Prophet] (the peace and blessing of God be upon him) didn't, on any account, allot the entirety of the water to upstream users excluding downstream users, so the mill owners should on no account take exclusive possession of the water for their mills, excluding the orchard owners, even if the latter were upstream and even if the [millers] built before the [garden owners]. What is left to be resolved, then, concerns what you asked about confiscation and summoning [the parties to present their pleas] (*al-tawqīf wa-l-iʿdhār*). In God is success. Said Muḥammad b. Rushd.

Muḥammad [b. ʿIyāḍ] adds:

This answer is the same Ibn Rushd gave to questions seven and eleven below.

Second answer to this sixth question:

The owners of the mill have the right to use (*al-intifāʿ*) the water during this season in which the orchard owners have need of it. When irrigation time comes, if the mill owner can't prove that the testimony of the orchard owners was self-interested, then what they established [as their need] should be adjudicated to them. In God is success. Said Muḥammad b. Aḥmad b.al-Ḥājj.

Seventh question concerning a point of this case:

Consider – may God bestow honor upon you – [what should be done] when the mill owner has recused all of the witnesses except for one, the [orchard owners] claim they can produce other witnesses ready to testify, and the owner of the mill claims that the remaining witness also testified in self-interest and asks that the confiscation be dissolved based on the the legal doctrine that just one witness is insufficient for the purpose. Should this be judged in his favor, or should the confiscation not be dissolved, according to the two maxims, unless all of them are recuse, since it is a decision that remains in effect? And thus no contrary decision, against implementing the decision to confiscate, should be taken, unless all the witnesses are recused. God suffices me.

The answer to this seventh question:

I studied and considered your question, and what I answered to the previous question applies to this one. In God is success. Said Muḥammad b. Rushd.

Muḥammad [b. ʿIyāḍ] adds:

He means the sixth question, above.

A second answer to the seventh question:

If the matter has proceeded as you have described, then the confiscation would be lifted according to the doctrine that requires two witnesses, and it would remain effective according to the doctrine that deems one witness [sufficient]. The first doctrine conforms to current judicial practice (*ʿalā al-qawl al-awwal jarā al-ʿamal wa-maḍā al-ḥukm*). This of course, in so far as confiscation is the correct approach. In God is success. Said Muḥammad b. Aḥmad b. al-Ḥājj.

Eighth question concerning a point of this case:

And may he – may God grant him success – give an answer concerning this case. If an upright (*ʿādil*) judge has judged the flow of water across a road for irrigation by owners of some orchards should be cut off because of the damage inflicted on the road. [And it was established] that someone caused this diversion and the judgment was passed on that person who caused [the diversion]. None of the litigating (*al-qāʾimīn*) [orchard owners] mentioned above appear [in the record], nor do those who sold [them the land], since most of [the litigating orchard owners] bought [their land] after the decision and summons to plea (*al-iʿdhār*). So the plaintiffs (*al-qāʾimūn*) argue now that the decision is not binding on them, since it was unknown to them and to those who sold to them. They bought the orchards with rights. The owner of the mill argued that those who sold the land or owned it back then had no water rights and that no one except those the judge mentioned and summoned could have had rights. For how then would he have found the man guilty (*al-maḥkūm ʿalayhi*) of causing the diversion? And why then did those who sold [the land] did not oppose the decision?

What if they claim that the road now has been repaired so that no damage will be inflicted on it, that it is different from when the judgment was passed? What if another [water] source has appeared in this road after the judgment? Does the judgment apply to it or is the case reopened? God gives success in the correct through His compassion.

The answer to this eighth question:

I have studied and thought of your question at length. And if the presiding judge established his decision to cut the flow of the water to the orchards through the road, because of the damage therein inflicted, through trustworthy evidence, containing no [demonstrable] bias (*madfaʿa*) in favor of the orchard owners, and there being no other road, then their right to the water is nullified. [This shall be the case] unless in their plea they offer to suppress the damage to the road by reinforcing the water's course in such a way that it is [clearly] known that the damage has been eliminated, or they furnish evidence of greater probity than that upon which the decision was based, that no such damage to the road exists. Or, they recuse the witnesses of the document upon which the judge personally established the [existence of] the damage. In these cases, they are more entitled to irrigate their orchards because of their need. If a water source appeared in the road after the decision, then [the case should be] reopened for reconsideration, God willing. And in God is success. Said Muḥammad b. Rushd.

Second answer to this eighth question:

The answer [to this question] is contained within the answer to the first question of the second card, God willing. God grants success with the correct through His glory. Said Muḥammad b. Aḥmad b. al-Ḥājj.

Muḥammad [b. ʿIyāḍ] adds:

He means the fourth question above.

Ninth question on a point of this case:

Give us your answer – may God bestow honor upon you – concerning a point of this matter. The owner of the mill has demanded the orchard owners to produce their ownership documents and in some of the documents they appear as having purchased with irrigation [rights] from a different location, not from this water. Should the mill owner's demand for this document be dropped? Or should it be admitted after [the document was presented] on account of its mentioning [water] rights? For [the orchard owner] says: among its rights are that to irrigate from this disputed location. And his opponent responds: when it is written that you irrigate from a different water [source] that indicates that you do not have right to this [disputed] water.

In some of the documents of purchase (*al-ashriyāʾ*) there appear [the land's] rights and facilities (*ḥuqūquhā wa-marāfiquhā*), while there is no mention of irrigation. Thus his opponent [the mill owner] says he has no [right] to irrigation, since if he did, the document would include it. Should the [the orchard owner] be barred from litigating until he provide evidence of his specific [rights] to irrigate?

The answer to this ninth question:

I have studied and considered your question, and there is no argument against the orchard owners in their documents of purchase, based on what I have answered above, concerning the first question. They therefore are not obliged to produce these, since their contents are irrelevant to the impending decision (*idh lā yūjibu muḍmanuhā ḥukm*[an]). In God is success. Said Muḥammad b. Rushd.

Muḥammad [b. ʿIyāḍ] adds:

He means the ninth question above.

[Second answer to the ninth question:

The demands of the orchard owners and what they have provided as evidence are not weakened by what appears in the documents you have described.][1]

Tenth question concerning a point of this case:

And give us your answer – may God bestow honor upon you – concerning the mill owner's demand for copies of these documents. His opponents say: "copies of the whole texts are of no use to you, and part that you need concerning irrigation has been copied and incorporated into the testimonies. There is no need for us to disclose all of our documents to you, since the only section that is of use to you is that on irrigation." Should this be enough or must the entire documents be taken [into account]. And what if they demand a copy of the record of the judge's decision to cut the water through this road. Should they be allowed access to look into it or not? Explain to us what you [would] decide to do in this case so that we can proceed accordingly, especially in this case, when it has been established that there is no mention of them in the record, as stated above.

The answer to this tenth question:

The orchard owners are not compelled to present copies of their documents of purchase to the mill owner, nor are they obliged to present any part of them, since they are irrelevant to any argument against them (*idh lā ḥujja ʿalayhim fī shayʾ minhā*). A copy of the register can only be of use in arguments among [the orchard owners] in appealing [the decision of cutting the water]. In God is success. Said Muḥammad b Rushd.

Muḥammad [b. ʿIyāḍ] adds:

This is the same answer as that given to the tenth question.

Second answer to this tenth question:

If the matter is as you have described, copies of the whole documents must be provided in order to set forth explaining the irrigation in detail. In God is success. Said Muḥammad b. Aḥmad b. al-Ḥājj.

Eleventh question concerning a point of this case:

Give us you answer – may God bestow honor upon you – [to what should be done] if no irrigation rights are established for the litigating [orchard owners], other than that they occasionally diverted water to their orchard more or less since the time in which this mill was built. They provided evidence that the water that supported and gave life to the orchards ran dry, running low and seeping away until it ceased to reach them, and that, were it not for said water, their orchards would have died, since the water is closer to them and that it is over abundant when it flows through the orchards.

So the mill owner argued that he had established full possession of the water through use (*aḥajja bi-ḥiyāzatihi*) and that he had spent much money building this mill on the water. Is this an argument in his favor if they have provided evidence that they have also [used this water], occasionally irrigating with it when needed, and

1 Included by Bencherifa.

before he did? He argued against them that they have no right to irrigate through the road, thus did the judge decide, and thus does he prohibit them from doing so. "And were you to provide evidence of possession through use (*law thabatat ḥiyāzatukum*), it would be unlawful possession (*ḥawz*[un] *bi-ghayri ḥaqq*), while I established possession lawfully and rightfully." Explain to us, may you be rewarded.

The answer to this eleventh question:

I have studied and considered your question, and the orchard owners are more entitled to irrigate their orchards than the owner of the mill, even if the mill were older than the orchards, because of what we said above concerning the first question, and because the fruit trees, if not watered at the right time, will perish, while the mill does not perish when water is cut from it. Only its profit (*al-manfaʿa*) is cut during this time. In God is success. Said Muḥammad b. Rushd.

Muḥammad [b. ʿIyāḍ] adds:

He means the sixth question above.

Second answer to this eleventh question:

If the matter is as you have described it, the judge's decision remains effective and nothing else is to be considered. In God is success. Said Muḥammad b. Aḥmad b. al-Ḥājj.

Bibliography

Primary Sources

al-Bakrī, Abū ʿUbayd. *L'Afrique Septentrionale*. Translated by Mac Guckin De Slane. Paris: Librairie d'Amérique et d'Orient Adrien-Maisonneuve, 1965.

al-Ḍabbī. *Bughyat al-multamis fī ta'rīkh rijāl ahl al-Andalus*, ed. I. al-Abyārī. Beirut, Cairo: 1989.

al-Ghazālī, Abū Ḥamīd. *Iḥyā' ʿulūm al-dīn*. 5 vols, ed. Ṣidqī Jamīl al-ʿAṭṭār. Beirut: Dār al-Fikr, 1999.

Ibn ʿAbdūn. *Risālat Ibn ʿAbdūn fī al-quḍāt wa-l-ḥisba*, ed. É. Lévi-Provençal. In *Trois traités hispaniques de hisba*. Cairo: 1955.

———. *Séville Musulmane au début du XIIe siècle: Le traité d'Ibn ʿAbdun traduit avec une introduction et des notes par É. Lévi-Provençal*. Paris: Édition G. P. Maisonneuve, 1947.

Ibn Abī Zarʿ. *Rawḍ al-qirṭās*. Translated by A. H. Miranda. 2nd ed. 2 vols, Valencia: Textos Medievales, 1964.

Ibn Buluggīn, ʿAbd Allāh. *El siglo XI en 1a. persona: las "Memorias" de ʿAbd Allāh, último Rey Zīrí de Granada, destronado por los Almorávides (1090)*. Translated by É. Lévi-Provençal and E. García Gómez. Madrid: Alianza Literaria, 1980.

Ibn Ḥawqal. *Kitāb ṣūrat al-arḍ*. Ed. J. H. Cramer. Leiden: 1938.

Ibn Khaldūn. *Kitāb al-ʿibār*. 7 vols, Beirut: Dār al-Kitāb al-Lubnānī, 1959.

———. *Histoire des Berbères et des dynasties musulmanes de l'Afrique Septentrionale*. 4 vols, Paris: P. Geuthner, 1925–1956.

———. *The Muqaddima: An Introduction to History*. Translated by Franz Rosenthal. 3 vols, Princeton: Princeton University Press, 1958.

Ibn al-Khaṭīb. *al-Iḥāta fī akhbār Gharnāṭa*, ed. Muḥammad ʿAbd Allāh ʿInān. 2nd ed. 2 vols, Cairo: Maktabat al-Khānjī, 1973.

Ibn Rushd. *Fatāwā Ibn Rushd: li-Abī al-Walīd Muḥammad b. Aḥmad b. Aḥmad b. Rushd al-Qurṭubī al-Mālikī*. 3 vols, ed. al-Mukhtār b. al-Ṭāhir al-Talīlī. Beirut: Dār al-Gharb al-Islāmī, 1987.

———. *Masā'il Abī al-Walīd b. Rushd al-Jadd*. 2 vols, ed. Muḥammad al-Ḥabīb al-Tajkānī. Casablanca: Dār al-Afāq al-Jadīda, 1992.

———. *al-Bayān wa-l-taḥṣīl wa-l-sharḥ wa-l-tawjīh wa-l-taʿlīl fī masā'il al-Mustakhraja*. 2nd ed. ed. Muḥammad Ḥajjī and Aḥmad al-Sharqāwī Iqbāl. Beirut: Dār al-Gharb al-Islamī, 1988.

Ibn Rushd al-Ḥafīd. *Bidāyat al-mujtahid wa-nihāyat al-muqtasid*. 2 vols, Cairo: Maktabat al-Kulliyāt al-Azhariyya, 1969.

———. *Bidāyat al-Mujtahid (The Distinguished Jurist's Primer)*. Translated by Imran Ahsan Khan Nyazee. Vol. I & II. Reading, UK: Garnet, 1994.

Ibn ʿIdhārī. *al-Bayān al-mughrib fī akhbār al-Andalus wa-l-Maghrib*, ed. G. S. Colin and É. Lévi-Provençal. Leiden: 1948–1951.

Ibn Simāk (attributed). *al-Ḥulal al-mawshiyya fī dhikr al-akhbār al-Marrakushiyya*, ed. Suhayl Zakkār and ʿAbd al-Qādir Zamāma. Casablanca: Dār al-Rashād al-Ḥadītha, 1979.

al-Idrīsī, Abū ʿAbd Allāh Muḥammad. *Nuzhat al-mushtāq fī iktirāq al-afāq* (*Description de l'Afrique et de l'Espagne par Edrisi*). Translated by R. Dozy and M. J. de Goeje. Leiden: E. J. Brill, 1866.

ʿIyāḍ b. Mūsā. *Tartīb al-madārik wa-taqrīb al-masālik li-maʿrifat aʿlām madhhab Mālik*. Rabat: Wizārat al-Awqāf wa-l-Shu'ūn al-Islamīya, 1970.

———. *al-Ghunya*, ed. M. Jarrār. Beirut: Dār al-Gharb al-Islamī, 1982.

al-Maqqarī al-Tilimsānī. *Azhār al-riyāḍ fī akhbār ʿIyāḍ*. Rabat: 1978–1980.

———. *Nafḥ al-ṭīb min ghuṣn al-Andalus al-raṭīb*. 7 vols, Beirut: Dār Ṣādir, 1968.

Mālik b. Anas. *al-Muwaṭṭa'*. 2 vols, ed. Muhammad Fu'ad Abd al-Bāqi. Cairo: Dar Iḥyā' al-Kutub al-ʿArabiyya, 1955.

al-Marrākushī, ʿAbd al-Wāḥid. *al-Muʿjib fī talkhīs akhbār al-Maghrib*. 7th ed. ed. Muḥammad Sāʿīd al-ʿAryān and Muḥammad al-ʿArabī al-ʿAlamī. Casablanca: Dār al-Kutub, 1978.

Muḥammad b. ʿIyāḍ and ʿIyāḍ b. Mūsā. *Madhāhib al-ḥukkām fī nawāzil al-aḥkām*. 2nd ed. ed. M. Bencherifa. Beirut: Dār al-Gharb al-Islāmī, 1997.

Muḥammad b. ʿIyāḍ. *al-Taʿrīf bi-l-qāḍī ʿIyāḍ*, ed. M. Bencherifa. Muḥammadiya: 1982.

———. *Madhāhib al-ḥukkām fī nawāzil al-aḥkām* (*La actuación de los jueces en los procesos judiciales*). Translated by Delfina Serrano. Madrid: Consejo Superior de Investigaciones Científicas, 1998.

Saḥnūn b. Saʿīd al-Tanūkhī. *al-Mudawwana al-kubrā li-l-imām Mālik b. Anas al-Aṣbaḥī. Riwāyat al-imām Saḥnūn b. Saʿīd al-Tanūkhī ʿan al-imām ʿAbd al-Raḥmān b. Qāsim. wa-yalīhā muqaddimat Ibn Rushd*, ed. Zakariyā ʿUmrān. Beirut: Dar al-Kutub al-ʿIlmiya, 2005.

al-Tādilī, Abū Yaʿqūb Yūsuf b. Yaḥyā. *al-Tashawwuf ilā rijāl al-taṣawwuf wa-akhbār Abī al-ʿAbbās al-Sabtī*, ed. Ahmed Toufiq. Rabat: Jāmiʿat Muḥammad V, Manshūrāt Kulliyyat al-Adāb wa-l-ʿUlūm al-Insāniyya, 1984.

al-Wansharīsī, Aḥmad. *al-Miʿyār al-muʿrib wa-l-jāmiʿ al-mughrib ʿan fatāwā ʿulamā' Ifrīqiyā wa-l-Andalus wa-l-Maghrib*. 13 vols. Rabat: Ministry of Culture and Religious Affairs, 1981–1983.

Secondary Sources

Abun-Nasr, Jamil M. *A History of the Maghrib in the Islamic Period*. Cambridge: Cambridge University Press, 1987.

Aillet, Cyrille, Mayte Penelas, and Philippe Roisse, (eds.) *¿Existe una identidad mozárabe? Historia, lengua y cultura de los cristianos de al-Andalus (siglos IX-XII)*. Madrid: Casa de Velázquez, 2008.

Ali-de-Unzaga, Miriam, and Gaiser, Adam. "Facets of Exchange between North Africa and the Iberian Peninsula." *The Journal of North African Studies* 19, no. 1 (2014): 1–6.

Anjum, O. "Islam as a Discursive Tradition: Talal Asad and His Interlocutors." *Comparative Studies of South Asia, Africa and the Middle East* 27, no. 3 (2007 Nov 1): 656–692.

Austen, Ralph A. *Trans-Saharan Africa in World History*. The New Oxford World History. Oxford: Oxford Uiversity Press, 2010.

Ávila, María Luisa, and Maribel Fierro, (eds.) *Biografías Almohades II*. Estudios Onomástico Biográficos de al-Andalus, vol. x. Madrid-Granada: Consejo Superior de Investigaciones Científicas, 2000.

Bearman, P. J., Rudolph Peters, and Frank E. Vogel. *The Islamic School of Law: Evolution, Devolution, and Progress*. Cambridge, Mass: Islamic Legal Studies Program, Harvard Law School: Distributed by Harvard University Press, 2005.

Bekir, Ahmed. *Histoire de l'école malikite en Orient jusqu'a la fin du Moyen Age*. Tunis: Imprimerie de l'U.G.T.T., 1962.

Bennison, Amira K. *Jihad and its Interpretations in Pre-Colonial Morocco: State-Society Relations during the French Conquest of Algeria*. London: Routledge Curzon, 2002.

———. "Liminal States: Morocco and the Iberian Frontier between the Twelfth and Nineteenth Centuries." In *North Africa, Islam and the Mediterranean World: From the Almoravids to the Algerian War*, ed. Julia Clancy-Smith, 11–28. New York: Frank Cass Publishers, 2001.

Berkey, Jonathan. *The Transmission of Knowledge in Medieval Cairo: A Social History of Islamic Education*. Princeton, N.J.: Princeton University Press, 1992.

———. *The Formation of Islam: Religion and Society in the Near East, 600–1800*. Cambridge; New York: Cambridge University Press, 2003.

Berque, Jacques. "Essai sur la méthode juridique maghrébine." In *Opera minora*, 273–358. Paris: 2001.

Bloom, Jonathan. *The Minbar from the Kutubiyya Mosque*. New York, Madrid [Rabat]: Metropolitan Museum of Art, Ediciones el Viso, Ministry of Cultural Affairs, Kingdom of Morocco, 1998.

———. "The Masterpiece Minbar." *Saudi Aramco World* (May/June 1998): 2–11.

Bonine, M. E. "The Sacred Direction and City Structure: A Preliminary Analysis of the Islamic Cities of Morocco." *Muqarnas* 7 (1990): 50–72.

Boone, J. L., J. E. Myers, and C. L. Redman. "Archeological and Historical Approaches to Complex Societies: The Islamic States of Medieval Morocco." *American Anthropologist New Series* 92, no. 3 (1990 Sep 1): 630–646.

Bosch Vilá, Jacinto. *Los Almorávides*. Introductory study by Emilio Molina López. Granada: Universidad de Granada, 1998.

Bovill, E. W. *The golden trade of the Moors: West African Kingdoms in the Fourteenth Century*. 2nd ed. Princeton: M. Weiner Publishers, 1995.

Brett, Michael. "The Islamisation of Morocco from the Arabs to the Almoravids." In *Ibn Khaldun and the Medieval Maghrib*, edited by Michael Brett, London: Ashgate, 1999.

Brett, Michael, and Elizabeth Fentress. *The Berbers: The Peoples of Africa*. Wiley-Blackwell, 1997.

Brunschvig, R. "Urbanisme medieval et droit musulman." *Études d'Islamologie* 2 (1976): 7–35.

Burkhalter, Sheryl L. "Listening for Silences in Almoravid History: Another Reading of "The Conquest That Never Was."" *History in Africa* 19 (1992): 103–131.

Būtshīsh, Ibrāhīm al-Qādirī. *Iḍā'āt Ḥawla turāth al-gharb al-islāmī wa-ta'rīkhihi al-iqtiṣādī wa-l-ijtimā'ī*. Beirut: Dār al-Ṭalī'a, 2002.

———. *Mabāḥith fī al-ta'rīkh al-ijtimā'ī li-l-Maghrib wa-l-Andalus khilāl 'asr al-murābiṭīn*. Beirut: Dār al-Ṭalī'a, 1998.

Calder, Norman. "Al-Nawawī's Typology of Muftīs and Its Significance for a General Theory of Islamic Law." *Islamic Law and Society* 3, no. 2 (1996): 137–164.

Carmona, Alfonso. "Le Malékisme et les conditions requises pour l'exercice de la judicature." *Islamic Law and Society* 7, no. 2 (2000): 122–158.

Chalmeta Gendrón, Pedro. *El "señor del zoco" en España: edades media y moderna: contribución al estudio de la historia del mercado*. Madrid: Instituto Hispano-Arabe de Cultura, 1973.

Conrad, David, and Humprey Fisher. "The Conquest that Never was: Ghana and the Almoravids, 1076. I. The External Arabic Sources." *History in Africa* 9 (1982): 21–59.

———. "The Conquest that Never was: Ghana and the Almoravids, 1076. II. The Local Oral Sources." *History in Africa* 10 (1983): 53–78.

Cornell, Vincent J. *Realm of the Saint: Power and Authority in Moroccan Sufism*. Austin: University of Texas Press, 1998.

Cressier, P., M. Fierro, and J.P. Van Staëvel, eds. *L'urbanisme dans l'Occident musulman au Moyen Age: aspects juridiques*. Madrid: Casa de Velázquez-Consejo Superior de Investigaciones Científicas, 2000.

Cressier, Patrice, Maribel Fierro, and Luis Molina. *Los Almohades: problemas y perspectivas*. Madrid: Consejo Superior de Investigaciones Científicas, 2005.

Dandash, 'Ismat. "Mawqif al-murābiṭīn min 'ilm al-kalām wa-l-falsafa." In *Aḍwā' jadīda 'alā al-murābiṭīn*, 83–99. Beirut: 1991.

de la Puente, Cristina. "La caracterización de Almanzor: Entre la epopeya y la historia." In *Biografías y género biográfico en el occidente islámico*, edited by María Luisa Ávila, and Manuela Marín, 367–402. Madrid: Consejo Superior de Investigaciones Científicas, 1997.

Deverdun, Gaston. *Marrakech, des origines à 1912*. Rabat: Éditions techniques nord-africaines, 1959.

Dutton, Yasin. *The Origins of Islamic Law: The Qur'ān, the Muwaṭṭa' and Madinan 'Amal.* London: Curzon Press, 1999.

El Hour, Rachid. "The Andalusian Qadi in the Almoravid Period: Political and Judicial Authority." *Studia Islamica* no. 90 (2000): 67–83.

———. "Biografías de cadíes en época almorávide: análisis de las fuentes árabes." In *Estudios onomástico-biográficos de al-Andalus, VIII*, 177–199. Madrid: Consejo Superior de Investigaciones Científicas, 1997.

———. "El cadigazgo en Granada bajo los Almorávides: enfrentamiento y negociación." *Al-Qanṭara* XVII (2006): 7–24.

———. "Córdoba frente a los Almorávides: familias de cadíes y poder local an al-Andalus." *Revista del Instituto Egipcio de Estudios Islámicos* XXIX (1997): 181–210.

Endress, Gerhard. *An Introduction to Islam*. New York: Columbia University Press, 1988.

Fadel, Mohammad. "Riba, Efficiency, and Prudential Regulation: Preliminary Thoughts." *Wisconsin International Law Journal* (Winter 2008):

Feldman, Noah. *The Fall and Rise of the Islamic State*. Princeton, N.J.: Princeton University Press, 2008.

Ferhat, Halima. "Famille et societe a Sabta d'apres l'ouvrage du cadi 'Iyāḍ Madhāhib al-ḥukkām (XIIème siecle)." *Hespéris-Tamuda* Vol. XXX, no. 2 (1992): 5–15.

———. *Sabta des origines au xivème siècle*. Rabat: Ministère des affaires culturelles, 1993.

Fernandes, Leonor E. *The Evolution of a Sufi Institution in Mamluk Egypt: The Khanqah (Islamkundliche Untersuchungen)*. K. Schwarz, 1988.

Fernández Félix, Ana. *Cuestiones Legales del Islam Temprano: La 'Utbiyya y el Proceso de Formación de la Socidad Islámica Andalusí*. Estudios Árabes e Islamicos: Monografías. 6. Madrid: Consejo Superior de Investigaciones Científicas, 2003.

Fierro, Maribel. "El tratato sobre el profeta del Cadí 'Iyāḍ y el contexto almohade." In *Legendaria Medievalia: En honor de Concepción Castillo Castillo*, edited by Raif Georges Khoury, Juan Pedro Monferrer-Sala, and María Jesús Vigerua Molíns, 19–34. Córdoba: Ediciones el Almendro–Fundación Paradigma, 2011.

———. "Ill-Treated Women Seeking Divorce: The Qur'ānic Two Arbiters and Judicial Practice among the Malikis in al-Andalus and North Africa." In *Dispensing Justice in Islam: Qāḍīs and Their Judgments.* Edited by Rudolph Peters, Muhammad Khalid Masud, David S. Powers. Leiden: Brill, 2006.

———. "Opposition to Sufism in al-Andalus." In *Islamic Mysticism Contested: Thirteen Centuries of Contrversies and Polemics*, ed. Frederick De Jong and Bernd Radtke, 184–197. Leiden: Brill, 1999.

———. "The Legal Policies of the Almohad Caliphs and Ibn Rushd's *Bidayat al-Mujtahid*." *Journalof Islamic Studies* 10, no. 3 (1999): 226–248.

———. "The Polemic about the Karamāt al-Awliyā' and the Development of Ṣufism in al-Andalus (Fourth/Tenth-Fifth/Eleventh Centuries)." *The Bulletin of the School of Oriental and African Studies* 55 (1992): 236–249.

———. "The Qāḍī as Ruler." *Saber religioso y poder político en el Islam. Actas del Simposio Internacional: (Granada, 15–16 October, 1991)* (1994): 71–116.

———. "La Religión." In *El retroceso territorial de al-Andalus: almorávides y almohades. Siglos XI al XIII*, ed. María Jesús Vigerua Molíns, 8:2, 435–546. Madrid: Espasa Calpe, 1997.

———. "Proto-Malikis, Malikis, and Reformed Malikis in al-Andalus." In *The Islamic School of Law: Evolution, Devolution, and Progress*, ed. Peri Bearman, Rudolph Peters, and Frank E. Vogel, 57–76. Cambridge: Harvard University Press, 2005.

———. "Sobre monedas de época almohade: I. El dinar del Cadí ʿIyāḍ que nunca existió. II. Cuándo se acuñaron las primeras monedas almohades y la cuestión de la licitud de acuñar moneda." *al-Qanṭara* XXVII, no. 2 (2006): 457–76.

Fierro, Maribel, and María Luisa Ávila (eds.). *Biografías Almohades I*. Estudios Onomástico Biográficos de al-Andalus, vol. IX. Madrid-Granada: Consejo Superior de Investigaciones Científicas, 1999.

Fórneas, J. M. "De la transmisión de algunas obras de tendencia ašʿarī en al-Andalus." *Awrāq* 1 (1978): 4–11.

Fromherz, A. "North Africa and the Twelfth-Century Renaissance: Christian Europe and the Almohad Islamic Empire." *Islam & Christian-Muslim Relations* 20, no. 1 (2009 Jan 1): 43–59.

Garcia-Arenal, Mercedes. *Messianism and Puritanical Reform: Mahdis of the Muslim West*. Leiden: Brill, 2006.

Garden, Kenneth. "Al-Ghazālī's Contested Revival: *Iḥyāʾ ʿUlūm al-Dīn* and its Critics in Khorasan and the Maghrib." PhD diss., University of Chicago, December 2005.

Glick, Thomas. *From Muslim Fortress to Christian Castle: Social and Cultural Change in Medieval Spain*. Manchester: Manchester University Press, 1995.

———. *Irrigation and Society in Medieval Valencia*. Cambridge: Belknap Press of Harvard University Press, 1970.

———. *Islamic and Christian Spain in the Early Middle Ages*. Princeton: Princeton University Press, 1979.

Goitein, S. D. *A Mediterranean Society: The Jewish Communities of the Arab World as Portrayed in the Documents of the Cairo Geniza*. 6 vols. Berkeley: University of California Press, 1967.

Gómez-Rivas, Camilo. "Qāḍī ʿIyāḍ (d. 544/1149)." In *Islamic Legal Thought: A Compendium of Muslim Jurists*, edited by Oussama Arabi, David Powers, and Susan Spectorsky, 323–338. Leiden: Brill, 2013.

Gottreich, Emily. *The Mellah of Marrakesh: Jewish and Muslim Space in Morocco's Red City*. Bloomington: Indiana University Press, 2007.

Guichard, Pierre. *Al-Andalus: estructura antropológica de una sociedad islámica en Occidente*. Barcelona: Barral Editores, 1976.

Hallaq, Wael. "From *Fataws* to *Furu'*: Growth and Change in Islamic Substantive Law." *Islamic Law and Society* 1, no. 1 (1995): 29–65.

———. *A History of Islamic Legal Theories: An Introduction to Sunni Usul al-Fiqh*. Cambridge: Cambridge University Press, 1997.

———. "Murder in Cordoba: Ijtihād, Iftā' and the Evolution of Substantive Law in Medieval Islam." *Acta Orientalia* 55 (1994): 55–83.

———. "Was the Gate of *Ijtihad* Closed?" *International Journal of Middle Eastern Studies* 16 (1984): 3–41.

Halm, Heinz. *Empire of the Mahdi: The Rise of the Fatimids*. Leiden: Brill, 1996.

Hendrickson, Jocelyn. "The Islamic Obligation to Emigrate: Al-Wansharīsī's *Asnā al-Matājir* Reconsidered." PhD diss., Emory University, 2009.

Hermosilla Llisterri, M. José. "En torno al Qāḍī 'Iyāḍ I: datos biographicos." *Miscelánea de Estudios Árabes y Hebraicos* XXVII-XXVIII (1978–1979): 149–174.

Herrero, Omayra. "Ṭāriq b. Ziyād: las distintas visiones de un conquistador beréber según las fuentes medievales." In *Biografías Magrebíes. Identidades y Grupos Religiosos, Sociales y Políticos en el Magreb Medieval*, edited by Mohamed Meouak, 141–186. Madrid: Consejo Superior de Investigaciones Cientíificas, 2012.

Hodgson, Marshall G. S. *The Venture of Islam: Conscience and History in a World Civilization*. Chicago: University of Chicago Press, 1974.

Huici, Miranda Ambrosio. *Historia política del Imperio Almohade*. Tetuán: Editora Marroquí, 1956.

Iskander, John. "Devout Heretics: The Barghawata in Maghribi Historiography." *The Journal of North African Studies* 12, no. 1 (2007): 37–53.

Kahera, A. I., and O. Benmira. "Damages in Islamic Law: Maghribī Muftīs and the Built Environment (9th-15th Centuries CE)." *Islamic Law and Society* 5, no. 2 (1998): 131–164.

Kassis, Hanna E. "A 5th/11th-Century Maghrebi Treatise on the Conduct of the Ideal Ruler." *The Maghreb Review* 17, no. 1–2 (1992): 84–94.

———. "La Moneda, Pesos y Medidas." In *El retroceso territorial del al-Andalus: almorávides y almohades. Siglos XI al XIII*, ed. María Jesús Vigerua Molíns, 303–342. Madrid: Espasa Calpe, 1987.

———. "Qadi Iyad's Rebellion against the Almohads in Sabtah (AH 542–543/AD 1147–1148) New Numismatic Evidence." *Journal of the American Oriental Society* 103, no. 3 (1983 Jul. - Sep.): 504–514.

Kennedy, Hugh. *Muslim Spain and Portugal: A Political History of al-Andalus*. London: Longman, 1996.

Lagardère, Vincent. "Abū l-Walīd b. Rushd Qāḍī al-Quḍāt de Cordue." *al-Qantara* VII (1986): 202–228.

———. *Les Almoravides jusqu'au règne de Yusuf b. Tašfin (1039–1106)*. Paris: L'Harmattan, 1989.

———. *Campagnes et paysans d'Al-Andalus* (VIII-XVe s.). Collection Islam et Occident; 9. Paris: Editions Maisonneuve et Larose, 1993.

———. "Communautés mozarabes et pouvoir almoravide en 519H/1125 en Andalus." *Studia Islamica* 67 (1988): 99–119.

———. "La Haute Judicature à l'Epoque Almoravide en al-Andalus." *al-Qantara* 7 (1986): 135–228.

———. *Histoire et société en occident musulman au Moyen Age: analyse du Miʿyār d'al-Wanšarīsī*. Collection de la Casa de Velázquez; 53. Madrid: Casa de Velázquez, 1995.

———. "Structures étatiques et communautés rurales: les impositions légales en al-Andalus et au Maghreb (XIe-XVe)." *Studia Islamica* (1994): 57–95.

———. "Une théologie dogmatique de la frontière en al-Andalus aux XIe et XIIe siècles: l'ašʿarisme." *Anaquel de estudios árabes* no. 5 (1994): 71–98.

Lapidus, Ira. *A History of Islamic Societies*. 2nd ed. Cambridge: Cambridge University Press, 2002.

———. *Muslim Cities in the Later Middle Ages*. Cambridge: Cambridge University Press, 1984.

Laroui, Abdallah. *L'histoire du Maghreb: Un essai de synthese*. 2nd ed. Casablanca: Centre Culturel Arabe, 2001.

Layish, Aharon. *Sharīʿa and Custom in Libyan Tribal Society: An Annotated Translation of Decisions from the Sharīʿa Courts of Adjābiya and Kufra*. Studies in Islamic Law and Society, v. 24, Leiden: Brill, 2005.

Le Tourneau, Roger. *Fez in the Age of the Marinides*. Norman: University of Oklahoma Press, 1961.

Levtzion, N., and J. F. P. Hopkins, (eds.) *Corpus of Early Arabic Sources for West African History*. Princeton: Markus Wiener Publishers, 2000.

Love, Paul M. "The Sufris of Sijilmasa: Toward a History of the Midrarids." *The Journal of North African Studies* 15, no. 2 (2010): 173–88.

Makdisi, George. *The Rise of Colleges: Institutions of Learning in Islam and the West*. Edinburgh: Edinburgh University Press, 1981.

Marcos Cobaleda, María. "Los Almorávides: Territorio, Arquitectura, y Artes Suntuarias." PhD diss., Universidad de Granada, 2010.

Marshall, D. A. "Behavior, Belonging, and Belief: A Theory of Ritual Practice." *Sociological Theory* 20, no. 3 (2002 Nov 1): 360–380.

Masud, Muhammad Khalid, Brinkley Morris Messick, and David S. Powers. *Islamic Legal Interpretation: Muftis and Their Fatwas*. Cambridge, Mass: Harvard University Press, 1996.

Messier, Ronald A. *The Almoravids and the Meanings of Jihad*. Oxford: Praeger, 2010.

———. "The Almoravids: West African Gold and the Gold Currency of the Mediterranean Basin." *Journal of Economic and Social History of the Orient* 17, no. 1 (March 1974): 31–47.

Messick, Brinkley. *The Calligraphic State: Textual Domination and History in a Muslim Society*. Berkeley: University of California Press, 1993.

Miller, James A. "Trading through Islam: The Interconnections of Sijilmasa, Ghana and the Almoravid Movement." In *North Africa, Islam and the Mediterranean World: From the Almoravids to the Algerian War*, ed. Julia Clancy-Smith, 29–58. London: Frank Cass, 2001.

Miller, Kathryn A. *Guardians of Islam: Religious Authority and Muslim Communities of Late Medieval Spain*. New York: Columbia University Press, 2008.

———. "Muslim Minorities and the Obligation to Emigrate to Islamic Territory: Two Fatwās from Fifteenth-Centruy Granada." *Islamic Law and Society* 7, 2 (2000): 256–288.

Monroe, James T. "Hispano-Arabic Poetry during the Almoravid Period: Theory and Practice." *Viator: Medieval and Renaissance Studies* 4 (1973): 65–98.

Moore, R. I. *The First European Revolution, c. 970–1215*. Oxford: Blackwell Publishing, 2000.

Müller, Christian. *Gerichtspraxis im Stadtstaat Córdoba: zum Recht der Gesellschaft in einer mālikitisch-islamischen Rechtstradition des 5./11. Jahrhunderts*. Leiden: Brill, 1999.

———. "Judging with God's Law on Earth: Judicial Powers of the Qāḍī al-Jamāʿa of Cordoba in the Fifth/Eleventh Century." *Islamic Law and Society* 7, no. 2 (2000): 159–186.

Nagendra Kr. Singh, ed. "The Almoravids." In *North Africa and African Continent*. Vol. 33, 313–340. New Delhi: Anmol Publications, 2005.

Nirenberg, David. *Communities of Violence: Persecution of Minorities in the Middle Ages*. Princeton, N.J.: Princeton University Press, 1996.

Norris, H. T. *The Berbers in Arabic Literature*. London: Longman, 1982.

———. "New Evidence on the Life of ʿAbdullāh b. Yāsīn and the Origins of the Almoravid Movement." *Journal of African History* 12, no. 2 (1971): 255–68.

———. *Saharan Myth and Saga*. Oxford: Clarendon Press, 1972.

O'Callaghan, Joseph F. *A History of Medieval Spain*. Ithaca: Cornell University Press, 1975.

O'Meara, Simon. *Space and Muslim Urban Life: At the Limits of the Labyrinth of Fez*. New York: Routledge, 2007.

Peters, Rudulf. *Jihad in Classical and Modern Islam*. Princeton: 1996.

Powers, David S. "On Judicial Review in Islamic Law." *Law and Society Review* 26:2 (1992): 315–341.

———. *Law, Society, and Culture in the Maghrib, 1300–1500*. Cambridge studies in Islamic civilization, Cambridge; New York: Cambridge University Press, 2002.

———. "Legal Consultation (*Futyā*) in Medieval Spain and North Africa." In *Islam and Public Law*, ed. Ch. Mallat, 85–106. London: 1993.

Rahman, Sayeed Sajjadur. "The Legal and Theological Thought of Ibn Abī Zayd al-Qayrawānī (310–386/922–996)." PhD diss., Yale University, 2009.

Rodriguez Mediano, Fernando. "El Género Biográfico Árabe: Apuntes Teóricos." In *Biografías y Género Biográfico en el Occidente Islámico*, edited by María Luisa Ávila and Manuela Marín, 17–33. Madrid: CSIC, 1997.

al-Sabtī, ʿAbd al-Aḥad, and Ḥalīma Farḥāt. *Al-Madīna fī al-ʿaṣr al-wasīṭ: qaḍāyā wa-wathāʾiq min taʾrīkh al-Gharb al-Islāmī*. Casablanca: al-Markaz al-Thaqāfī al-ʿArabī, 1994.

Schimmel, Annemarie. *And Muhammad is His Messenger: the Veneration of the Prophet in Islamic Piety*. Chapel Hill: University of North Carolina Press, 1985.

Serrano Ruano, Delfina. "Explicit cruelty, implicit compassion: Judaism, forced conversions and the genealogy of the Banu Rushd." *Journal of Medieval Iberian Studies* 2, no. 2 (2010): 217–233.

———. "Los Banū ʿIyāḍ: de la caída del imperio almorávid a la instauración de la dinastía nazarí." In *IX*, ed. M. Luisa Ávila and M. Fierro, 351–406. Madrid-Granada: Consejo Superior de Investigaciones Científicas, 1999.

———. "Las demandas particulares como limitación de las construcciones privadas en el Occidente islámico medieval." In *L'Urbanisme dans l'Occident musulman au Moyen Âge: Aspects juridiques*, ed. P. Cressier, M. Fierro, and J. P. Van Saëvel, 17–38. Madrid: Casa Velázquez-CSIC, 2000.

———. "Legal Practice in an Andalusī-Maghribī Source from the Twelfth Century CE: The Madhāhib al-ḥukkām fī nawāzil al-aḥkām." *Islamic Law and Society* 7, no. 2 (2000 Jan 1): 187–234.

———. "Ibn Rušd al-Ŷadd." In *Biblioteca de al-Andalus: de Ibn al-Dabbag a Ibn Kurz*, edited by Jorge Lirola Delgado and Jose Miguel Puerta Vílchez, 617–26. Almería: Fundación Ibn Tufayl de Estudios Árabes, 2006.

———. "ʿIyāḍ b. Mūsà." In *Biblioteca de al-Andalus*, edited by Jorge Lirola Delgado, 404–34. Almería: Fundación Ibn Tufayl de Estudios Árabes, 2009.

———. "Why did the scholars of al-Andalus distrust al-Ghazāli? Ibn Rushd al-Jadd's fatwā on Awliyāʾ Allāh." *Der Islam* 83, no. 1 (2006): 137–156.

———. "Dos fetuas sobre la expulsión de mozárabes al Maghreb en 1126." *Anaquel de Estudios Árabes* 2 (1991): 163–182.

———. "Ibn Rušd al-Qurṭubī al-Mālikī, Abū l-Walīd Muḥammad b. Aḥmad b. Aḥmad, *Fatāwī Ibn Rušd*, taqdīm wa-taḥqīq wa-ŷamʿ wa-taʿlīq al-Duktūr al-Mukhtar al-Ṭāhir al-Talīlī. *Masāʾil Abī l-Walīd Ibn Rušd (al-ŷadd)*; taḥqīq ʿan sitt nusaj jaṭṭiyya maʿa dirasāt ʿan l-muʿtallif wa-l-kitāb Muḥammad al-Ḥabīb al-Tiŷānī." *al-Qanṭara* xv (1994): 531–534.

———. "Los almorávides y la teología ash'arí: ¿Contestación o legitimación de una disciplina marginal?" In *Identidades Marginales*, ed. C. de La Puente, 461–516. Madrid: Consejo Superior de Investigaciones Científicas, 2003.

Shabana, A. *Custom in Islamic Law and Legal Theory: The Development of the Concepts of ʿurf and ʿādah in the Islamic Legal Tradition*. New York: Palgrave Mcmillan, 2010.

Shatzmiller, Maya. *The Berbers and the Islamic State*. Princeton, N.J.: Markus Weiner Publishers, 2000.

———. *Her Day in Court: Women's Property Rights in Fifteenth-Century Granada*. Harvard Series in Islamic Law. Boston: Islamic Legal Studies Program, Harvard Law School, 2007.

———. "Women and Property Rights in al-Andalus and the Maghrib: Social Patterns and Legal Discourse." *Islamic Law and Soceity* 2, no. 3 (1995): 219–257.

Stewart, Frank H. "Tribal Law in the Arab World: A Review of the Literature." *International Journal of Middle Eastern Studies* 19, no. 4 (1987): 473–90.

Toledano, Henry. *Judicial Practice and Family Law in Morocco: The Chapter on Marriage from Sijilmāsī's al-'Amal al-muṭlaq*. Boulder: 1981.

Triki, Hamid. "Retrato Historico de una Metropolis Medieval. Siglos XI-XII." In *La Architectura del Islam Occidental*, 93–106. Granada: 1995.

———. "Marrakech." In *Le Prix Aga Khan d'Architecture: Cèrèmonie de remise des prix 1986, Maroc*, 4–38. 1986.

Urvoy, Dominique. *Pensers d'al-Andalus: la vie intellectuelle à Cordoue et Séville au temps des empires berbères (fin XIe siècle-début XIIIe siècle)*. Paris [Toulouse]: Editions du CNRS Presses Universitaires du Mirail, 1990.

Vallvé Bermejo, J. "Suqūt al-Barghawāṭī rey de Ceuta." *Al-Andalus* 28 (1963): 171–209.

Vidal Castro, Fransisco. "Aḥmad al-Wansharīsī (m. 914/1508). Principales Aspectos de su Vida." *al-Qanṭara* XII (1991): 315–52.

———. "El *Mi'yār* de al-Wanšarīsī (m. 914/1508). I: Fuentes, manuscritos, ediciones, traducciones." *Miscelánea de Estudios Árabes y Hebraicos* 42–43 (1993): 317–61.

———. "El *Mi'yār* de al-Wanšarīsī (m. 914/1508). II. Contenido." *Miscelánea de Estudios Árabes y Hebraicos* 44 (1995): 213–46.

———. "La Expansión en el Magreb y al-Andalus." In *Mauritania y España: Una Historia Común: Los Almorávides, Unificadores del Magreb y al-Andalus (s. XI-XII)*, ed. Amor Ben Hamadi, 75–98. Seville: Fundación el Legado Andalusí, 2003.

———. "Las obras de Aḥmad al-Wanšarīsī (m. 914/1508) Inventario analítico." *Anaquel de Estudios Árabes* III (1992): 73–112.

Viguera Molíns, María Jesús. "Historia Política." In *El retroceso territorial de al-Andalus: almorávides y almohades, siglos XI al XIII*, ed. María Jesús Viguera Molíns, Madrid: Espasa Calpe, 1997.

———. *Los reinos de taifas y las invasiones magrebíes: (al-Andalus del IX al XIII)*. Madrid: Editorial MAPFRE, 1992.

al-Warāgilī, Ḥasan. *Abū l-Faḍl al-Qāḍī 'Iyāḍ al-Sabtī*. Beirut: Dār al-Gharb al-Islamī, 1994.

Wilbaux, Quentin. *La médina de Marrakech: formation des espaces urbains d'une ancienne capitale du Maroc*. Paris: L'Harmattan, 2002.

Zomeño, Amalia. *Dote y matrimonio en al-Andalus y el norte de África: estudio sobre la jurisprudencia islámica medieval*. Madrid: Consejo Superior de Investigaciones Científicas, 2000.

Index

ʿAbbādī dīnār 61–62
ʿAbbūd b. Saʿīd al-Tanūkhī 124
ʿAbd Allāh b. Yāsīn 11–13, 32, 42
ʿAbd al-Muʾmin 120, 149
ablutions 99–101
 see also tayammum
Abū ʿAbd Allāḥ b. ʿIsā al-Tamīmī 118
Abū ʿAbd Allāh al-Tuṭīlī 60, 70
Abū ʿAlī al-Ṣadafī 118
Abū Bakr al-Bāqilānī 87
Abū al-Maʿālī 87
Abū Bakr b. Fawrak 87
Abū Bakr b. Rizq 68
Abū Bakr b. ʿUmar 13–15, 32, 50–52
Abū Ḥanīfa 102
Abū al-Ḥasan al-Ashʿarī 87–93
Abū al-Ḥasan b. al-Wazzān 25
Abū Ḥurayra 108
Abū ʿImrān al-Fāsī 11–12
Abū Isḥāq al-Isfaraynī 87
Abū al-Walīd al-Bājī 87, 133
Abū Yaḥyā b. Rawāda (governor of Cordoba) 24
Abū Zakariyyāʾ Yaḥyā b. ʿUmar b. Buankayn 12
Abū al-Zinād 71
ʿāda (custom) 37–38
adultery 82–83
Aghmāt 13–14, 31, 50–51
Alfonso I of Aragon 17, 22, 24, 81
Alfonso VI of Castile-Leon 16, 115
Algeciras 113, 119–120
ʿAlī b. Ḥammūd 114
ʿAlī b. Yūsuf b. Tāshufīn 15–18, 22–25, 46–47, 49, 86–87, 89, 93–94, 97, 115, 117
Almería 118
Almohads 17–18, 80, 84, 91, 120–121, 149–151
Almoravids
 attitudes toward theology 87–93
 capture of Ceuta 114–116
 collapse 149–151
 commercial revolution of 48–49
 connection to twelfth-century renaissance of Latin West 18–19
 dīnārs 59–62
 effect of encounter with more urban north (north and south division) 14–15, 31–32
 effects on economy of Far Maghrib 104
 first Berber-Islamic empire 3, 15
 founding of capital at Marrakesh 49–56
 high level contacts with Cordoba 86–87
 historical background of rise in the Maghrib 9–18
 in Almohad historiography 89, 91
 in al-Andalus 16–17, 23–24
 neglect of social history of 5
 question over corruptibility of rulers 107–112
 referred to as *mulaththamūn* (veiled ones) 107–108
 sponsorship of Mālikism 76
ʿamal (judicial practice) 34–38
al-Andalus 2, 4, 14, 41–42, 49, 76, 86–87, 93–96, 118
apostasy 79–84
ʿaqd (document; contract) 74, 146–147
Ashʿarism 86–93
Atlas Mountains, High 50
Awdaghusht 10, 12, 15

Badajoz 115
Balearic Islands 17
Balyūnsh 115, 124, 126–128
al-Bakrī 10n28, 11, 26–27
Banū Aghmār of Azemmour 18n78
Barghawāṭa 4, 10n28, 13, 48
Barghawāṭī dynasty 113–116, 124
bayʿ (sale) 67–70
Berbers 13, 20, 27–28, 54
 definition 1n2
 dominant ethnic group of Maghrib 1–2
 first empire of 3
 pre-Islamic trade 30
Berque, Jacques 34n124
Butshīsh, Ibrāhīm 20

Cairo 4
cattle-raiding 107–111

Ceuta 3, 5, 14, 20, 40, 44, 97
city of ʿIyāḍ b. Mūsā 116–121
great mosque of 16
historical background 113–116
Christians
in Marrakesh 80–82
commercial law *see* Mālikism
confiscation (of disputed property) 138
conversion 79–84
Cordoba 3, 14, 22–25, 36, 38, 47 , 76, 114, 115, 118, 128
rebellion of 515/1121 17, 23–24
Cornell, Vincent 21
criminal law
murder 101–104
theft (as compared to usurpation) 108
customary law *see* Mālikism

Dār al-Islām 16–17
Daran Mountains 51
Dāy 31, 121
dīnār 65–67
see also Almoravid dīnārs
dirham 63, 65–67
divorce *see ṭalāq*
Draʿa 57
drawing of lots 106
Dukkāla 51

Ebro valley
northern border of Almoravid Empire 1, 17
empire
Berber-Islamic 3
definition of 1n1
Egypt 41–42
evidence 82–83, 131–133
documentary 146–147

Far Maghrib 3–5, 41–42, 44
relationship with al-Andalus 8–9
Fatimid Imamate 3–4, 4n11, 11, 14, 85n1, 114
fatwā(s)
breakdown by region and subject in al-Wansharīsī 39–41
character and studies of those by Ibn Rushd al-Jadd 25–26
containing place names in the Far Maghrib 30
definition 5–6, 5n18
studies of 6, 6n21
Ferhat, Halima 20
Fez 3, 3n9, 5, 15, 36, 38, 87
first Islamic city of the Far Maghrib and spiritual axis 3, 3n9, 5
fortification 15, 52
Fierro, Maribel 21, 32n122

Ghana, kingdom of *see* Soninke Kings of Ghana
al-Ghazālī 18n78, 58, 84n114, 89–91, 119
gift-giving 107–111
gold
ṣarf (exchange) 60–62
fatwās concerning buying and selling of 59–65
mint 59
see also trade
Granada 25, 115–119
grazing rights 105–106

ḥadd punishments 82, 102, 108
ḥajj 93–99
al-Ḥakam II 47n4
ḥākim 36–37
Haylāna 51
Hazmīra 51
historiography
marginalization of Maghrib in 1–2, 2n4, 2n6, 17
of Islamic social institutions 6–7
ḥukm (binding legal decision) 66, 125, 127

Ibn Abī Zayd al-Qayrawānī 85n1
Ibn Ḥabīb 75
Ibn al-Ḥājj 24, 118, 128, 132, 134, 137, 144, 146–147
Ibn Ḥamdīn, Aḥmad 23–24, 84n114, 118
Ibn Ḥawqal 10n28, 28–29
Ibn ʿIdhārī 13, 50–51
Ibn al-ʿImād 119
Ibn Khaldūn 121
Ibn al-Mawwāz 69
Ibn Qasī 17
Ibn al-Qāsim 72, 103
Ibn Rushd al-Ḥafīd (Averroës) 22
Ibn Rushd al-Jadd
biography 21–26

commentary on *al-ʿUtbiyya* 69–70
fatwās to the Far Maghrib 86–112
fatwās to ʿIyāḍ b. Mūsā 131–148
fatwās to Marrakesh 59–84
influence as legal reformer 70n80
Ibn Shihāb 71, 73
Ibn Tūmart 17–18, 25, 84, 90
Ibrāhīm b. Tāshufīn 15n60, 18, 119
al-ʿIdwa (the other shore) 93, 97, 99–101, 104
Ifrīqiya 41–42
importance to rise of Almoravids 11
Iḥyāʾ ʿulūm al-dīn see al-Ghazālī
ijāza (transmission license) 116–118
ʿIkrama Mawlā b. ʿAbbās 27
ʿilla (*ratio juris*) 96, 140
Iraq 34n125, 41–42
ʿIsā b. Mazīd al-Aswad 27
Isḥāq b. ʿAlī 15n60, 18, 120
Islam, diffusion of 9–13, 27–29
Islamic social and urban institutions 6–7, 14, 56
continuity between Almoravids and Almohads 18n78
in Sijilmāsa 30
Islamization
and urbanization 3, 3n7
ʿIyāḍ b. Mūsā 32, 38–42, 57
biography 116–121
in Dāy 31
on Mālikī *ʿamal* 35
riparian dispute presided over 122–148

Jawhar b. Sakkum 11
jihād 17, 93–99
espoused by Almoravids as legitimating practice 1, 16
Judāla 11–12
judge *see* qāḍī
judgment *see ḥukm*
judicial review *see* Mālikism

kalām (theology) 87–93
Khawārij *see* Midrārids
Kutubiyya Minbar 46–48, 55

Lagardère, Vincent 19, 40–41
al-Lakhmī al-Qayrawānī 72
Lamtūna 12–13
land (private, communal, and stolen) 104–107
partitioning of 106
Laqqūt b. Yūsuf 14n58
Laraoui, Abdallah 18–19

mahdī 18
Maghrāwa 10, 13–14
Mahdia 4
Mālik b. Anas 35, 39, 108, 117n12
al-ʿUtbiyya 69
Mālikism 5, 48
absent from Sijilmāsa 30–32
ʿamal, ʿurf, and *ʿāda* 34–38
commercial law 49, 56–57, 65–70, 106–111
comparative development of establishment in the Far Maghrib 39–42
diffusion in Far Maghrib 30–33, 58
diverse levels of literacy in Far Maghrib 71, 138–139
eastern 34n125
impact of Ibn Rushd al-Jadd on 25
impact of ʿIyāḍ b. Mūsā on 117–119
in Ifrīqiya, as background for rise of Almoravids 4, 11
interaction with customary law and practice 33–38, 104–112
judicial review 127–133
reasons for development in the Far Maghrib 8–9, 48–49
repressed by Almohads 18n78, 149–151
resolution of contradicting opinions 70–76
symbolic authority of 76–84, 87–93
ʿulamāʾ, comparative regional numbers 41–42
ʿulamāʾ, working with Almoravid state 54, 57
water law 121–122
water (irrigation) rights arbitration 136–148
al-Manṣūr, Almohad caliph 149
Marrakesh 5, 22, 25, 44, 46–49, 58–59, 115, 116, 120, 128
comparison to Sijilmāsa, its predecessor 29–33
development under Almoravids 53–59

Marrakesh (cont.)
legal questions originating from 59–84
foundation 14, 49–53
great mosque of 46–47, 53
ramparts 15, 53–55
al-Marrākushī 89, 91
Masjid al-Tūb 52
maṣlaḥa (public interest) 102, 127
Masmūda 50
maẓālim courts 131
Mecca 41–42, 97
Medina 34–35, 41–42
Midrārids 4, 10n28, 27–29
mint (*sakka*) 29, 32, 114
Mozarabs 17, 22, 24, 81
al-Mudawwana 71–73, 75
muftī 5–7, 24, 30, 32, 34–36, 44, 48, 57, 62, 67, 70, 71, 73, 76, 77, 85, 86, 93, 101, 111, 121–124, 128–138, 140–147
Muḥammad b. Ismāʿīl 128, 132, 134, 137, 146
Muḥammad b. ʿIyāḍ 119–120
Muḥammad b. Marzūq, Shams al-Dīn 47
Muḥammad, the Prophet 46
muḥtaṣib (inspector) 124–127
Murcia 118
al-Muʿtadid b. Abī al-Qāsim 114
al-Muʿtamid b. ʿAbbād 16, 115
Muʿtazilism 88
Mūsā b. Ḥammād 57, 70, 73–74, 79–84, 128, 138–139

Nafīs 50
nafy al-ḍarar (avoiding harm) 130–134
nawāzil
definition 5, 5n18

oath-taking 66–70, 101, 103
Oran 3
orthodoxy and orthopraxy 4, 12, 48, 92

Powers, David S. 20, 124, 131
property 107–112
see also land
qāḍī
as compared to *ḥākim* 36
protector of private property and public interest 133–134
role as mediator in dispute 140
supervision of gold trade 62–65

Qāḍī ʿIyāḍ *see* ʿIyāḍ b. Mūsā
al-Qāʾim bi-Llāh ʿAbd Allāh 114
Qarawiyyīn Mosque 15
Qaṣr al-Ḥajar 52–53
Qayrawān 3, 11, 12, 38, 85n1
qiṣāṣ (law of retaliation) 102–103
Qubbat al-Barudiyyīn 55

reconquista 4
recusal *see* testimony
religious identity 79–84
repudiation *see ṭalāq*
Reverter 80
ribā restrictions 60–62, 67, 109
ribāṭ
origins of term associated with rise of Almoravids 12
riḥlat al-ṭalab fī al-ʿilm 23
ritual law 77–79, 99–101

salt trade 10
Saḥnūn b. Saʿīd al-Tanūkhī 71, 119
Ṣanhāja 1, 4n12, 9–13, 15, 56–57, 84, 107
ṣarf (exchange) 65–76
see also gold
Senegal and Niger river valleys
souther border of Almoravid empire 1
diffusion of Islam there 13
Serrano, Delfina 21, 22–26, 90, 119
Seville 114, 128
al-Shaʿrānī 119
Sharīʿa 36–38
Shatzmiller, Maya 20
shūra (court council) 119
Sijilmāsa 4, 5, 10–13, 26–33. 59
Soninke Kings of Ghana 10, 12, 14–15
Ṣūfism 5, 17, 18n78, 21, 84, 91
Sufrīs *see* Midrārids
Sulaymān al-Mustaʿīn 114
Suqūt al-Barghawāṭī 113–115
Sūs 57
Syria 41–42

taifa states 16
Tafīlālt 26, 57
ṭalāq (divorce) 70–76
Tangier 3, 87n4, 113, 115, 120
Tansīft Valley 51
Tāshufīn b. ʿAlī 15n60, 18, 80, 119–120

tawātur 35
tayammum (performing ablutions with sand) 77–79
testimony 73, 80, 103, 108, 124–126, 128, 137
  contradicting 71–73, 131–133, 142
  recusal 73–76
Tin Māl 18
Tlemcen
  great mosque of 15–16, 47, 55
Toledo 36, 38
  fall to Alfonso VI 16
Trade
  of gold 10, 13, 15, 27, 49, 59
  trans-Saharan routes 10, 12, 26–33

ʿulamāʾ *see* Mālikism
ʿUmar b. al-Khaṭṭāb 54, 92
Umayyad Caliphate of Cordoba 16n64, 47, 114
  struggle with Fāṭimids 3, 4n12, 14

urbanization (and urban development)
  and Islamization in the Maghrib 3, 3n7, 30–33
  promoted by Almoravids 15–16
  of Far Maghrib 26–33
  under the first three Almoravid Amīrs 50–59
ʿ*urf* (customary law) 37–38
  see also Mālikism

Wajjāj b. Zalwī 11–12
al-Wansharīsī, Aḥmad 39–41
Warīka 51
wars between Muslims and Christians
  Almoravid role in 4
  effect on frontier and identity 98–99
water law *see* Mālikism
Western Sahara
  birth-place of Almoravids 1, 9–13
Wilbaux, Quentin 53
witness *see* testimony

Yaḥyā b. Abī Bakr al-Ṣaḥrāwī 120
Yaḥyā b. Ibrāhīm 9–13
Yaḥyā Diyāʾ al-Dawla 113, 115
al-Yasaʿ Abū Manṣūr b. Abī al-Qāsim 27
Yemen 41–42
Yūsuf b. Tāshufīn 13–17, 52–54, 115, 118
Yūsuf I, Almohad caliph 149
zakāt 63
Zallāqa, battle of 16
Zanāta 3, 4n12, 10
Zaynab bint Isḥāq al-Nafzāwiyya 14, 51–52
Zirids 85n1

www.ingramcontent.com/pod-product-compliance
Lightning Source LLC
LaVergne TN
LVHW010626300926
849162LV00001B/82